THE BUMPER

JOKE

BOOK

WOLFE PUBLISHING LIMITED
10 EARLHAM STREET LONDON WC2

The Mini Ha-Ha books have proved to be very popular throughout the world, and we have received many requests for them to be presented in a more durable format. To meet this demand, we have prepared selections from the series, printed and bound in a more permanent form for easy reference.

Also available in this series:

THE SECOND BUMPER JOKE BOOK

© Wolfe Publishing Limited 1970, Reprinted 1971
SBN 72340171 3

PRINTED IN GREAT BRITAIN
BY EBENEZER BAYLIS AND SON LTD.
THE TRINITY PRESS, WORCESTER, AND LONDON

Contents

BEST
Irish
JOKES

Compiled by

TONY BUTLER

Introduction

THE GREATEST WITS have been Irish—Swift, Sheridan, Wilde, Shaw. Even in the very distant past the humour and satire of the Irish bards or minstrels were famous. The influence lives on.

'The Irish,' said Dr Johnson, 'are a very truthful race. They never speak well of one and other.' The ability to laugh at themselves has been a great advantage, and it has been suggested that in the world everything may be serious but not hopeless while in Ireland everything is hopeless but not serious.

It may help to know that politics and religion tend to be related in parts of Ireland and Nationalists are usually Roman Catholic while Orangemen and Unionists are generally Protestant. In the Republic of Ireland a magistrate is known as a District Justice and the police force is called the Garda Siochana or Civic Guard. Poteen, which is mentioned in some jokes, is an illegally distilled spirit not uncommon in the west of Ireland. Gaelic is still the language of the home in several areas and Irish words like 'amadan' (fool) or 'slainte' (health) are used to flavour everyday speech in English.

Gratitude is due to the publishers of *Dublin Opinion* for permission to use material from that publication; to David Marcus for a quotation from his Dolmen Press translation of *The Midnight Court* and to Myra Scally, Jim Shanahan, Gerry Gallivan, Joe Macauley, Brendan Tighe and many others who allowed access to their private collections of Irish jokes and limericks.

The grocer complained to Tadgh Brophy about the eggs.

'In every dozen, Tadgh,' he said, 'there's one or two shells with nothing in them.

'Is that so?' Tadgh nodded grimly. 'Well, leave it to me. I'll fix it.'

When he returned to the farm he went into the hen house and glared at the roosting fowl.

'Come on,' he sternly growled; 'admit it. Which of ye is on the Pill?'

The greyhound was a grave disappointment to everyone in Thurles and they lost a fortune on him.

'There's only one thing that will improve that dog, Paudeen,' urged a neighbour. 'Put some lead in his left ear.'

'And sure how would I do that?' asked Paudeen.

'With a shotgun.'

'Mick you're working very hard carrying bricks up and down the ladder at that speed.'

'Be quiet. I have them all fooled. Sure they're the same bricks all the time.'

They were holding hands at the pigsty in the sheltering shadow of the manure heap.

'I tell you, Cait, I bet you've been out with worse lookin' fellas nor me.'

Silence.

'I said, Cait, that I bet you've been out with . . .'

'Shut up, I'm thinking.'

County Wexford is noted for its free-and-easy lovers and its intense interest in music. A young woman from that county found herself in an interesting condition without a husband to share her interests. She came to Dublin and, by mistake, rang a Doctor of Music to make an appointment. The musician's maid took the phone call.

'I'm sorry, miss, but Dr Sheehy can't come to talk at the moment. He's very busy orchestrating *The Boys of Wexford*.'

9

There was silence for a moment.

'I'm delighted to hear it but it's too late for me.'

Father Scally stopped Owen on his way into the church.

'Owen, could you come back tomorrow night for confession? We have hundreds in the church at the moment. You haven't committed a murder since the last time?'

'Indeed I haven't, Father. I'll come back tomorrow night.'

On his way out he met Declan.

'Go home, Declan, and come back tomorrow. They're only hearing the murderers tonight.'

'I've been drinking whiskey all week to cure my sciatica.'

'I can give you a cure, Mr Cummisky.'

'Shut up. I don't want to hear it.'

The foreman loaded Fitzpatrick's wheelbarrow to the sky with lead piping.

Fitzpatrick scratched his head. 'Would you mind, sir,' he said, 'tying a couple of concrete blocks to my ankles.'

'What for?'

'To stop me breaking into a run.'

An Irish alibi is the proof that you were in two places at the one time.

Winston Churchill once travelled on the Tralee–Ballybunion railway. The train stopped at one station and showed no sign of moving. Winston asked a porter if anything could be done to get the journey under way again and mentioned who he was.

'Look, sir, if you were the stationmaster's son, it wouldn't make any difference.'

The peculiar humour of the Irish Bull was blamed by Sir Richard Steele on the climate of the country. In the reign of James the First, a good Welshman, Sir John Davies, was scarcely in the country before he started sending reports with such gems as: 'Most Mighty Prince, the gold mine that was lately found discovered at Ballycurry turns out to be a lead one.'

'Paddy,' jeered the Yank as he pointed to two stone dogs on entrance piers to an estate, 'how often do you feed those animals?'

'Every time they bark,' grinned Paddy.

The Wicked Landlord had robbed the poor farmer's daughter of her Virtue but he wanted to be just. He sent for the mother of the girl to come to him.

'Mrs O'Shaughnessy, you must know I can't marry your daughter, but I wish to compensate her. I'll settle five thousand pounds on the child and give a further two thousand pounds to your daughter. For yourself, I have five hundred pounds.'

She was a little breathless as she started to leave.

'The blessing of the revolving Indian saint of Inishbofin be on you, the blessing of the Holy Hermits of Clonmacnoise fall on you and all who belong to you . . .'

She paused as an awful thought struck her.

'Oh, heavens, sir . . . if she had a miscarriage will you give her another chance?'

The three thugs attacked Slattery and it was a fierce struggle. Finally they got him down and took three shillings and a half-penny from his pocket.

'What the hell did you put up a fight like that for three shillings and a halfpenny?' asked one of the disgusted hijackers.

'Sure I thought you were after the ten pound note in me sock.'

He was a small farmer who had managed to live for many years on ten acres and faith in the Lord. Now he was preparing to pass on to Green Pastures. He could hear the family whispering about the funeral arrangements.

'Will we have two cars with the hearse?'

'Sure, what do we want them for? The pony and car will do.'

'Maybe we should get a few wreaths?'

'Waste of money. We'll do without.'

He struggled and sat up.

'Bring me my trousers, let ye. I'll walk to the graveyard and ye can cut out the hearse.'

The Birmingham landlady wanted to please her Irish lodger. The first day she gave him two slices of bread for his package lunch. He didn't seem satisfied, so she gave him four slices the next day and then six slices and had to go on until he was getting ten. Even this wasn't enough so, in despair, she cut the loaf in half and put ham between the pieces. When he came in that evening she asked: 'Had you enough today, Colum?'

'It wasn't bad,' he said grudgingly, 'but I see you're back to the two slices again.'

Mrs Redmond went into the confession box and was about to start when she noticed an unfamiliar face behind the shutter.

'You're not Father Donlon. What are you doing there?'
'I'm the french polisher, M'am.'
'Well, where is Father Donlon?'
'I couldn't tell you, but if he heard anything like the stories I've been listening to, he's gone for the police.'

'If I married you, Kate, would your father give the dowry?'
'Yes, Mike.'
'And do you think he'd let us live here if we got married?'
'Yes, Mike.'
'Would he let me be the manager of the public house as well, if we married, Kate?'
'Yes, Mike.'
'Will you marry me, Kate?'
'No, Mike.'

The maid picked up the phone and muttered something before slamming it down.
'Who was that, Marie? I'm expecting a trunk call.'
'Only some mad idiot, Mr Slattery. He said it was a long distance from California. I told him we knew.'

The Roman Catholic parish priest of a Belfast church was amazed to find two bigoted and drunken Orange Protestants outside his window at two o'clock in the morning.
'What do you want?' he called.
'Well, we wanted ye to tell us if it was the Pope that called the Ecumenical council?'
'Look, come back in the morning and I'll discuss it when you're sober.'
'Sure, when we're sober, we don't give a damn about the Pope.'

The Captain was annoyed by the noise of a card game from the privates' barracks as it was keeping him awake. He rang the corporal and ordered him to break it up.
It was two hours before the corporal reported back that it was over.
'Surely, Mullarkey, it didn't take two hours to break it up?'
'And why wouldn't it? Sure I only started with sixpence.'

Flanagan had won a great deal of money and bought himself a piano. One day Burke saw him pushing it on a handcart along the street.
'What's this, Flanagan! Are you taking it back?'
'Not a bit of it. I'm going for me first lesson.'

The great Rabelaisian poem of *The Midnight Court* by Bryan Merriman was written in Irish in the 18th century. Bawdy and uninhibited, it tells of a dream trial where the women of Ireland plead for marriage. This is an extract from a translation by David Marcus published by the Dolmen Press:

> *We have thousands of women who's keep you busy*
> *With breasts like balloons or small as a bud*
> *Buxom of body and hot in the blood*
> *Virgins or whores—whatever's your taste—*
> *At least don't let them go to waste;*
> *It's enough to make us broken-hearted—*
> *Legs galore—and none of them parted.*

The Co. Donegal farmer was convinced he'd swallowed a horse and he couldn't be persuaded otherwise. Eventually they got him to a psychiatrist who gave him an injection, put him to sleep and brought a big white gelding to the bedside.

'There you are, Finnegan. I removed the horse.'

Finnegan shook his head sadly.

' 'Tis fooling me you are. Sure my horse is a Connemara pony.'

Strolling through Ireland's supreme honeymoon resort, Glengarriff, Francis Xavier Muldoon was a picture of bliss.

'But, Muldoon,' asked the local barkeeper, 'how is it you come here on your honeymoon without the wife?'

'Are you mad, man?' said Muldoon. 'Sure if she came, who'd look after the shop?'

The oldest inhabitant of Castlebar was interviewed some years ago and asked if he had his life to live again was there any major change he'd make.

He thought about it.

'Indeed there is . . . indeed there is,' he whined.

'And what would it be?'

'Sure and I'd part me hair in the middle so I would.'

Then there was the notice outside an Irish dance hall which proclaimed that 'Ladies and gentlemen are welcome, regardless of sex.'

'There's a ladder in these stockings.'

'What do you want? A marble staircase?'

The company commanded by Captain O'Shaughnessy was surrounded by the enemy under a tropical sun. Supplies were running down and a radio message told its own tale.

'Ammunition low and we're run out of food and whiskey.'

'Any water?' Headquarters radioed back.

'This is no time to be thinking of washing,' came the prompt reply.

At a political meeting addressed by one of Ireland's more dignified statesmen a heckler insisted on shouting: 'Who is the woman you're living with in Dublin?'

He was ignored and once more yelled: 'Who is the woman you're living with in Dublin?'

His friend pulled his arm anxiously.

'Shut up. That's his wife.'

'I know. I know . . . but I'm going to make him admit it.'

In Miami the local was explaining to Seamus the time-lag between Ireland and the United States.

'Look at it this way, Seamus, while we're lying here in the sun all the folks at home are asleep in bed.'

Seamus shook his head bitterly: 'There you are again. No justice for Ireland.'

He staggered home from the pub, wandered into the cemetery, fell into a newly-dug grave and went into a sound sleep. A factory horn woke him the next morning and he staggered to his feet and looked around.

'Heavens above,' he whispered to himself, 'the Day of Judgement and I'm the first up.'

The family gathered around the baptismal font and the ceremony commenced.

'And now,' said the priest, 'what name are you giving the child?'

Patrick Eamonn Sean Fergus Oscar Phelim Michael Pascal Xavier Thomas,' announced the proud god-mother.

The priest turned to the altar boy: 'Quick, get more Holy Water.'

She was shocked with the maid.

'Marie,' she said, 'I find your bra hanging from the light and your slip on the fridge and I'm told you did a striptease for my son. Is it indeed true that while I was absent you entertained him here last night?'

'Well, I hope so, Mam . . . I did me best.'

Tadgh took a correspondence course in body-building and finished in three months. He wrote to the school: 'I have now finished the course. Please send on the muscles by return.'

A meek little country man came to town and visited the local health office. He explained the problem.

'We all live in one room out in Newtownmoneenluggagh. Meself and six brothers. One of 'em keeps three greyhounds in with him and Tadgh has his mountain goat with the weak chest that can't go out in the field and Colman keeps his wolfhound in the room so that we have to let Padraig have his five budgies. Of course, Francis only has his goldfish so they don't matter. But the air is terrible and the smell is shocking.'

The Health Officer was sympathetic but saw no difficulty.

'Surely it would be easy to open a window and let in some air.'

'Open the window, he says! Sure what about my fifteen pigeons?'

Paudge, Liam and Francis were shifting furniture but when Paudge struggled with a huge oak wardrobe he noticed that Liam was missing.

'Francis, where's Liam? He should be helping us with this.'

'And sure so he is,' protested Francis, 'He's inside holding the clothes hangers in place.'

It has been said with some truth that an Englishman thinks and speaks; a Scot thinks twice before he speaks and an Irishman speaks before he thinks.

She didn't approve of smoking and when the newcomer got into the carriage and lit his pipe she couldn't help letting him know.

'Do you know that my husband is sixty years of age and he never puts a pipe in his mouth?'

'M'am, I'm sixty-five and never put it anywhere else.'

A favourite Irish joke of P. G. Wodehouse tells of the English butler who served an aristocratic family during the 'Troubles' in the Green Isle. When they came to the great oak door their leader told the butler: 'We've come to shoot his Lordship. Get him.'

Imperturbably he replied: 'He's not here, sir; perhaps you could call again.'

The I.R.A. men burst into the house and set fire to everything that could burn. As they rushed out afterwards the butler was still standing with quiet dignity. He bowed as they swept by.

'Gentlemen,' he called after them, 'may I tell his Lordship who called?'

'Did you hear that I'm engaged to an Irish lad?'
'Oh, really!'
'No, O'Reilly.'

They were an innocent honeymoon couple right from the heart of Connemara and they were shown to their hotel room. It had twin beds.

'Oh, Colum,' wailed the bride, 'why can't we have a room to ourselves.'

President Kennedy owed more than a little of his wit to his Irish blood. On one occasion a little boy asked him how he became a hero.

'I couldn't help it,' he replied; 'the Japanese sank my boat.'

The short-sighted Trinity professor was thrilled when his first shot brought down something in the distance.

'What,' he cried, 'is the name of the species I have successfully shot?'

'Well,' said his beater, 'between curses he says his name is Murphy.'

A Belfast newspaper once reported the launching of an aircraft carrier and recorded: 'The Duchess smashed the bottle against the bow and amid the applause of the crowd she slid on her greasy bottom into the sea.'

Read any good tombstones lately? Try this:

This monument is erected in memory of Tim O'Donovan who was accidentally stabbed as a token of affection by his loving wife.

They were making a match, but the farmer's son wasn't too happy.

'But, da,' he protested. 'The girl has a shockin' limp.'

'It's a wife you're marryin',' growled the father, 'not a bloody show jumper.'

'Excuse me, sir,' said the farm labourer to his boss, 'I've been watching the bull chase your wife around the meadow for the past hour.'

'You fool, why didn't you tell me before.'

'Why? Does she get tired quickly?'

16

'Father Cassidy, the church is on fire!'
'Holy smoke!'

Finlay was sent sprawling by the motor car. The anxious motorist looked down at him.

'Here,' he said, 'I'll give you five pounds and if you let me know your name and address I'll send you more.'

Finlay sat up on one elbow.

'Oh, and is it trying to knock me down on the instalment plan you are?'

The monastic background of Ireland has given a host of jokes to the world. This is a typical one:

Three hermits had been living at Clonmacnoise for four years when one of them spoke.

'That was a fine black horse that went by.'

Three years later one of the others said, 'It was a white horse.'

Ten years afterwards the third member had his say.

'If there's going to be bickering I won't stay.'

Women begin by resisting a man's advances and end by blocking his retreat.—OSCAR WILDE.

Mrs O'Grady was weary with the demands of her small son. When he came for his fifth apple it was too much.

'Look, Sean, you can't have another. The way you go on you'd think they grew on trees.'

The priest was gravely concerned with the moral state of Uinsinn.

'Uinsinn, do you entertain immoral thoughts about women?'

'Not a bit, Father. They entertain me.'

'What's he charged with?' asked the judge.

'Bigotry, Your Honour. He married three women.'

'Don't be absurd, Guard. That's not bigotry that's trigonometry.'

The first week they were married Mick gave his wife all his money and kept only five shillings for himself.

On the next payday she said to him: 'Mick, it must have been hard to manage on five shillings. I don't know how you did it.'

'You will,' he said grimly, 'it's your turn for the five bob this week.'

'If you feed hens different foods it will affect the eggs,' explained the agricultural adviser to the farmer.

'I know that,' replied Flaherty; 'a cousin of mine in America fed his hens sawdust and when the eggs were hatched six of the chickens had wooden legs and four of them were woodpeckers.'

The road was dark and the moon high as they drove slowly along a country road.

'Could you drive with one hand?' she asked in a soft sultry voice.

'Oh, yes . . . yes I could. Easily,' he stammered as his heart leaped to the call.

'All right. Here's an apple. Have a bite.'

—*Dublin Penny Journal*, 1833

Thomas Moore, the Irish poet, often told of a journey from Sandymount into Dublin. On the way the travellers passed the body of a highwayman who had died from a shot in the forehead.

An old woman looked down and shaking her head said: 'Well, thank God, it missed his eye.'

The doctor was amazed.

'Mr Rafter, your wife's baby weighs only fifteen ounces.'

Rafter waved a modest hand.

'What would you expect, Doctor? We're only married a fortnight.'

Mrs. Hennessy met an old school chum in Paris and decided to impress her.

'You know,' she sighed with an air of deprivation, 'we've been here a week and I haven't been to the Louvre yet.'

Her friend lifted a shocked eyebrow.

'Well, don't wait any more, see a doctor.'

They met after the new baby had been christened.

'What did you call her, Mam?'

'Hazel.'

'Are you daft! With an Irish saint's name for every day of the week, you have to call her after a nut.'

They were crossing O'Connell Bridge.
  'Hello, Casey, how are you?'
  'Not too bad, Mullarkey, but my name isn't Casey.'
  'Well mine isn't Mullarkey so it mustn't be either of us.'

He had been bitten by a mad dog but medical help arrived quickly.
  'Doctor McDermot,' he said, 'get me a sheet of paper.'
  'You're all right, man. You don't need to make a will'
  'I don't want to make a will. I want to write a list of all the people I'm going to bite.'

The Inspector spoke to the new Civic Guard.
  'Guard O'Shaughnessy, you'll be going on night duty soon and I hope you're prepared for it.'
  'Don't worry, Inspector. My mother is coming around with me until I settle down.'

The tinker whined outside the farmer's door.
  'Give us twopence for a bed, sir.'
  'Let me see it first.'

Two little girls were talking about religious knowledge.
  'I'm past Original Sin,' boasted the first one.
  'That's nothing,' answered the other. 'I'm beyond Redemption.'

The circus elephant was dead and the three men sat glumly and sad on the wagon outside his tent.
  'I know the elephant is a big loss,' said the clown, 'but why do you three take it so bad?'
  'We've got to dig the grave.'

There was the Cork farmer who won a large prize on a milking contest and told the reporters: 'I owe my success to udders.'

Mrs Mulligan brought her dear departed husband's photograph to the dealer.
  'Could you enlarge this?'
  'Certainly, madam.'

'And could you remove his hat?'

"We could touch it up for you—but which side was his hair parted?'

'Is it mad you are! Sure won't you see that when you take off his hat.'

The racehorse owner was annoyed with the running of his horse at the Curragh. He turned on the jockey.

'Flaherty, could you not have raced faster?'

'Of course I could, boss, but you know we're supposed to stay on the horses.'

Over the old gate of Bandon, Co. Cork the following slogan was carved in the past:

> *Turk, Jew or Atheist*
> *May enter here*
> *But not a Papist.*

Someone, probably a Papist, wrote a reply:

> *Who wrote it, wrote it well*
> *For the same is written,*
> *On the gates of Hell.*

The Irish Teachta Dala or M.P. heard that his wife had given birth to triplets. Instinctively he shouted: 'I demand a recount.'

After each drink Murphy took a frog from his pocket, put it on the bar counter and stared at it. Eventually the barman asked him what he was up to.

'You see,' said Murphy, 'so long as I can see one frog I'm sober. It's when I see two that I have to do something.'

'And what do you do?'

'I pick up the two of them, put them in my pocket and go home.'

Peadar woke up in a hospital bed and he knew that he was suffering from more than the normal hangover. Groaning with pain, he turned over to find his faithful friend Terence beside the bed.

'What happened to me, Terence?'

'You went up on the roof of "The Silver Swan" and bet you could jump off and fly over the city.'

'Why didn't you stop me?' groaned Peadar.

'Sure I had a ten bob bet on you.'

An Irish joke that was to have many American variants in gangster jokes originated in the lawless days of the last century when the assassination of landlords was a national sport.

"Well, they certainly killed his lordship. Twenty-five bullets in him, no less. Have they buried him?'

'Buried him is it? They've sent him to be smelted.'

Dublin's Zoo is famous for the lions it breeds but even the most contented beasts will stray. Two of them escaped and fled into the city. They met after several nights and while one was worn and starving the other was sleek and fat.

'I'm feeling awful,' said the starved one; 'I haven't eaten for days.'

The fat one sympathised.

'Come on with me,' he said, 'I'm hiding in Government Building and I eat a Civil Servant every day.'

'Isn't it dangerous?'

'Not a bit. They never miss them.'

A story which has gone the rounds for the past hundred years or so is a classic Irish joke which must be repeated. Two men were waiting for the local landlord to pass by so that they could ventilate his hide with buckshot. He was a long time in coming and an awful thought occurred to Mick.

'Paddy,' he said, 'say a prayer that nothing's happened to the poor man.'

His cigar, his suit and everything about him proclaimed prosperity as he entered a bar in a small town in County Mayo.

'Well, well,' he said, 'fifteen years ago I left and all I had was five shillings that John Conroy loaned me. Ah, I suppose that poor John has passed on by now and how I wish I could meet him . . .'

'Here I am . . . here I am. I'm still living here,' said John eagerly as he pushed his way forward.

'I'm glad to see you, John, and I was going to ask if you wouldn't mind lending me fifteen bob to make it the even pound I owe you.'

The two drunks stopped under the O'Connell Monument and Shane held out his cupped hands.

'Guesh whash I have?'

'Yoush gotta a elephant.'

'No, 'snoshanelephant. Guesh again.'

'Ish anostrich.'

'Guesh again.'

'Ish a horse.'

'Yesh, but wha' colour?'

21

The two little girls were in a restaurant and before the meal, little Denise prepared to bless herself. Her sister nudged her.

'You don't have to say grace, Denise. We're paying for this.'

'What were you saying to that man just now?'

'He wanted to give me the winner of the Irish Grand National.'

'And would you not take it?'

'Of course not. Sure we've only a very small garden.'

'I'm going up to the Phoenix Park to tell something to my brother in the Three Day Bicycle Race.'

'Heavens, don't you know that ended two days ago?'

'I do. That's what I want to tell me brother.'

Shaun was the most popular man in Co. Tipperary and when he said he might go to Rome to see His Holiness the Pope everyone encouraged him.

'Shaun,' said the parish priest, 'bring us back an account of all you see.'

When Shaun arrived at the airport he found a priest waiting for him.

'Shaun,' the priest said, 'I have someone to meet you here.'

He whispered the names of two of Ireland's leading bishops and Shaun went to meet them.

'Shaun,' they said, 'tell His Holiness that we send him our best wishes through you and tell him your visit has our full approval.'

When Shaun arrived in Rome he was met by a big car and whisked away to meet an important cardinal.

'I will bring you, Shaun,' said the cardinal, 'to His Holiness, the Pope, and he's looking forward to meeting you.'

When Shaun met His Holiness he was greeted warmly.

'Shaun,' said His Holiness, 'I'm going to bless the crowd in St. Peter's Square and will you come out on the balcony with me.'

As the crowd cheered a short-sighted American bishop looked up.

'I can recognise Shaun,' he said, 'but who's the man that's talking?'

Then there was the Irish shopkeeper who said his eggs were so fresh the hens hadn't missed them.

James O'Neill, the father of the Irish-American playwright Eugene O'Neill, was a man who displayed Irish commonsense. At at early age he gave Eugene some solid advice: 'Nothing I say, son, will keep you from drinking. Nothing I say will keep you from cards and dice.

You'll go after the girls as well, no matter what I think. But with women, boy, keep this thought of your father in mind—one at a time, one at a time.'

The little housewife was waiting for confession and two acrobats from a visiting circus went in ahead of her. The first when he emerged, purged of his sins, turned six double somersaults. The second was also in an elated state; when he came out he walked on his hands for five or six yards. When the timid housewife's turn came she pleaded in alarm: 'Oh, Father Duff, before I tell you about myself and the plumber's mate promise me you won't give me a penance like the last two.'

'My people,' boasted McCourt, 'can trace their ancestors back to the Kings of Tara.'
    'I suppose they were in the Ark with Noah as well.'
    'Not at all. They had their own boat.'

The priest was instructing the class in religious knowledge. 'Like the fat and lean in bacon,' he said, 'some people are good and some are bad. Now, Eileen, if you were bacon, what would you be?'
    'Streaky, Father.'

'Come over, Macauley, we've a party,' said Carthy on the phone.
    'I can't go. We have a bad case of laryngitis here.'
    'Heck, bring it over—we'll drink anything.'

'Oh, Mrs Carey, my husband went out six months ago for a loaf of bread and never came back. What should I do?'
    'Well, since you ask me I'd say not to wait any more. Send one of the children down for another one.'

The smugglers on the border between Northern Ireland and the Republic of Ireland are usually slick and fast. One pig smuggler who was caught red-handed explained afterwards: 'The sow squealed on us.'

Mr Clarke stared at the young suitor with surprise.
    'You want to marry my daughter? Why, she's only a girl.'
    'I know, sir. That's why.'

The reporters as usual were gathered around the centenarian.
    'To what, Mr Grogan, do you attribute your great age.'

'The Irish climate.'
'You mean it's healthy?'
'No, but t'would put years on you.'

If there are thirteen cows in a field you can always recognise the Irish bull. He'll be the one that's standing.

'Mr Corrigan, I'd like to have a day off to attend my mother-in-law's funeral.'
'So would I, Flynn, but she's an absolute picture of health.'

The bricklayer fell twenty feet from the scaffold on to a heap of rubble.
'Get him water . . . get him water . . .' shouted the foreman.
The bricklayer raised himself indignantly.
'And how far do you have to fall to get a drop of whiskey?'

'Tell me, Kieran, how long cows should be milked?'
'The same length as short ones, sir.'

The Belfast sales manager had a busy week in the country and on Saturday evening he was exhausted when he dropped into the local bar to have a quick one before going home.
'Give me something to pick me up,' he asked.
'Brandy? Vodka? Tullamore Dew? Bushmills?'
'No, no. I need something different.'
'Well,' said the barman with hesitation, 'the only thing that might do it would be our parish priest's special.'
'I'll try it,' said the sales manager and he had to admit that the first made him feel a new man while the second and third sent him home floating on air.
He was telling a friend about it, 'It was terrific,' he said, 'and the next morning I jumped out of bed and gave all the family their breakfasts, packed them into the car and took them to an early Mass. It was when we came out that the trouble started.'
'In what way?' asked his friend.
'Sure we're not Roman Catholics. We're Presbyterians.'

Then there was the keeper at the level crossing in Co. Kilkenny who kept the gates half open because he was half expecting a train.

The blind farmer was often taken for a walk in the fields by a kind neighbour. However kindly the neighbour might have been he was undoubtedly a coward. When a bull charged towards them one day he abandoned the blind man.

The bull, puzzled by a lack of fear, nudged the farmer in the back. He turned very quickly, caught the bull by the horns and threw it to the ground with a bump that left it breathless.

'Aidan,' said the neighbour, 'I never knew you were so strong.'

'Faith, and if I could have got that fella off the handlebars of the bicycle I'd have thrashed him properly.'

'Isn't it a pity that the Maguires have no children, Mr Flynn?'

'It is indeed, but I hear that sterility is hereditary on both sides of their family.'

The English buyer looked dubiously at the steeplechaser offered to him.

'Are you sure it's a good jumper?' he asked.

'Good jumper, is it . . . why, we have to give notice to air traffic control when he's running.'

And we should not forget the Irishman who said he would rather die than be buried in a Protestant cemetery.

The drunk staggered into his car and fumbled with the keys while a big Civic Guard—an Irish policeman—stared across at him. Finally he went over and spoke to the driver.

'You're not seriously thinking of driving that car the way you are.'

'Look, oul son, I'm in no fit condition to walk.'

If you think there are only two sexes take note of the little lad who waited outside a school as small girls and small boys trooped in.

'Why don't you go in with the boys?' asked a sympathetic passer-by.

'I'm not a boy,' grumbled the small one, 'I'm a Mixed Infant.'

It was a favourite story of Brendan Behan and it was supposed to have happened in a Dublin municipal housing scheme some years ago. One house had been the centre of various infections and the local doctor decided to call and see for himself what was wrong. The household, he noted, could be more easily ploughed than washed; they were so coated with Mother Earth.

'Do you,' he asked the woman who came to the door, 'have a bath in the house?'

'We do, doctor,' she sniffed, 'but thank God we haven't had to use it for the past ten years.'

The Co. Cork hurler arrived at the gates of Heaven and the shadowy figure guarding the entrance had a word to say.

'Is there anything you have done that might keep you from entering Paradise?'

'Well, now you see, sir,' said the embarrassed hurler, 'I played for St. Finbarr's in Cork and in the last game I missed the ball with my stick and I kicked it into the goal and we won, see. And St. Finbarr's shouldn't have got the match, see.'

'Pass within!' said the shadowy figure.

'But, St. Peter, I don't think I should.'

'I am not St. Peter. He is off duty, so pass within.'

'Well, and who are you then?'

'St. Finbarr.'

They rescued Shamus when he was on the brink of drowning and gave him the kiss of life and pumped him as dry as they could. When he was somewhat recovered they brought him a noble glass of smooth, rich Irish whiskey.

He looked at the drink and then asked reverently: 'Turn me over again, lads, and get more water out first.'

As elsewhere there are some people in Ireland who look on insurance as a source of income rather than protection. It happened in Limerick one time.

'Clancy, my poor fella, I'm powerful sorry to hear about your shop being burned down last Tuesday.'

'Shut up will you . . . that's next Tuesday.'

Memory, they say in Ireland, is the thing a man forgets with when he owes anyone money.

The tourist was in a great hurry but the only transport available to take him to the railway station was an old Irish sidecar. As they moved slowly along the tourist grew frantic.

'Hit that damn horse in a place he'll feel.'

'Peace,' said the driver; 'I've hit everywhere it hurts except the most important and I'm saving that for the big hill.'

He was returning from London after a year in exile. His two brothers were at the crossroads to meet him and the first thing he noticed was their long beards.

'Mick . . . Colum! What did you grow beards for at all?'
Colum shuffled angrily.
'Sure what did you expect? Didn't you take the bloody razor blade with you?'

Poteen is an Irish illegal brew that can burn holes in steel plate. Oisin Flaherty after a pint of it saw so many animals in his room that he put a sign on his house 'Flaherty's Zoo'. The local Garda sergeant went to reason with him and was no sooner in than he was offered a glass of the Mountain Dew, as it is called. When he staggered out thirty minutes later he raised his hand for silence.
'Ish all right, men. The worst's over. He sold me half the elephants.'

'Was your father very shy, Ronan?'
'Shy? My mother told me that if he hadn't been so shy I'd be five years older now.'

Casey had come to comfort the last hours of his friend Burke.
'Casey, I want four black horses to pull the hearse,' instructed Burke.
'Don't be so old-fashioned,' scoffed Casey; 'You should have a motor hearse.'
'All right, but make sure that I have six wreaths of fresh flowers.'
'Plastic ones are better, Burke, and they last longer.'
'Maybe you're right, but see that there's a granite tombstone on the grave . . .'
'Marble is better, Burke, and . . .'
The corpse-to-be sat up indignantly.
'Look, Casey,' he said, 'whose funeral is this? Yours or mine?'

Long courtships are notorious in Ireland and after a fifteen-year-courtship Shaun went to see the father of his girl.
'I've been going with your daughter now, Mr Cummisky, for fifteen years.'
'You have indeed, Shaun.'
'D'ye think there'd be any objection if I married her?'
'None at all, Shaun,' said the relieved father. 'For a moment there I thought you were going to ask for a pension.'

Swift wrote many gusty poems as for instance *The True English Dean*. It tells of a case of 1730 in which a Dean of Ferns was charged with rape. Its lively humour may be judged by this stanza:

The dean he was vexed that his whores were so willing
He longed for the girl that would struggle and squall:
He ravished her fairly and saved a good shilling
But here was to pay the devil and all.
His troubles and sorrows now come in a heap
And hanged he must be for committing a rape.

An Irish political prisoner escaped from jail by digging a tunnel that emerged in a school playground. As he emerged to the open air he couldn't help shouting at a small girl, 'I'm free . . . I'm free.'

'That's nothing,' she said scornfully; 'I'm four.'

The Football and Hurling Finals are national events that bring close on 100,000 people to the great sports stadium in Dublin, Croke Park. Overcrowding is not uncommon; both O'Brien and Cosgrove were knocked down. As they lay under the feet of the fans Cosgrove started to cheer.

'What are you cheering for?' gasped O'Brien as he tried to avoid the feet around him.

'We've scored a goal,' said Cosgrove, 'Donegan is jumping up and down on my face with joy.'

On another occasion two fans had a little dispute.

'Who are you pushing?'

'I don't know. What's your name?'

The tinker was in court charged with stealing an overcoat.

'My man,' said the District Justice, 'three years ago you were before me charged also with stealing an overcoat.'

'Of course,' said the tinker. 'How long do you think overcoats last?'

And there was that Dublin householder who rushed the decoration of his home so that he'd have it finished before the pot of paint ran out.

They were completely drunk but when they saw the black crêpe on the door they decided to go in and show respect for the dead.

They tiptoed into a darkened room lit only by two candles on a grand piano. Heads down, they went over and knelt beside it, said a prayer and tiptoed out again.

As they staggered away Aongus shook his head at Fergus.

'I'll tell you one thing, Fergus. . . .'

'Whash that?'

'That corpse had the finest set of teeth I ever saw.'

Many English students come to Trinity College in Dublin and on one occasion a harassed professor was interviewing one of them.

'And, Bassett-Claghorne, do you know anything about ethics?'

'No, thir. I'm from Thuththex.'

A classical Belfast joke tells of a new policeman who found a dead horse in Chichester Street, Belfast.

'How do you spell Chichester?' he asked some of the people around him; but no one knew.

'All right, then. Give me a wee hand to pull the animal into Mary Street.'

Kennedy came along the road to find his friend Finnegan lying in the ditch where the playful impact of a ten-ton lorry had landed him. As he lay on his back groaning and moaning the rain came pouring down and the lightning flashed about him.

'Kennedy, Kennedy—get me a rabbi. Get me a rabbi.'

'Are you mad, Finnegan? Sure you're a Roman Catholic and what would you want a rabbi for?'

The victim opened his eyes reproachfully: 'Arrah, Kennedy, you wouldn't think of asking a priest to come out on a night like that.'

Health, they'll assure you in parts of Ireland, is a wonderful thing to have especially when you're sick.

The little boy had been sitting close to the confession box door for a long time before Father Casey noticed him.

'Have you been listening to confessions all evening?' thundered the priest.

'Oh, no, Father. I'm only here since the woman who slept with the sailor came out.'

'And why, Johnny, do you think your daddy is kind to animals?'

'Well he told us, teacher, that he'd like to kill the man who scratches horses.'

On the rough trip to the Aran Islands the tourist lay over the rail and suffered.

'Cheer up, mo cairde,' said a member of the crew, 'sure no one ever died of sea sickness yet.'

'Ah, sure,' gasped the victim, 'isn't it the hope of dying that keeps me alive.'

They had been in jail for some years and Hugh's only pleasure was to go over the agricultural price lists in the papers each week.

After a long and careful calculation one evening he turned to Rory with awe in his voice.

'By the holy saints of Clonmacnoise—if we were only stealing turkeys in Co. Cavan these days we'd be making fifty pounds a week.'

She was only a poteen maker's daughter but he loved her still.

At one period of the eighteenth century there was an Irish hang-man in London. On one occasion he was given an expensive present by the condemned man just before the execution.

'Long life to your honour,' he cried delightedly as he pulled the bolt.

He walked into Flavin's Bar and asked for a glass of water. He drank it and walked out. The next day he was in again and he asked for a glass of water, drank it and was getting ready to go.

'Here,' complained the barman, 'you come in here, ask for a glass of water; drink it and then walk out . . .'

'What do you want me to do . . . stagger?'

The two tinkers were making camp for the night.

'Yerra, man, what do you want with that length of drainpipe you're carrying?'

' 'Tis I'm going to use it for a pillow.'

'Sure t'would be as hard as the hob of hell.'

'Is it a fool you take me for? I'm going to stuff it with straw first.'

At the seed shop the farmers were complaining about the devastation caused by leather-jackets.

'All my crop was destroyed,' groaned one.

'So was mine.'

The storekeeper shook his head.

'It's going to be worse, far worse. The damn creatures were in here last night and wanted to know who planted potatoes last spring.'

He wasn't an expert stick-up man, but he tried.

'Stick up your hands or else,' he warned.

'Or else what?'

'Don't mix me up now—this is my first job.'

'Hey, Dermot, you look very tired.'
'Don't talk. I couldn't sleep last night I was dreaming that much.'

The mustard plaster is a remedy that has never been popular in Ireland. The fact that is is considered to be an English treatment may have something to do with it. In any event, Mrs Carey was recommended to try it by a returned exile. When they met again an enquiry was inevitable.
"Well, Mrs Carey. Did you try the mustard plaster on your husband?'
'Indeed I did, but he wouldn't have it. Even when I made it into sandwiches he wouldn't eat it.'

The Boston taxi driver backed into the stationary fruit stall and in a second he had a cop beside him.
'Name?'
'Brendan O'Connor.'
'Same as mine. Where are you from?'
'Co. Leitrim.'
'Same as me. . . .'
The policeman paused with his pen in the air.
'Hold on a moment and I'll come back and talk about the old county. I want to say something to this fella that ran into the back of your cab.'

'Please, Mister, will you ring that doorbell for me?'
The gentleman obliged with a beaming smile.
'Now, sonny, what else should I do?'
'Run like hell.'

It was a terrible mine disaster and Tadgh was one of the few survivors.
'Tell me about what's happening,' he gasped in hospital.
'It's terrible,' said the nurse. 'Eighty Englishmen killed and your friend Rafferty.'
'Oh,' moaned Tadgh. 'Isn't it awful about poor Rafferty.'

If one could only teach the English how to talk and the Irish to listen, life might be civilised.—OSCAR WILDE.

The Irish Fleadh Ceoil is a Mardi Gras with a brogue. It can be rough sometimes and on one occasion the crowd moved in on a ballad singer with a menacing air.
'Get the illegitimate! Bury the so-and-so!'
'Wait,' called an anxious voice above the din, 'don't waste him. Kill a fiddler as well.'

31

From poverty his business instincts had enabled him to become one of the wealthiest men in Ireland. When he arrived at a Galway hotel in the middle of a blazing June day the manager was a little confused to see the skis, snowshoes, toboggans and winter sports equipment that was brought in.

'Pardon me, sir,' he apologised, 'but you must know we have no snow in Galway at this time of the year.'

The tycoon waved his hand.

'Don't you be bothering about it,' he said, 'I'm having the snow sent on with my heavy baggage.'

The small man watched nervously as the muscular hotel guest struggled into an overcoat.

'Excuse me,' he said, 'are you Aidan O'Gorman?'

'No,' said the big man. 'Why did you ask?'

Well that's Aidan O'Gorman's overcoat you're putting on.'

Who's Aidan O'Gorman?'

'Me.'

Clusky's barns were on fire and eventually the local fire brigade pulled in.

One of the more enthusiastic members jumped off the engine and started to rig up the pump and the hose.

'Hold on . . . hold on,' advised the brigade captain, 'let the fire burn up a bit bright so we can see what we're doing.'

The Kerryman had a remarkable range of general knowledge and the visitor asked him how he knew so much.

'This is the way of it,' he said; 'I picked up a bit here and I picked up a bit there and I was too lazy to forget it.'

Then there was the little boy who wanted his hair cut the same way as his Daddy's With the hole in the top for his head to come through.

Pat was not accustomed to the thin bread of his London boarding-house.

'Did you cut them yourself?' he asked the landlady pointing to the heap of slices.

"I did, Pat," she answered.

"All right then, I'll shuffle and deal.'

It was three o'clock in the morning when the telephone rang beside the bed of O'Gorman, the publican.

'Mr O'Gorman,' said the alcohol-saturated voice of Cleary, 'what time do you open in the morning?'

'Ten o'clock, Cleary,' snapped O'Gorman and hung up.

At seven o'clock the phone rang and it was Cleary again, 'Wash time dush you open?'

'Ten o'clock but you're not going to be let in.'

'I'sh don't want to get in. I want to gesh out . . .'

Then there was the Spiddal man with two wooden legs whose house went on fire. He was burnt to the ground.

Murray was muttering to himself with fiendish glee when his friend Hyland asked him what it was all about.

'I'll tell you, Hyland. That amadan O'Rourke keeps slapping me on the back. Well, I've put a stick of dynamite under my coat and this time he'll blow his arm off.'

The late President Kennedy had a nice rural wit that may have come from his Irish ancestry. Addressing a Californian crowd on one occasion he said: 'I appreciate your generous hospitality. As the cow said to a farmer once, "Thank you for a warm hand on a cold morning." '

An Irishman was caught by cannibals on one occasion, and finding that his blood was almost pure alcohol they drew off a pint each day for the chief. He got fed up in the end with this and put his foot down: 'Ate me if you want to, you hungry gombeen men, but stop sticking me for the drinks.'

An Englishman thinks seated; a Frenchman, standing; an American, pacing; and an Irishman, afterward.—AUSTIN O'MALLEY.

The Civic Guard watched her as she backed into one car with a loud bang; drove out and scraped another with a metallic shriek and went back in again to hit a motor-cycle with a thump.

Slowly he strolled over and stood beside her, scratching his head.

'Excuse me, missus,' he asked, 'but do you always park by ear?'

Ernest Blythe, politician and Abbey Theatre director, recorded another instance of stout defiance of Roman Catholic fasting laws by an Orangeman. His family employed a loyal, Protestant workman who made it a solemn rule never to eat fish on Fridays.

Although they were amateurs, the Wexford farmer took a chance and lent them two guns and three dogs. Half-an-hour later they were back.

'What do you want?' he asked. 'More ammunition?'

'Oh, no. More dogs.'

The old lady offered the bus conductor a five-pound note.

'Look, missus, is that all you have?'

'Oh, no,' she answered brightly, 'I've got fifteen-pounds-seven-and-six in my post office account.'

'What a lovely coloured cow.'

'It's a Jersey.'

'Is it? I thought it was its skin.'

On one occasion it was proposed in New York that a gondola should be introduced to Central Park. An Irish councillor supported the idea with enthusiasm.

'Let's get two gondolas,' he said. 'A male and a female.'

Moore Street in Dublin is famous for its street dealers, most of whom have tongues that would file stainless steel.

'I want to complain about the bananas you sold me yesterday. They were awful hard to skin.'

The dealer drew herself up.

'Look, mam, what do you want at the price? Zip fasteners?'

The Coventry landlady gave her new Irish lodger little else except rabbit pie for a whole week.

He was sick in the end.

'Terence,' said she, 'will I get a doctor?'

'Oh, no,' he groaned, 'see if you can borrow a ferret.'

The two tinkers had been walking all day along the Connemara roads. Wearily they came to a signpost. One examined it.

'How far is it to Clifden?'

'Only ten miles . . .'

'That's good. Sure it will be only five miles each.

This Irish joke was, in its original form,told by the Edgeworth's about 150 years ago in their *Essay on Irish Bulls*.

34

If all the world's economists, quipped George Bernard Shaw, were laid end to end they wouldn't even reach a conclusion.

The two mercenary soldiers were trudging through a nasty patch of jungle.

'And you tell me, Murphy, you joined up because of a girl in Ireland. Why don't you forget her?'

'Forget her? How can I forget a girl with a name like Gobnait ni Mhathghamhna?'

—'TILL' CARTOON IN DUBLIN OPINION.

In Ireland they still have match-making and it sometimes happens that the bride and bridegroom see little of each other before the wedding.

At one rural event the priest turned to the bride at the end of the ceremony.

'Now,' he said, 'here is your very own husband.'

Blushing, she held out her hand.

'I'm pleased to make your acquaintance, sir,' she whispered modestly.

The Uileann Pipe is a fearsome and unusual Irish musical instrument. The player has a bellows under his arm which he moves in and out to fill the bag. Roughly speaking, you would imagine he was wrestling with an octopus in its last death agonies.

The English visitor had listened with fascination to a performance on one of them.

'I say,' he asked the player, 'would you mind playing *The Rose of Tralee* for me?'

'Again?' asked the indignant musician.

On an Irish radio show for children the following dialogue is supposed to have taken place.

'And you tell me that your father's horse fell into a hole. And did your Daddy shoot the horse in the head?' asked the compère.

'Oh, no, sir. He shot the horse in the hole.'

The farmer's wife told Brigid, the family servant, that five shillings would be deducted from her wages if the family had to cook their breakfast themselves. A few mornings later Brigid staggered down long after the day had started.

'Brigid, we had to get our own breakfast again.'

'Well, sure amn't I payin' you for it?'

35

The Irish policeman was doing his best to stop a suicide from jumping off a New York skyscraper.

'Think of your sweetheart,' he shouted at the man.

'I haven't got one,' came the reply.

'Think of your father and mother,' pleaded the cop.

'I'm an orphan,' wailed the suicide.

'Think of the saints of Ireland,' begged the Law.

'Why should I? I'm English.'

'Jump, you bastard, jump.'

The farmer and his son were both lazy. As they sprawled in their chairs one day the father said:

'Paudeen, go out and see if it's raining.'

'Ah sure, can't you call in the dog and see if he's wet?'

J. P. Mahaffy, the Irish wit and scholar, was once involved in a tedious argument on the social inequalities of women.

'After all, Mahaffy, what is the difference between you and a woman?'

'I cannot conceive,' was the suave reply.

It was the first time she had left West Cork to travel by train. The journey to Dublin had been under way for two hours when looking around she reached up with the handle of her umbrella and pulled the communication cord.

When the train stopped an excited train guard entered the carriage.

'You pulled the communication cord,' he said to her; 'what do you want?'

'Would you kindly bring me a bottle of lemonade, sir, and a package of plain biscuits.'

Paddy had a rough time with a tax inspector and couldn't make much headway. Finally with a sigh of resignation he suggested, 'Look, why don't you keep the income and give me the tax.'

It was almost finishing time at the quarry when the dynamite went off and Clancy sailed high into the air.

'I'm not waiting any more for Clancy,' said the foreman after a while as he prepared to go home, 'but when he comes down tell him he's not getting overtime for the past hour-and-a-half.'

The London visitor wanted to return to the Co. Cavan farm again for a holiday but he wrote to say that he had been annoyed by the pigs on his first holiday. The farmer rushed to reply: 'Don't worry at all. We haven't had a pig since you were here yourself.'

O'Hara fell from the scaffold and dropped two storeys. They gathered around him and the foreman asked: 'Did the fall hurt you, Peadar?'

The victim felt his aching bones.

'It wasn't the fall hurt me. T'was the sudden stop.'

'And have you made your will, Shamuseen?'

'Indeed I have. All of me fortune goes to the doctor that saves me life.'

It was a lonely part of Connemara; a place of small wealth and low population. The tourist stopped beside a workman on the road and asked a few questions.

'And what occupation have you?' he asked, to keep the conversation going.

'Me, is it?' answered the man; 'why I'm a piano tuner.'

The tourist was astonished.

'I hardly imagined there would be enough pianos in this district to keep you busy.'

'And who, might I ask,' answered the man, 'would keep the telegraph wires tightened if I wasn't around?'

To quote Sir Boyle Roche: 'Happy are the parents that have no children.'

The new recruit from Belfast was being fooled by others in his company.

'Come on, Joe, Climb up the searchlight for us.'

Joe chuckled.

'Is it a fool of a man you take me for. I know that trick.'

'What trick?'

'When I'd be half way up the light—you'd switch it off.'

'What sort of a builder is Cassidy?'

'Well, he has only one man working for him but he'd send in an estimate for the repair of the Great Wall of China.'—*Dublin Opionion.*

The farmer was giving his last instructions to the lawyer.

'. . . and put Paddy down for £2,000. Put Shane down for £3,000 and see that another £3,000 goes to Liam . . .'

'Just a moment, Mr Carey,' whispered the puzzled lawyer, 'where is all this money to come from?'

'To hell with them,' muttered Carey, 'let them work for it the way I had to . . .'

She noticed that he was buying his second cinema ticket although he had been at the box-office a short time before. It was, however, when he came back a third time that she said something.

'This is the third ticket you've bought, sir.'

'I know . . . I know. There's a big fella inside the door there and he keeps tearing them up on me.'

She followed her husband to the public-house.

'How can you come here,' she said, taking a sip of his pint of stout, 'and drink that awful stuff?'

'Now!' he cried, 'And you always said I was just out enjoying myself.'

'When we got to the Cliffs of Moher my husband's face fell almost 300 feet,' sighed Mrs. Dermody.

'Was he disappointed?' asked her neighbour.

'Not at all. He slipped.'

'Mary,' complained the mistress to her new maid from the country, 'I can write my name on the dust on the piano.'

'Oh, Mam, isn't it wonderful to have the education,' marvelled Mary.

Brendan Behan told the story of how he got a job in London with a street repair gang. The first job he went to they were down in a hole singing *Happy Birthday* around the foreman.

'Is it the foreman's birthday?' asked Brendan.

'No, Brendan. It's the third anniversary of the hole.'

> *On an upright Judge*
> *In church your grandsire cut his throat;*
> *To do the job too long he tarried;*
> *He should have had my hearty vote*
> *To cut his throat before he married.*
> —DEAN SWIFT.

Mrs Mulligan was delighted with the letter from her son who had emigrated to London.

'He has a great job,' she boasted to her neighbours. 'The best. He's working in a crematorium burning Englishmen and getting paid for it.'

The gillie was tired of the amateur fisherman as they drifted amongst the glorious islands of Lough Corrib. At last when his eager companion caught a small salmon and wound it frantically to the tip of the rod he could put up no more with the wild appeals about what should be done next.

'If you don't mind me suggesting it, sir,' he muttered sarcastically, 'I think you should climb up the rod and gaff him yourself.'

She who hesitates is won.—OSCAR WILDE.

A worried defendant once asked an Irish judge what was the maximum penalty for bigamy.

'Two mothers-in-law,' was the suave reply.

'How is your son the doctor doing in Dublin, Mrs Lenihan?' asked the curious neighbour.

'Grand, to tell you the living truth. He's making so much money that he doesn't have to operate on every patient now.'

A farmer had enjoyed a sunny holiday at Lisdoonvarna and with that economy that marks the Irish farming community, he dropped dead as soon as time came to pay his bill.

A driver whose breath would burst a breathalyser drove his car right into an old cottage on the Cork Road. As he drew up neatly beside the fireplace he leaned out and questioned the old lady sitting in the armchair.

'Shay, ish this the road to Dublin?'

Timidly she shook her head.

'No, sir, you'll have to turn right over there by the piano and keep straight on when you pass the scullery table.'

It was the old man's 105th birthday and all the reporters of Co. Mayo gathered around with the same old question: 'How do you account for your long life?'

'Vitamin pills,' the old man cackled.

'Vitamin pills?' they cried.

'Yus,' mumbled the ancient one. 'I haven't missed them for a day since I turned the century.'

Flannery was boasting about his cousin in America who was so big when he died that they couldn't get a coffin to fit him.

'Wasn't that extraordinary?' he asked.

Cummins was not impressed.

'Flannery,' he said, 'if they let the air out of your cousin they could have buried him in a matchbox.'

'Would you buy a raffle ticket for a poor widow?'

'Deed I won't. What would I do with her if I won?'

The American tourist had been complaining a great deal about the food.

'Here,' he said to the waitress, holding out a piece of meat for inspection, 'do you call that pig?'

'Which end of the fork, sir?' she asked sweetly.

Liam was dozing on the bridge when the interviewer came to see him.

'Look, I've been told that you drink fifty-seven cups of tea each day. Is that correct?'

'Oh, that's right,' yawned Liam.

'Doesn't it keep you awake?' asked the interviewer.

'Well, it helps'

There are still parts of Ireland where the train service is not as good as it should be. On one occasion a tourist complained bitterly of the slowness of the train.

'Why,' asked the harassed conductor, 'don't you get off and walk?'

'Because I'm not in that big of a hurry.'

The golf course was haunted by a malicious leprechaun who exploited the desperate ambitions of the poorer players. He slipped up beside one unfortunate man who was ploughing the fairway in a club competition.

'Look,' he said, 'if you agree never to court a woman, flirt with a girl or marry, I'll help you win.'

'Done,' shouted the young golfer with the desperate abandon of his breed.

When the golfer was in the clubhouse changing and receiving the congratulations of the members the leprechaun popped up on the shelf of the locker.

'Hey,' said the little elf, 'I have to have your name for my records. What is it?'

'Father Murphy,' grinned the golfer as he adjusted his Roman collar.

Heat,' explained Rafferty to his friend Mulligan, 'makes things expand and cold makes them contract.'

Mulligan laughed with a sneer.

' 'Tis mad you are entirely. Mad,' he said. 'Who ever heard the like of that.'

'Well,' replied Rafferty, 'how do you account for the longer days in summer and the short ones in the winter?'

Large families are very common in Ireland but Mrs Finnegan's was different. As she herded them into a cinema she explained to the cashier which of them was entitled to half-price.

'Those two,' said Mrs Finnegan, 'are under ten, those two are under eleven, those two are under twelve, those two are under thirteen and the older twins won't be fourteen until next week.'

'In the name of St. Agnes, the virgin martyr,' said the dazed cashier as she punched the tickets, 'do you and your husband have twins every time?'

'Not at all,' blushed Mrs. Finnegan, 'sure lots and lots of times we don't have any children at all.'

He had the sort of face that, once seen, never remembered.—OSCAR WILDE.

When George Moore, the Irish author, was eighty, he was asked how he had managed to have such a long life. 'I believe,' said Moore, 'that it is due to the fact that I never smoked, drank or touched a girl—until I was ten years of age.'

Prosperity is coming to the Irish farmer in many ways, although he would be the last to admit it. When the harvest is bad he complains of poor crops and when it's good he moans about the cost of fertilising the ground again. Mary and John decided to buy a car after many years and they went into the dealer to pay for it. John threw two socks on the counter.

'There you are,' he said, 'there's £500 in one pound notes in these.'

The salesman opened them.

'But, Mr O'Shaughnessy, these are all five pound notes.'

John turned to his wife: 'You dirty old idiot, I knew you'd bring the wrong socks.'

Paddy strayed into a rather sleazy nightclub in London where the one big attraction was the strip dancer who performed in a cage with a lion. In the finale when she was down to her last sequin the moth-eaten lion placed its paws on her shoulders and licked her face.

'Well, Paddy,' said the club manager, 'could you do better than that?
'Get that lion out of it, sir, and I'll have a try.'

Then there was the old lady who thought her horse was certain to win the Irish Derby because the bookie told her it would start at twenty to one and the race didn't begin until a quarter past.

Turlough took his lantern and made his way across the bog to the shebeen where the poteen was being distributed. It was a good evening but in the morning there was a loud knocking at the door.
'What is it?' he called.
'Here's your oul' lantern and will you give me back me canary and cage.'

The greyhound had been a disaster at the track and the two owners were disgusted.
'Throw him in the canal,' said one.
'Don't waste time,' said the other, 'we'll just run away from him.'

The clerk at the Irish International Airways office had been patient as the fussy customer rejected each suggested tourist area.
'Can you not think of some other country?' asked the traveller.
'No, sir, I couldn't. Those are the only countries that have been discovered so far.'

It was his last confession and he didn't want to tell a lie.
'Oh, Father,' he told the priest who was attending him, 'my name is Patrick Murphy but I'm not Irish at all.'
'Don't worry,' consoled the priest, 'when you get to St. Peter, give him your name—and then keep your mouth shut.'

The Roman Catholic fast on Fridays has always been a target for opponents of the Church. Even Dean Swift in the eighteenth century had a crack at the subject:

> *Does any man of commonsense*
> *Think ham and eggs give God offence?*
> *Or that a herring has a charm*
> *The Almighty's anger to disarm.*
> *Wrapped in His majesty divine,*
> *D'you think he cares on what we dine?*

42

When she opened the door a forlorn tinker stood on the door-step.

'Please, me good woman, could you spare me a bit of creamy cake?'

She was shocked.

'Now, wouldn't bread be much better for you?'

He shuffled his feet: 'I know, mam. But today's me birthday.'

Two Canadians—one huge and the other very tiny—were cutting down a tree with a crosscut saw under the indignant eye of Seoirse. Finally he could stand it no longer as he watched them pull the saw backwards and forwards. He hit the biggest one a straight right to the chin.

'You big bully,' he yelled, 'give it to the little fella if he wants it.'

The old lady picked a winner almost every day of the week and the bookie was curious.

'How do you do it, Mrs Casey?'

'I stick a pin in the paper and that's how.'

'But you backed four today. How was that?'

'I couldn't find a pin so I used a fork.'

The honeymooners looked at the list of mealtimes in their hotel.

Breakfast 6.30 *a.m. to* 11.30 *a.m.*
Lunch   12.30 *p.m. to* 3.30 *p.m.*
Dinner   6.30 *p.m. to* 9.30 *p.m.*

'Kevin,' wailed the bride, 'sure we'll be kept in atin' so long we won't have time to go anywhere.'

It has been claimed that it is very difficult to produce a limerick about the city of Limerick. Gerry Gallivan, a major Irish playwright, has succeeded with this effort:

As two rustic cats went to Limerick
The brighter hick spoke to the dimmer 'ick;
'I know I can't fail,
    if I cut off my tail,
For this is the age of the gimmerick.'

The customer put five shillings on the bar counter and staggered away. Colum put it in his pocket and turned to find the accusing eye of the boss glaring at him.

'Would you believe it at all,' Colum said blandly, 'he leaves a five shilling tip and doesn't pay for his drink.'

They were drunk after the annual college dinner and wanted to leave the hotel.

'Look, son. Howdjwegetout?'

The porter pointed along the passage.

'Turn to the right at the next passage and go down two steps and you'll be in the main hall.'

They staggered on together; turned right and fell down the lift shaft to the basement.

As they sorted themselves out Paddy rolled over.

'Look, Tadgh. If that fella thinks I'm going down the other step, he's crazy.'

<hr/>

Dr Kelly wanted to console the patient and he assured him soothingly: 'My man, within six weeks of amputating your legs I'll have you on your feet again.'

<hr/>

The visitor thought he would like a little music and he stopped to query a passing peasant.

'Say, is there anyone around here that would sing *Galway Bay* for me if I gave them ten shillings?'

'Sing it! Why for ten bob they'd swim it.'

<hr/>

The happy-go-lucky Irish maid was about to serve her first dinner.

'And Nuala,' said the lady of the house, 'you must make absolutely sure that you serve from the left and take away from the right.'

'Lord, Ma'am, aren't you awful superstitious.'

<hr/>

The doctor was not very good and his lady patient seemed to have a bad cold. Nothing he gave her was any use and she was growing dissatisfied.

'Can you do nothing to cure me, Doctor?'

'I tell you what to do,' he replied. 'Go home and have a hot bath and without drying yourself stand in the nude where there is a strong draught.'

'Will that cure me?' she asked with surprise.

'No, but it'll give you pneumonia—and I can cure pneumonia.'

<hr/>

An Irish judge, infuriated by the noise and disturbance in the public gallery, ordered the court room to be cleared.

'All the blackguards that aren't lawyers will have to leave,' he cried.

<hr/>

He was a good lodger and Alf didn't want to get his Irish up too quickly but he couldn't tolerate it any longer.

'Look, Paddy, I don't wanna complain but will you flippin' well put down your boots a little quietly. Let's leave the ceiling up, mate.'

Paddy was contrite, but as he was going to bed he forgot and threw one boot down with a crash. Immediately he realised his mistake and he put the other down gently. He had been asleep for an hour or two when he was awakened by a pounding on his door. It was his landlord.

'For blinkin' Pete's sake, Paddy, throw down that other boot . . .'

Country feuds in Ireland can be almost Sicilian in their vendetta qualities. A parish priest, disgusted with the conduct of his flock, addressed them from the pulpit.

'You're at each other's throats all the time. 'Tis a great pity ye are not heathens and you might start acting like Christians.'

Flanagan, the railway porter, had a soft spot in his heart for lovers. When he saw the young couple holding hands and embarrassed by all the people on the platform he had a bright idea.

'Here,' he said to them, 'let ye slip under the last carriage there and you'll find a fine comfortable mat under it that I was lying on to clean the axles. Youll be snug, safe and private in there.'

They gratefully accepted his offer. It was late in the evening when he remembered them.

Shaking them by the shoulders he said: 'Come on, you'll have to go. The train left two hours ago and I have to shut the station now.'

Gaelic football is not a game for the gentle and the refined. In Co. Kerry it is played with particular zest.

'Remember,' said the captain of a team as they prepared for a match, 'if you can't kick the ball, leave the marks of your boots on the other team. Now, where's the ball?'

'Forget about the bloody ball,' said one enthusiastic player: 'Let's get on with the game.'

The Irish missionary was preaching to the African tribe.

'And I say to you that you must love your fellowmen!'

'Moolagumbi!' shrieked the natives.

'White man and black man must learn to co-operate.'

'Moolagumbi!' chanted the crowd.

The missionary told the chief how pleased he was with the reception.

'I am glad, O man of Ireland,' said the chief, 'but be careful as we pass my cattle that you do not step into the moolagumbi.'

Sign on Dublin fruit vendor's stall: 'God helps them that help themselves but God help those that get caught.'

45

One optimistic farmer in Co. Offaly gave hot water to his hens. He wanted them to lay boiled eggs.

Carson, the barrister and politician, asked a reluctant witness:
'Is it true, miss, that you are a prostitute?'
'That's my business,' was the indignant reply.
'I see. Well, please tell the court your hobbies.'

The Protestant football team was playing in Dublin and was leading by one goal. Suddenly the church bells of the city rang out for the Angelus. The referee stopped the game and the Roman Catholic players and spectators stood in contemplation. Immediately the game was resumed the Dublin team scored seven goals in quick succession, and won.

The dazed Protestant captain congratulated his opponent, 'We've been out-played, out-scored and out-manœuvred in our time but by the holy bones of King Billie's horse, this is the first time we've been out-prayed.'

Then there was the Irishman who was asked the difference between an explosion and a collision. 'In a collision,' he replied, 'there you are but in an explosion where are you?'

Michael and Tod were nailing up the side of a wooden bungalow. Tod noticed that Michael was examining the nails and throwing away every second or third.
'What's wrong with those nails?' he asked.
'Sure the heads are on the wrong end.'
'You straw-headed idiot, sure they're for the other side of the house.

Wealth may not bring happiness but it seems to bring a pleasant kind of misery.—*Dublin Opinion.*

He had been in a bad road smash and Fagan had him carried into the bar. The injured man opened his eyes and looked around.
'You've been in a bad smash,' said Fagan, 'and I had you brought in here to bring you to.'
'Very well,' groaned the victim, 'make both of them double whiskies.'

The stick-up man was the old-fashioned type. He put the gun in Willie Byrne's ribs and said: 'Your money or your life.'

'Take me life, sir,' cried Willie; 'I need the money.'

It was the end of a long friendship as Dara and Killian said good-bye.

'Dara, when I'm in Australia will you come to the pub and have two drinks, one for me and one for you in memory of old times.'

'I will too, Killian. And you'll do the same for me.'

'I will that, Dara.'

And so night after night Dara went through the ritual. One large Irish for himself and then another for Killian in Australia.

Came the day, however when he ordered only one drink. The barman was curious.

'If ye'll forgive me intrusion, Dara, why have you given up one of the drinks.'

'Simple, oul son, simple. I'm on the wagon now.'

The doctor was puzzled.

'I'm very sorry but I can't diagnose your trouble, Mahoney. I think it must be drink.'

'Don't worry about it, Dr Kelly; I'll come back when you're sober.'

Then there was Rafferty's attempt to drown his troubles in drink. He found they could swim.

Another Brendan Behan story told of a good Dublin street dealer—they often wear big black enveloping shawls—who came down the road with one breast bare.

'Hey,' Brendan shouted at her. 'Make yourself decent.'

Her eyes popped as she swung the shawl about her and then the penny dropped: 'Holy Joseph, I left the baby on the bus.'

'Harnett, do you plead guilty?'

'I couldn't say, your honour. I haven't heard the evidence yet.'

In Ireland a candidate for the Dail (the Irish Parliament) has to be willing to do many things. Calling on McCann, a small farmer, one enthusiastic office-seeker, found him milking a cow.

'Get up,' said the candidate. 'I'll do that for you while you're listening to me. By the way, has my opponent been near you yet?'

'He has,' said McCann; 'he's working the two teats on the other side at the moment.'

Doctors in Roscommon are busy men and he was a little absent-minded as he sat down to breakfast. His wife put her hands over his eyes and when he opened them there was a new pen in front of him.

'For our wedding anniversary, Padraig,' she smiled.

'Well, thanks,' he said with embarrassment, 'and when it's yours I must give you something.'

'Why am I cut ten shillings in my wages?' raged Byrne.

'You were paid ten shillings too much last week,' answered the foreman, 'but I didn't hear you complain about that.'

'Of course, I didn't,' said Byrne. 'Anyone can make one mistake but two in a row is a little too much.'

An Irish magician made a feature of sawing a woman in half. After his retirement a friend asked him what had happened to his assistant.

'She's living now in Belfast and Dublin,' he answered.

The Mexican bandits had captured Declan and several others. The first victim they hung over a cliff but the rope broke and he fell into the lake and swam away. Declan looked on with horror.

'For the love of Mike,' he pleaded, 'tie that knot properly. I can't swim.'

The whistle went for lunch on the London building site and the foreman noticed that O'Grady was limping badly as he went to the canteen.

'O'Grady, what's the matter with you?'

'Sure I have a nail in my boot.'

'Well, take it out.'

O'Grady looked at him in wide-eyed horror.

'Is it take it out in my own time you want me. D'ye think I'm mad?'

The salesman persuaded Mrs Casey that his ointment would clear up the warts on her husband's face. Two days later she was back looking for a refund.

'Did it not clear up his face?' asked the saleman.

'It did indeed. The warts are still there but his face is gone.'

In rural Ireland there are spare-time barbers who shave and cut hair only on market days. Pierce had survived a rather close shave, and, still shaking, he asked for a drink of water.

'What for, Pierce?'

'I want to see if my neck leaks.'

The foreman was tired looking at his street-digging crew.

'Come on,' he said, 'we'll do it a new way. Jump out of the trench when I tell you and jump in again when I tell you.'

They were doing this for a minute or so when Phelim got curious.

'Will ye tell us what the bloody hell you're up to?' he asked.

'I'll tell you,' growled the foreman, 'you take more dirt out on your feet than you do with a shovel.'

In England people actually try to be brilliant at breakfast. That is so dreadful of them! Only dull people are brilliant at breakfast.—OSCAR WILDE.

An Irishman was in the dock for drunkenness.

'Where did you get the money to buy all that whiskey?' asked the District Justice.

'My friend Haggis McTavish gave it to me.'

'Three months for perjury,' rapped the judge.

The Coventry landlady politely asked her new lodger from Clare if he'd like his eggs on toast. Equally polite and accommodating, he answered: 'Well, mam, if you haven't got a plate they'll do that way.'

The American had been fishing for two weeks at Ballinahinch without getting a bite. On the last day of his vacation he caught a small salmon.

'Turlough,' he said to his gillie as the fish was gaffed, 'that salmon cost me five hundred dollars.'

'Well now sir,' comforted Turlough, 'aren't you the lucky man you didn't catch two.'

The motorist was honest and when he hit the cock wandering on the road he stopped and went back to the cottage.

'I'm afraid I killed your cock, Madam, but I'd very much like to replace him.'

'Whatever you want,' said the sour-pussed farmer's wife. 'Go around the side there and you'll find the hens in the back.'

She gave the tinker a sixpenny piece with a great flourish.

'There, it gives me great pleasure to give you that.'

He looked at it.

'Give us five bob, mam, and have a real good time.'

The flood had devastated the farm area and McCormack's piggery was swept away.

49

'Tell me,' he asked the agricultural inspector, 'were Butler's pigs all drowned?

'They were.'

'Did Carey lose all his too?'

'He did.'

McCormack sighed with relief.

'Ah, so things are not as bad as I thought.'

Tadgh Cafferky boasted how he kept his money in a sock under the mattress.

'Sure,' advised his brother, 'you lose interest that way.'

"Deed I don't. I put a bit aside for that as well.'

The farmer's cow was stolen and he was complaining loudly. His cousin from Dublin consoled him.

'Don't worry, Phelim. They can't get far with it. Didn't I see you drain its fuel tank last night.'

Slattery swung his sledge hammer with cheerful abandon and struck his workmate a fearful thump on the side of the head.

'Slattery, Slattery, be careful,' begged Donegan, 'you're after making me bite my lip.'

Then there was the student at Trinity College who was most indignant when he failed in history. Half the questions, he told everyone, were about things that happened before he was born.

It was a typical shop selling Roman Catholic religious goods and there were many statues of the saints. With savage energy, a Protestant Orangeman shattered them with his stick.

In court he explained why.

'Me Lord. I couldn't pass the place by and not do something. If there's one thing I hate, it's bigotry.'

A Dublin description of meanness: 'He wouldn't give you a slide if he owned the Alps.'

He was from one of the more remote parts of Co. Down and used his knife exclusively. The waitress thought she'd be kind.

'Pardon me, sir, but why don't you use your fork?'

'I tried that, Miss, but it leaks.'

'How can you tell your twins apart, Mr Hayden? They look exactly alike to me.'

'Well, if I put my finger in Michael's mouth and he bites me I know it's his brother Shane.'

The professor mislaid his umbrella and went from shop to shop looking for it. When he finally traced it, he was most grateful.

'You are the only honest shopkeeper in Dublin,' he told the proprietor. 'All the others denied having it.'

The stout was awful and the farmer complained bitterly to the owner of the public-house.

'What are you complaining about?' said the barkeeper indignantly. 'You've only got a pint but I've got 78 barrels of the bloody stuff.'

Respect for the dead is a great Irish quality and when O'Reilly had to bury his mother-in-law he went round to the local to borrow something to do the thing decent.

'Lend us a tenner, Mr Ryan,' he pleaded.

Even publicans in Ireland respect the traditions and Casey searched the till to get the money.

'O'Reilly,' he said, 'I have only nine pounds fourteen. Will that do?'

'It will. You can give me a pint of stout, five cigarettes and a razor blade to make up the difference.'

'Mr Kelly . . . Mr Kelly! Will you lend your corkscrew for me daddy?'

'It's all right, sonny. I'll bring it over meself.'

The world, they say in Dublin, isn't round or flat—it's just plain crooked.

'You know,' said the dismal farm labourer to his employer, 'I feel very guilty working for you.'

'How so?' asked the farmer with surprise.

'Sure I have a feeling I'm doing a pair of horses out of a job.'

The teacher opened the letter that young Colm brought her.
Dear Teacher,
  Please stop giving Colm those sums about bottles of whiskey at two shillings a bottle. It keeps his father awake at night . . .

'What's your name,' he asked the boy on the winding white road to Fanad.

'James Doherty.'

'You should say "sir".'

'All right. Sir James Doherty.'

He had killed the farmer's hen but he offered to pay for it.

'I'll give you a pound,' he assured the cottager.

'You'll have to make it two pounds,' said the old woman with a mournful shake of her head. 'Two of my fowl are destroyed by you.'

'What do you mean?' he asked indignantly.

'Ah then when my cock finds out you killed that hen he'll die of shock.'

It was outside the church after Mass and the tinker was making his way from group to group.

'Look,' one man said to him, 'go over and see the parish priest and he'll look after ye properly.'

The tinker had a long conference with the parish priest but when he left him his face was a picture of woe.

'Well, didn't he give you a few shillings?' asked his adviser.

'Give me anything, is it? He talked me into a subscription for the altar.'

The farmer showed the city labourer how to milk the cows and sent him into the fields.

'How many did you milk?' he asked when the labourer came back.

'Twenty, but there's one thing . . .'

'What's that?'

'I think you should have given me a bucket.'

'Are you sober, Flanagan?'

'Yes, sir. Often.'

'Why in the name of Heaven,' asked the weary passenger, 'did they build the railway station three miles from the village?'

'Ah,' nodded the porter, 'they must have thought it would be a good thing to have it near the trains.'

'I'm afraid, Mrs Moylan, your husband will never work again,' said the doctor sadly.

'I'll go in and tell him. It might cheer him up.'

'You're doing fine, Mullarkey and you tell me you're only playing golf for a month.'

'Oh, yes but it took me four years to learn.'

The new farm labourer was from the city and didn't know too much about the work. He had been milking for some time when the farmer went along to see how he was doing. To his surprise the labourer was feeding the cow with milk.

'What in the name of the Seven holy men of Pogmohone are you doing?'

'The cow dropped its dirty tail in the pail and I'm putting the milk through her again.'

The Guard stopped the little man who was tearing down the street and then let him go. The publican came pounding up a few minutes later.

'Why didn't you stop that man?' he protested.

'He told me, Byrne, that you were racing him for the price of a drink.'

'I was. He didn't pay for it.'

Mrs Mulligan was in the witness box. The prosecution counsel indicated her husband.

'Do you mean to say that a physical wreck like your husband could give you a black eye?'

'He wasn't a physical wreck when he gave it to me.'

Then there was the Irish farmer who complained when his neighbour put up a wind-generator. He said there was only enough wind for his own.

The tourist stopped his car at the top of the Long Hill on the road from Glendalough.

'Tell me,' he asked a passer-by, 'is it dangerous here?'

'Not here,' said the Wicklow man, 'it's at the bottom that the accidents happen.'

The visitor complained of the long muddy avenue to the hotel.

'Well now,' soothed the proprietor, 'if it was any shorter it wouldn't reach the house.'

BEST
Scottish
JOKES

Compiled by

A. and B. ELLIOT

An Englishman, lecturing on his travels, was speaking rather disparagingly about the Scots in Canada, and the mixing of the race with the Indians. He was haughty and insulting about it. 'You'll find,' he said, 'a great number of Scots half-breeds, and French half-breeds, but you cannot find any English half-breeds.'

There was a Scot in the audience who had the answer: 'Oh well, ye see,' he announced, 'the squaws had to draw the line somewhere.'

Although it was the village custom to 'stand your hands' in the pub when there was a new arrival in the family, it was generally known that—having seven daughters—Dougal didn't prescribe to this too heartily. But there he was, greeting every new arrival in the bar with: 'Drink up, lads, they're on me!'

'Another girl?' asked Roddy sympathetically.

'No, indeed,' with a grin, 'we've got a boy at last!'

There was a general murmur of 'Well done!' and 'It had to happen some time!'

'Oh, that's great,' said friend Roddy, 'and who does the wee fellow look like?'

'Good God, man,' Dougal blurted out, 'I haven't the faintest idea. We haven't looked at his face yet.'

Jock and Tam were in high fettle. With their wives away visiting an ailing friend down in Arran they were free until the following day.

They bought two bottles of malt whisky and a 4lb sirloin steak. What a night they were going to have!

They left the steak in the kitchen and went 'ben the room' to sample the whisky.

It took quite a few drams before they decided it was up to scratch and suddenly they both felt decidedly hungry. However, search as they would, there was no sign of the steak.

Jock happened to notice the cat licking his whiskers with an uncommonly satisfied air. 'The damned scoundrel!' he exploded, but Tam stopped his raised boot.

'We'll soon find out,' he said grimly and, seizing the cat by the scruff of the neck, hauled it upstairs and dumped it on the bathroom scales. The pointer, sure enough, registered exactly four pounds.

'Told you,' he triumphed, 'there's our steak—but where's the ruddy cat?'

What excitement there had been in Edintrose. Not only had the multi-storeyed flats been completed in record time but they were now fully occupied and the City Factor's staff were very pleased with themselves.

'Aye', said the chief, opening his morning mail, 'a monument to mankind.' Suddenly he stared in disbelief, 'Read that, Morrison,' he laughed, 'a Mrs McBain complaining about rats—and her up on the fourteenth floor. *There's* a woman with a sense of humour!'

However, two days later the same tenant repeated her complaint, this time in more forceful language. 'The woman's daft,' avowed Morrison. He decided, however, to send Brodie, the vermin exterminator, to keep the peace.

'Sit down here, my man,' says she, 'and keep your eye on that wee hole in the skirting-board.' Brodie, with a quiet laugh, did as he was told. Five minutes had passed when suddenly a nose poked itself through the hole. It was a brown trout—maybe a two-pounder!

The woman glared at him, 'Just you keep your eyes open for the rats, mister—we'll talk about the rising damp later.'

Fiona was almost eighteen and as bonny a lass as you could wish for. She sidled up to her father, sitting in his favourite chair, and put her arms round his neck. 'Dad,' she began, 'will it be all right to go to Rothesay with my boy-friend for the holiday week-end?'

'Oh, I don't know,' said her father, 'with your mother visiting your Aunt Lizzie in London, I'm not sure. . . .'

'Come on, Dad,' she wheedled, 'don't be so old-fashioned.'

'Well, I'll tell you what, lass, just as long as you promise not to let him come into your room. You know how your mother worries.'

When she arrived back on the Monday night his first question was, 'Now, did you keep your promise?'

'Oh, aye,' said Fiona, 'I just went to his room—let *his* mother worry.'

There's the story about the time Queen Victoria was making one of her many visits to Balmoral.

In the city of Perth lived a Major McAndrew, the proud possessor of a magnificent vine, who wondered if, when the Royal train stopped there, he might be allowed to offer Her Majesty some of his delicious grapes. He was delighted when he received word that the Queen would be pleased to accept such a gift.

When the great day arrived he carefully selected his choicest bunches and lovingly put them into a nicely garnished basket. Handing them over to the Queen's lady-in-waiting caused great excitement for the fortunates who happened to be in the station on that day.

The Major, however, was ecstatic when he received a personal note from Her Majesty praising him highly for his delectable gift. He lost no time in showing it to his faithful old gardener who read each word slowly and carefully.

'That's grand, sir,' said the gardener slowly, 'but she says nothing about sending back the basket.'

The Highland village was grief-stricken. Word had come from America that McNab was dead. 'No! What did he die of?' one old crony asked. 'A broken heart, it's said,' replied another.

'Poor laddie, how was that?'

'Well,' he went on, 'they say that he was heartily sick and tired of hearing tales of his country's parsimony, so one night he stood treat to all in the pub in New York—only to find that they thought he was Irish all the time.'

To illustrate his point, a lecturer on temperance and the evils of drink had put two glasses in front of him—one filled with water, the other with whisky. He then produced a big fat worm which he put into the water. It swam about contentedly. He took it out and put it into the whisky. After a few convulsive wriggles the worm died.

'That,' said the doctor, 'is what happens to your insides when you drink whisky!' His audience was quite impressed, but none more so than one old lady who waylaid him at the end and asked what particular brand of whisky he had used, 'Because,' she said, 'I've been that bothered with worms for years.'

Two Scots had enjoyed a very good international match at Wembley. Having finished all the whisky they had taken with them, they found their way to the West End and found a likely-looking pub.

'What kind of whisky have you got?' asked Angus. 'McGonogle's,' came the reply.

'Who ever heard of McGonogle's whisky?' they asked in unison.

'Sorry, Mac,' said the barman, 'only McGonogle's.'

'Oh well, I suppose it's better than nothing,' they decided: 'Give us a couple of glasses.'

Angus tossed his back and, with a grimace, turned to his friend, 'Jings, I'll be glad when we've had enough of this.'

McSouter, all the way from Tain, was in Glasgow on his first visit. Unluckily for him he was set about by three thugs as he went for an evening stroll. Although he fought valiantly he was eventually overcome. The trio of 'neds' struggled to get their breath back.

After such extraordinary resistance they expected a rich booty indeed. Imagine their disbelief when his pockets disgorged only 6s. 10d.

'Heavens!' said one of them, 'Thank God he didnae have a pound on him or he would have killed us for sure.'

Bruce and Alex had been down to Perth and were returning to their native Inverness. They had been drinking most of the day and had difficulty in finding the correct train home.

With some aid from a few sympathisers they eventually made it and managed to get an empty compartment.

'Good,' said Alex, 'we'll just have one for the road.'

'Best suggestion I've heard yet,' replied Bruce flopping into his seat.

Soon the alcohol overcame them both and they fell sound asleep. Darkness fell and a short time later they awoke just as they were hurtling through a small station at which a train was standing.

Rubbing the sleep from his eyes Alex mumbled, 'There must be something wrong in that wee village we've just passed. Did you notice the lights were on in every house?'

'Aye, I did that,' came from Bruce, proving he could be as observant as his sleepy friend, 'I suppose it's because there was such a big fire in the first one.'

A creditor in Edinburgh wrote a stiff letter to a firm in Aberdeen demanding immediate payment of a long overdue account. They received the following reply:

Dear Sir,

Please note that at the end of every month we place all unpaid accounts in a large pile on a table. Out of this we draw six and pay these. Any more impudence from you and yours won't even go into the shuffle at all.'

At the last census a collector called upon two old ladies in Perth to pick up their form. He noticed that neither of them had filled in her age and pointed this out.

'Oh,' said one, 'we didn't think that was necessary; but tell me, have the Hills next door given their ages?'

'Indeed they have,' he replied.

'Well then,' came the cautious reply, 'we're as old as they are.'

So the collector wrote on their form, 'As old as the Hills.'

A motorist had lost his way in the Highlands and was relieved to see an old worthy sitting on a gate. 'Can you tell me where this road leads to?' he asked.

'Aye,' came the reply, 'one end leads to my croft and the other end goes straight on.'

A minister, visiting his native parish in the Highlands, had gone for a walk on the Sunday afternoon. An old woman who was a strict Sabbatarian reproved him.

The minister said, 'But, my good woman, did not the Master walk on the Sabbath Day *and* pluck the ears of the corn?'

'Oh well, maybe,' said the wife grudgingly, 'but I'm no thinkin' any more o' Him for that.'

'What do you think of the new minister, Sandy?'

'During the week, invisible; on Sunday, incomprehensible.'

A well known Scottish minister consulted an eminent doctor who told him he must go to Algiers or some winter resort on the Riviera.

'Impossible,' said the clergyman. 'I have too much work to get through.'

'Well,' said the doctor, 'you must make your choice. It's either Algiers or Heaven.'

'Dear me,' sighed the man of God, 'then I suppose it must be Algiers.'

Andrew was a regular attender of all football matches at one of the larger Glasgow grounds. It wasn't that he was a strong supporter of the home team, but, like many of his kind, he loved to shout his disgust at the display of a right winger, whose standard of play was, according to Andrew, hopeless.

'Look at him!' he kept shouting, 'couldnae kick a hole in a wet newspaper!'

Comments of that nature poured from him most of the game till suddenly the victim, in a desperate clearance, kicked the wet and heavy ball hard into the terrace, hitting Andrew full in the face.

There followed a stunned silence. But only for a moment. Putting his cap back on his head, Andrew started again.

'Well,' he shouted, 'I'll say this much for you—you're no' deef.'

Or the one about the Scot who went into a tailor's in Leeds and asked to be shown the best suit in the shop.

The Jewish proprietor was soon back with a nice Donegal tweed. 'Look at this one,' he said, 'and it's *not* £50! Not even £40—£30 and it's yours.' The Scot felt it carefully.

'I wouldn't give you £25 for it—not even £20! £18 is my price.'

'Right you are,' said the Jew, 'that's the way I like to do business. No haggling.'

Not all Scots are as lacking in emotion as many of our alien detractors make us out to be.

I remember fine getting into a game of poker in a commercial hotel one wet night and half-way through, one of the boys (I think he had a Royal Flush) slumped to the floor—dead.

You may not believe me, but we finished the hand standing up.

A young servant lassie was being considered for a situation at the farm. Her prospective employer brusquely informed her that she would need to produce a reference from her previous place. Next day he saw her again and asked her if she now had 'her character'.

'Aye, I have that,' she replied, 'but I've got yours as well—so I'm not coming.'

Young Hughie, all the way from Sutherland, had been appointed Scottish representative with an agricultural implements firm in London.

It was his first visit ever to the 'big smoke' and after an exciting day with his sales director (slap-up dinner and all that sort of thing) he had a couple of hours to put in before the train took him back north.

He inevitably finished up in Soho. His eyes were popping out of his head at the mind-boggling displays outside the strip-joints when, suddenly, a coloured girlie sidled up to him.

'Say honey,' she began, 'how'd you like to come home with me?'

'Away ye go, lassie,' said Hughie, 'what would a man like me be doing in Africa?'

Dougal toiled for many months clearing some very rough ground as an extension to his garden. At long last he began to see some of the fruits of his labour. With pardonable pride he was admiring his display of flowers and vegetables when the minister passed by and smiled his approval.

'My, my, Dougal, I must say that you and the Creator between you have done a grand job.' But Dougal was not too pleased about the division of credit.

'Ay, maybe so—but you should have seen it when the Creator had it to Himself.'

The Edinburgh Festival was in full swing and none more so than the pipe-band marching along Princes Street.

Out in front the drum-major was revelling in the crowd's adulation and with an exaggerated swagger was catching the mace from high in the air.

Just as he was leading them into The Mound the traffic-lights suddenly turned to red. Soon there was an embarrassing gap between the marking-time musicians and our stalwart friend.

He had the usual entourage of local children, one of whom yelled at him, 'Hey, mister, you've lost your band!'

He gave a quick backward glance, 'Ach!' he muttered, striding on, 'it doesn't matter—I know the tune backwards.'

The Texan oil-millionaire had fallen into the burn on a famous Scottish golf-course. Old George, about to play off the 16th, saw the mishap. By the time his legs had carried him to the spot he was nearly too late to save the almost-drowned tycoon.

Still, he did manage to pull him out. After thanking him over and over, the American asked what favour he could bestow on him—anything he cared to name.

The Scot stole a look at the rich man's golf-bag and, gazing sadly at his own collection of decrepit old niblicks and what-have-you, said, 'Well, sir, I could do with one or two decent golf clubs.'

A week later, he received the following telegram:

SORRY STOP COULDN'T GET ST. ANDREWS STOP BUT TITLE DEEDS OF WENTWORTH CASTLE, HOYLAKE AND CARNOUSTIE BEING POSTED YOU TODAY.

Then there was the foursome at Western Gailes. At the short 14th, Alec had played a beautiful iron shot and was about to putt out for a birdie two.

Just then a funeral procession came round the bend of the road and he sprang to attention, cap in hand, and stayed that way until it was nearly out of sight.

Touched by this unusual respect his partner enquired, 'Someone you know?' 'Aye,' said Alec, 'and she was a good wife to me.'

He had been terribly out of sorts for quite a while and his Glasgow doctor advised him to get away from the rat-race of city life.

'Take a couple of weeks in the country, Mr McNiven. Get yourself plenty of fresh air.'

He plumped for Skye (where else was fresh air so plentiful?) and off he went. He found a nice wee hotel near Dunvegan and after dinner excused himself, having put in a 6 a.m. call for next morning.

When the knock came he was up like a shot. Ten minutes later he was walking along the loch-side.

Suddenly a farming type came into view. 'Grand weather,' said the Glaswegian as he passed.

'Aye, it is that!' came the reply: 'But it was damnt cauld this mornin'.'

They had been having an awful time down at Leith Docks. Pilfering was always to be expected but so many things had 'walked' that the authorities were really perturbed. So they arranged for a dozen plain-clothes men to try to catch the culprits.

One of them, near the entrance, had to check and search every docker going in and out of the area. He had a vague unease about one character who kept passing him with a wheelbarrow full of straw. He searched him thoroughly—even going through the wheelbarrow with a fine toothcomb. But nothing.

Weeks later, his special assignment over, he chanced to meet this very fellow in a city pub.

'Look, Mac,' he said, 'the job's over and I can't touch you now, but I know you were on the fiddle. Tell me,' he whispered, 'what in the name of the wee man were you stealing?'

'Wheelbarrows,' beamed Mac.

A Scot who had made a fortune remained the same genial 'rough diamond' that he had always been. At one society function he seemed very nervous as he sat down to dinner—maybe the array of cutlery did it. When, after soup, one of the liveried waiters tried to remove his spoon, he gruffly ordered the man to leave it.

'Another spoon will be supplied for the dessert, sir,' explained the attendant quietly, 'a much smaller one.'

'Maybe,' barked the guest, 'but I'll just have the old spoon. Ma mooth's as big for pudden as it is for soup.'

Two old cronies were in a reminiscent mood.

'Well,' said Tam, 'we've been friends for the last thirty years and never fallen out.'

'No, never a word between us,' said John.

'But there's just one thing I never liked to bring up in case we would quarrel,' remarked Tam.

'And what was that?' queried John.

'Oh, I still don't like to mention it, but I can't stand your wife!'

'Well,' said John, 'we'll no' quarrel about that. To tell you the truth, I can't stand her myself.'

During a railway strike there had been great difficulty in finding substitute engine-drivers. On a Fife section a young fellow undertook to drive the local train but on his very first day, in trying to draw up, he ran past the station. Upon putting back, he drove as far past the platform the other way. The station-master, seeing him preparing for a third attempt, shouted, 'Just stay where you are, Dougal; we'll shift the station.'

Sitting in a train, a Scotsman offered his snuff-box to an aquiline-nosed young aristocrat immediately opposite. The lad spurned his offer, adding that he did not indulge in such filthy practices.

'Man, it's a pity,' said the Scot. 'Ye've grand accommodation.'

A Scotsman had just got a position in a large commercial house in London and a friend, meeting him shortly afterwards, asked, 'Well, and how are you liking England?'

'Fair enough,' he replied.

'And how to you like the English?'

'Oh well,' said the Scot, 'I haven't met many of them yet. Y'see, all my dealings are with the heads of departments.'

Mac made his way unsteadily along the office corridor. He looked intently at the letters on the glass door and, with narrowed eyes, turned the handle and walked in.

'Ish thish Alcoholicks Anonymush?' he lisped.

'Yes, sir! D'you wish to join?'

'No—tae resign.'

The laird was instructing his gardener on cutting the grass.

'Remember,' he said, 'an inch at the bottom's worth two at the top.'

The job completed, the gardener was being given his usual dram in part payment. However his employer had contrived to fill only half the glass.

'Fill her up, man!' said the gardener. 'Remember? An inch at the top's worth two at the bottom.'

A Scot died and left his cousin all the money that his cousin owed him.

The boy was nervously clutching Jock by the hand as they marched into the Buchanan Street hairdressers.

'Just sit there and read the comics, son. I'll go first.' And he flopped into the chair.

'Trim, sir?' said the barber, 'Aye, the lot!' said Jock. 'When you've cut it I'll have a shampoo—then a shave and face massage. And anything else you can think of,' he added.

The barber was jubilant and got to work with a will. About an hour later Jock arose—a credit to tonsorial art and smelling like the inside of a beauty parlour.

'Just give the lad a back and sides,' he instructed. 'I'm away for some cigarettes.

Suitably shorn, the boy went back to his reading. After what seemed an age the barber remarked, 'My, but your father's been away a long time.'

'Oh, that's no' my Daddie,' he volunteered, 'that's just a man who offered me threepence if I'd come in and get my hair cut.'

The old couple had gone into an Edinburgh restaurant and ordered gigot chops. The waiter noticed that the woman hadn't touched hers.

'Something wrong, Madam?' he enquired politely, 'perhaps overdone?'

'No, no, laddie,' she smiled, 'I'm just waiting for Willie to finish. He's using the teeth first.'

Hughie was quite a character and this was his umpteenth appearance for poaching—salmon, no less.

His friends were so worried that they hired a very able young lawyer who very convincingly proved his client's innocence—he hadn't been within ten miles of the river.

Case dismissed and everybody happy, when up speaks our worthy to the magistrate: 'And does that mean I can keep the fish, sir?'

An officer was visiting a Scottish gun battery. During his tour of inspection he addressed a smart-looking soldier: 'What would you do if the First Gunner got his head blown off?'

'Nothing sir,' came the smart reply.

'Why nothing?' asked the nonplussed officer.

'Well sir, ye see,' he replied hesitantly, 'Ah'm the First Gunner.'

Two old cronies were discussing the good old days.

'Aye,' said Tam, 'nearly all our old friends are gone, but Jock's the one I miss most.'

'How's that, Tam,' asked the other.

'Because I married his widow.'

Campbell and MacDonald had been good friends for years but one evening, when out for their customary stroll, MacDonald was very quiet and uncommunicative, so his friend asked what was the matter.

'Well, if you must know,' said MacDonald, 'it's that terrible massacre at Glencoe by the Campbells that I'm thinking about.'

'Oh, man, but that was hundreds of years ago,' remonstrated Campbell.

'That might be,' replied MacDonald, 'but I just heard about it yesterday.'

Another old Scot was smoking in the waiting-room of a railway station. A porter approached him. 'Don't you see that notice on the wall—"No smoking allowed!"?'

'Yes, I do,' said the Scot. 'But I can't keep to all your rules. There's one on this wall—"Wear Spirella Corsets".'

An Englishman and a Scot were arguing about the respective parts their countries had taken in the Great War.

'Why,' said the southerner, 'there were five Englishmen killed for every Scot.'

'Aye, ye're right there, man—just like Bannockburn.'

A Highlander of advanced years decided to get married and asked his minister's counsel.

'Well, Donald, I trust you have got yourself a handmaid from the Lord.'

'Indeed, I don't know if she's hand-made or machine-made—but she's very well put together.'

An English tourist, trying to take the micky out of a country Scot, pointed to a scarecrow in a field, dressed up like a man, and sneered, 'One of the natives, I suppose?'

'Naw, naw,' was the reply, 'just a summer visitor.'

A Londoner, holidaying in a lonely part of the Western Isles was treated, day after day, to a diet of fish. Determined to introduce a little variety as well as a little spice, into his diet, he sent to London for a parcel of sausages and handed them over to his landlady.

At breakfast, when he lifted the cover, he found the dish filled with fried sausage-skins. He asked his landlady for an explanation and was told, 'That's a' that was left, sir, after I gutted them.'

The little car was bowling along the road on the outskirts of Bridge of Allan when a policeman at a junction motioned the driver to pull in. Alec did so.

'Excuse me, sir,' he said, 'but would you mind blowing into this breathaliser?' Alec, expressing annoyance at the delay, assured the officer that he and his wife were just returning from a children's Christmas party, having picked up their four-year-old son. Didn't he think it was a wee bit daft asking him to take the test?

The policeman however, insisted.

'This is nonsense!' protested Alec's wife, Agnes, from the back seat where she was trying to pacify her fretful son. 'Can't you see that wee Tommy is dying for his bed?' But the officer was adamant, and Alec, anxious to be on his way, grabbed at the contraption.

He looked at the policeman in astonishment when, after two mighty puffs, the breathaliser turned green. 'There's something the matter with this lot,' he said. 'Why don't you try another out on the wife here? She's never touched the stuff in her life.'

As this was one of the first tests the policeman had done he didn't want to be too heavy-handed about it, so he agreed to let Agnes blow into a fresh one—which turned even greener.

'I'm afraid we'll all have to go down to the station and sort this one out,' he said.

'I'll tell you what,' said Alec, having another go, 'if wee Tommy blows into one and the same thing happens, will you agree there's something wrong and let us go home?'

This seemed a reasonable request and the policeman was only too ready to agree. You can imagine his astonishment at the same tell-tale colour.

'I'm sorry, sir, to have wasted your time,' said the crestfallen lawman, 'I won't detain you any longer. This batch *will* have to be checked,' he added, waving them a weary farewell.

Not until he was in top gear did Alec slowly let out his breath.

'Well, woman,' he crowed, 'maybe now you'll believe it was a good idea to give the lad a double whisky before we left.'

A well-known Scottish league team manager had stuck faithfully to his club for many years—through good times and bad.

When his fame was at its height he was approached by the chairman of a London club who offered him quite a big inducement if he would travel south. The Englishman concluded, 'You'll never get better terms than these, but if there's anything else, apart from the money, we'll do all we can to help.'

'Right then,' said the Scot, 'I'll take the job but only on one condition.'

'OK, you name it!'

'You let me away every Saturday to support my own team.'

There was the domestic problem of the Borderer whose sister had been living with him and his wife for many years. Two women is one too many in any house and finally the situation became impossible.

One of them *had* to go—and it turned out to be the wife.

'What did ye expect?' he asked at his friend's surprise. 'You surely didn't think I'd send my sister away in favour of a strange woman.'

During the war, a young Scots soldier was asked how it came about that he was the only Scotsman in an English regiment. 'Och,' he said with a smile, 'they've just put me in this lot to stiffen them up.'

Angus, down from Aberdeen, was obviously enjoying his holiday in London. When he returned to his hotel each evening he was full of the wonders of the place.

Another guest, infected by Angus's delight asked him, 'Is this your first time in London?'

'Aye, it is that,' was the reply.

'You seem to be having such fun that I presume you haven't had a holiday for a considerable time,' said the chatty gent.

'It's not only that,' smiled Angus, 'but it's my honeymoon as well.'

'In that case,' asked the guest, taken aback, 'where is your wife?'

'Oh, she's been here before.'

Two farmers were discussing the weather. Said the first, 'Man, that shower will do a lot of good; it'll bring things out o' the ground.'

'God forbid,' said his neighbour, 'I've three wives there.'

Hamish, about to leave on holiday, was told by a friend that the best thing to bring luck was to throw a coin over every bridge he passed. On returning home he was asked how he had got on.

'I got on fine!' he said. 'Passing over the Dee and the Tay was nae bother, but when I came to that Forth bridge the string got caught on the girders and I lost ma penny.'

Two Highlanders stood looking at the imposing front of a large building in London. The corner stone bore the date in Roman characters, 'MCMIV'.

'Would you look at that, Alex,' said his companion proudly. 'I've never heard of McMiv before, but here's a Scotsman who's got his name on one of the finest buildings in London. You just can't keep our lads down, can ye'?'

A Scottish farmer, about to re-marry, was reminded by his friend how his first wife swore she would crawl out of her grave and haunt him if he ever took another woman.

'Aren't you just a wee bit scared?' he was asked.

'Not in the least,' he smiled drily, 'she'll have a long crawl—I buried her upside-down.'

Graham and Jean scrimped and saved until they had enough money to buy a little car, an ambition of theirs for most of their married life.

Graham took driving lessons and it was agreed that he would teach Jean, thereby making a great saving. On the day of her first lesson he patiently explained about gear changing, clutch control, accelerator, foot and hand brakes, etc. All went quite smoothly until they were coming to a set of busy traffic lights. To Jean's horror she found that the brakes wouldn't work.

Frantically she shouted to her husband, 'What on earth shall I do?'

'For a start,' he gulped, 'hit something cheap.'

A golfer was being buried and his old clubmates stood around the grave mourning their pal, wind and rain adding to their misery.

Hamish, feeling he had to contribute something more than the service just finished, commented, 'Oh, well, Angus wouldn't have played on a day like this anyway.'

Jock decided to brave the inner sanctum of his employer's office and in a very disgruntled voice said, 'I've been here five years doing the work of three men for one man's wage, and I think it's time I had a rise.'

'Well, Jock,' said his boss, 'I couldn't do that, but if you'll just tell me the names of the other two I'll sack them.'

A Scot went to see a psychiatrist. The preliminaries over, the head-shrinker was gently leading him to the couch.

'Tell me,' he said, 'when did you first start to enjoy treating your friends?'

A beggar, sitting at the side of the road with his hat on his knees, was approached by a Scot, who, after much fumbling in his sporran, finally threw in a penny.

'Well, my good man,' he condescended, 'and how did you come to be in such miserable circumstances?'

'By being over-generous like yourself, sir,' came the reply, 'giving away vast sums of money to the poor and needy.'

The Londoner wasn't over-impressed by the Scot's spirited dissertation on the beauty of his native land. In a final display of churlishness he sneered, 'Take away your mountains and your lochs and what have you got?'

'England,' was the withering reply.

She was a farmer's daughter and had invited her first boy-friend to tea. Everything went well until father got on about what had to be done the following day.

'Aye,' he said, 'we'll have to spread dung on the field at the road-end and maybe some more dung on the one at the other side of the barn.' And so it went on all through the meal.

Morag was affronted and at washing-up time she turned to her mother: 'That was terrible—couldn't he say "manure" or something?'

'Wheesht, lass,' said her mother, 'it's only in the last fortnight that I've managed to get him to say "dung".'

He was dying and a few of his closest relatives were at the bed-side.

'Mind now, Maggie,' he croaked, 'Jock McKay owes me £25.'

'Poor dear husband,' his wife nodded, 'sensible to the very end.

'. . . and another thing, remember to pay back the £40 that Roderick Fraser lent me.'

'My, my,' said Maggie, 'there's his mind wandering again.'

Craigie had never been out of Barra before and here he was at Carnoustie with his cousin, seeing his very first golf tournament.

The basic rules having been hurriedly explained to him, he joined in the general gasp of dismay as the favourite's tee-shot landed in a deep rut.

'Man, is *he* in trouble!' said the cousin. However, the shot was played out beautifully—into a huge bunker at the edge of the green.

'Oh, no, now he's *really* in trouble!' groaned his relative. A glorious wedge-shot lifted the ball with its sandy shower slap bang into the hole.

'Trouble did you say?' from Craigie, 'let's see him hit it out o' *that*.'

The commercial traveller joke you're always hearing about happened to a pal of mine, McDougall. He ran out of petrol on a lonely road in Wester Ross and asked at the only farmhouse in sight, 'Can you put me up for the night?'

The farmer said he could, 'If you don't mind sharing a room with my 18-year-old son.'

'Man alive!' gasped McDougall. 'I'm in the wrong joke.'

A wealthy American, falling in love with the Scottish countryside, decided to make it his home and bought himself a fine country mansion in the heart of Perthshire. To give himself something to do he decided on poultry-rearing and wrote to an English firm for a hen-house.

About ten days later the local station-master phoned him to say that it had arrived and that he could pick it up at his convenience.

Off he went in his truck taking two of the gardeners to help. Finding no-one at the station he decided to have a look himself and, sure enough, farther up the line he found it. Using a block-and-tackle it took him less than ten minutes to get it on board and they started the return journey.

Suddenly, along the road a bit, they saw the station-master waving his arms like a whirling Dervish. Pulling up to him the Yank explained, 'Okay, Mac, don't get all het up just because me and the boys picked up the hen-house ourselves.'

'Hen-house be damned,' he yelled hysterically, 'you're awa' wi' Strichan Junction.'

Prestwick Airport wasn't always the bustling place it is today, and at one time they put on ten-minute 'flips' in a two-seater bi-plane at 7/6d. per passenger. There was quite a queue when I got there and immediately in front of me was a middle-aged couple. He was sporting an old kilt and Glengarry while his better half was more soberly attired. From the odd snippets of conversation I gather that this was their first-ever holiday, that they were from Auchteraber (that's what it sounded like), and he was grumbling about 'a' this expense.

At last it was their turn and as the young pilot, a southerner, sauntered up with a 'Next please.'

Our friend ventured, 'How much is it for the two o' us?' 'We're married, ye ken!' he added hopefully.

The pilot looked at them with amusement. 'Well, actually, old boy, there's no reduction, but I'll tell you what—I'll loop-the-loop and if you don't yell out I won't charge you a penny.'

'Right you are, lad.'

There were a few chuckles as the bizarre trio got aboard. Up the plane soared and in a few seconds was almost out of sight. I could just make *one* loop-the-loop, but my neighbour swore he did it three times.

The plane made a perfect three-point landing and taxied to within twenty feet of us. The pilot jumped out and ran to help his passengers.

'Well, old boy,' he said admiringly, 'my congratulations! You must have nerves of steel—not even a squeak.'

'Aye, ye're right!' was the shaky reply. 'Mind you, it was touch and go when Morag fell out.'

Donald visited his doctor complaining of seeing striped camels when he tried to get to sleep.

'Have you ever seen a psychiatrist?' asked the doctor.

'No, never,' replied Donald, 'just striped camels.'

A country Scot called on a doctor to ask his advice. The doctor told him he must stop drinking and smoking. The man said nothing and quietly rose to depart.

'Friend,' the doctor reminded him gently, 'you haven't paid for my advice.'

'No,' said the man, 'and what's more, I'm not taking it either.'

Sandy and Murdo were serving on the same ship. Sandy died at sea, and when his body was lowered overboard it was loaded with some pieces of coal.

'Well, well,' said Murdo, 'I knew fine where he was going, but I never thought he would have to take his ain fuel.'

Mrs Morrison told her husband that they had important guests coming to tea. On hearing this he rose with alacrity and removed the umbrellas from the hallstand.

'For goodness' sake,' said Mrs M, 'surely you don't think anyone is going to take them; they're very respectable people.'

'Oh, that's no' what's bothering me,' said Mr M—'it's just that they might recognise them.'

Jock McGillivray, the ventriloquist, was momentarily out of work and had gone to spend a few days at his sister's place.

He was on the way down for his morning dram when a big shaggy dog fell in at his side. Jock gave him a friendly pat and motioned him to run along but the dog persisted in following.

When he got to the 'local' the brute was still with him—sitting at his heel as he ordered his drink. For a laugh Jock looked down at him and said, 'Well, and are you for the usual?'

'Oh, no thanks, I've had enough this morning,' the dog appeared to say.

The barman was flabbergasted, especially as the conversation went on for quite a time. When his wits did return he made Jock an immediate offer of £20.

'Not on your life!' said Jock, still having his fun. 'Man, I've had him since he was a pup and a better friend you couldn't find.'

There were nods of approval from the now-crowded bar but the barman was a persistent fellow and raised his offer to £50.

Jock shook his head, and then it came—'£100?' Jock was startled. He put on a woebegone expression. 'Man,' he said, 'being out of work I'd be daft to refuse. Quick, let's have the money afore I change my mind.'

'Mind now,' he added, making for the door, 'take good care of him.' With a last look at the dog—'Farewell, old pal!'

'Old pal, my Aunt Fannie!' was the withering reply, 'after what you've just done I'll never speak to another human as long as I live.'

Miners have always been known as great gamblers and at one time whippet-racing was their favourite sport.

At one meeting, in Fife, many years ago, the last race was just coming up. There were only three runners, and the odds were 'evens the field bar one', which was a rank outsider at ten to one.

Hughie approached a rather flamboyant bookie, 'Would you take £50 at 10 to 1?' he queried.

'Delighted, old boy!'

'Maybe you'd take £100 at the same odds?'

'Of course! Honest Harry, that's the name.'

To everyone's surprise the outsider won by a neck in a very slow race.

The bookie was paying Hughie on his winning bet. He grumbled, 'I suppose you didn't know that the winner—curse his hide—belongs to me?'

The miner laughed, 'Aye, I did that! But what you didn't know was that the other two dogs belong to me.'

Stopping at a country farmhouse on a Sunday, a party of four motorists asked the farmer's wife if they could have a glass of milk.

She hesitated a little but provided the milk which was greatly enjoyed. The motorists then asked about payment. 'Dear me,' said the horrified wife, 'you surely don't think we could *sell* milk on the Sabbath! Just give the bairns a half-crown each on the way out.'

And what about the day Lady Luck smiled on the two lads from Forfar. They had won the pools at last—to the tune of £75,000. The usual riotous celebration over, family and cronies dismissed, they looked at each other.

'Well, man,' enquired Duncan, 'and what have you a fancy for?'

'You'd never guess,' said George shyly, 'something I've always dreamed about—a Cadillac convertible!'

'Now there's a thing,' said his pal, 'I'd fine like one myself. Tell you what, the Motor Show is on in London—let's take a look at it!'

Off they went. It was early morning as they walked along Euston Road. Suddenly George stopped in amazement in front of a shop window. 'Would you just look at that!' he managed. Donald followed the direction of his shaking finger and soon saw the reason for all the excitement. 'A whole tray of them—Forfar Bridies!'

In less time than it takes to tell they were on their way again, mouths full of meat, potato, and pastry. At last they reached the Motor Show, and within half an hour it was done. Two gleaming 'Caddies'—one white, one blue.

George fumbled in his pocket for his cheque-book, but Donald a restraining hand on his arm. 'Fair's fair, man. These are on me—after all, you bought the Bridies.'

A Scot and a Jew decided to team up in business and bought themselves a second-hand bus. Sandy tossed a coin to see who should be driver and who'd collect the fares. Solly landed with the conductor's job and immediately insured his partner for £5000.

A week later the Scot died of a twisted neck, so Solly collected the insurance, bought two more buses and brought his twin brothers into the business.

Next day he advertised for three Scotsmen, with capital, capable of driving a bus and who would . . . Go on, finish the story yourself.

I remember being on an Aberdeen tramcar some years ago when a woman got on and sat opposite me. She looked at the woman on my left and the conversation went something like this:

'Oh, it's you—isn't it? I hardly knew ye.'

'Aye, it's me—an' that's you! How are you?'

'Och, no' sae bad.'

The opening speaker gave a closer scrutiny, and saw her mistake. With an apologetic smile she ended lamely, 'My, it's no' you at a'.'

'Naw, that's right, it's no' nane o' us.'

Old Miss Campbell had lived her threescore years and ten and was told by her family doctor that her days were numbered. She took the news philosophically and went calmly about settling her affairs. Her last call was to the undertaker.

'Now, Miss Campbell,' said the truthful man, 'there's the question of the shroud.'

'Well, Bob, it's no' a garment that I've had much to do with. Perhaps you could give me some advice?'

'Usually,' said Bob, 'I supply the married ladies with a rich, dark purple but, of course, you'll have the pure white that we keep for maiden ladies like yourself.'

'Oh, I see!' She reflected a while. 'You can make me up a white one right enough, but put a few splashes of colour here and there. I wouldn't like folk to think I'd been neglected altogether.'

McNab, hungry as always, went into a London restaurant and ordered dinner. After what seemed an age the waitress at last brought his soup.

'My, are you the same lassie that took my order?'

'I am that, sir.'

'Jings, you don't look a day older.'

MacPherson and McTavish had been boyhood friends. Mac-Pherson had done well in America and McTavish had prospered at home by opening, of all things, a bank. MacPherson, on returning home for a holiday, was quick to look up his old friend to discuss their good fortune.

'Did you not find it difficult to start your bank?' he asked.

75

'Not really,' came the reply. 'The first day I opened a man came in and deposited £20. Next day, another put in £30 and by that time I had so much confidence in myself that I put in 10/- of my own money.

Young Robert had been on holiday at the seaside and brought a barometer as a present for his mother.

'What a nice thought, son' she said, 'It's a great thing to tell the weather by but it's a pity to have wasted your money. What d'ye think the good Lord gave your father rheumatics for?'

Landlord to tenant: 'I've come to tell you that I'm going to raise the rent.'

Tenant to Landlord: 'Thank God, because I can't.'

Of course everybody knows that it was a Scotsman who invented the briefcase.

According to legend Sir Harry Lauder, the famous Scots comedian, was leaving the stage door of the Alhambra Theatre in Glasgow when a woman rushed up to him, shaking a box in front of his face.

'Come on, Sir Harry,' she beamed, 'it's flag day—give till it hurts.'

He looked at her in horror. 'Madam,' he replied, 'the very idea hurts.'

MacGregor was telling Stewart how MacDonald had gone to London and made £10,000 in one week. Stewart didn't believe him and called on the local gossip, Fraser, to verify the statement.

'Aye, it's true enough,' said Fraser, 'but it's wrong in four places.'

'How d'ye mean,' asked the astonished Stewart.

'Well,' said Fraser, 'in the first place, it was Sheffield, he went to, not London. In the second place, it wasn't a week but a year. In the third place, it wasn't £10,000 but £5,000. And in the fourth place— he didn't make it—he lost it.'

Ever since the Englishman had found out Gordon's nationality he had bored him to tears with the corniest remarks and things like 'Hoots, mon!'

The Scot started in to tell him about the night he dreamt he had died and gone straight to hell.

'It would be full of your kinsmen, eh?' was the jibe.

'Aye, ye're right—quite a lot! Satan took us on a conducted tour and when we came to this big door he asked us to open it and have a look inside. Well, we couldn't see a thing for smoke. Nearly choked us, it did. "What in Hell's name is in there?" I asked Satan.

"Ruddy Englishmen!" he coughed. "They're too damned green to burn."'

Many years ago a middle-aged farmer from Buchan married a pretty young thing and they were driving home after the wedding reception.

Suddenly the horse reared up on its hind legs.

'Whoa there, lass!' he cautioned. 'That's once!'

A few minutes later it shied again.

'Whoa, lass, dammit!' he yelled. 'That's twice!'

When the horse reared up for the third time he picked up his gun, walked round to it and without a word shot it right between the eyes.

His young bride was horrified. 'You big bully!' she managed, 'just because the poor animal . . .'

'Whoa, there, lass!' he chided. 'That's once.'

A Scot, down in Leeds on business, saw a shop window with the invitation 'EVERYTHING SOLD BY THE YARD'.

Thinking to have a bit of fun he boldly entered and demanded, 'I'll have a yard of whisky.'

The Yorkshireman gave him a hard look but rising to the occasion reached under the counter, brought out a bottle, dipped his finger in the neck and drew a long wet line along the counter.

'Anything else, Mac?'

'No, that's all,' smiled the Scot, 'just wrap it up and I'll take it with me.'

Maggie's first confinement had produced triplets. With understandable pride she was telling her best friend how this only happened once in every 200,000 times.

Her friend's eyes widened—'Beats me how you ever found time to do any housework.'

That's nearly as bad as the Scotswoman—expecting child number five—was horrified to read in the paper that every fifth person born in the world was Chinese.

Harry Lauder used to tell the story of how one wifie—I think she was from Deeside—sat through his show one night listening to all his jokes and patter without the vestige of a smile.

The next day she confided to a mutual friend, 'Must be the greatest comic in the world—took me all my time to keep from laughing.'

Late one night, many years ago, I was having a last quick one in Lauder's Bar, Glasgow, when an immaculately dressed fellow walked up to George, the barman, and ordered, 'The usual, old boy!' as he started to peel off his chamois gloves. A large pink gin was placed before him.

About halfway through his drink another dandy (silver-mounted cane and all) sauntered up and, having greeted George in a like fashion, was served with an identical mixture.

He gave the first dude an appreciative look, 'Beautiful suit you're wearing, old boy! Who's your tailor?'

'Finklebaum and McLean,' was the reply.

'Good heavens, I've gone there for years. What's your name, old man?'

'Cruikshanks—Peter Cruikshanks.'

'By Jove! That's what they call me. From out of town?'

''Smatter of fact, no—live over at Riverbank Terrace, next to the bridge.'

'Good Lord!—not number 18?'

Nodding in agreement, our first man finished his drink and with a 'maybe run into you some other time' took his farewell.

His inquisitor seemed lost in thought for a few moments then, draining his glass, he too was off.

All this had been a bit much for me. Turning to the barman I asked, rather stupidly, 'What d'you make of that? Same name—same tailor—like the same drink—live in the same house—it beats me!'

'It's dead simple,' he yawned, 'they're faither and son. Come in here every night but they're too drunk to recognise each other.'

She had the whole compartment to herself as the train got ready to leave Waverley Station, Edinburgh, so she took out all her embroidery threads and spread them across the opposite seat. It would pass a pleasant hour putting them into their shade sequence.

Just as the train was moving a big, burly docker opened the door and sat down.

She was flabbergasted at his appearance and expressed her annoyance. 'Don't you know better than to come in here—invading a lady's privacy. In any case I am just getting over a severe attack of an infectious disease and it might be dangerous for you travelling in the same compartment,' she added lamely.

'Don't worry about me, missus,' he said, 'I'm cutting my throat in the Haymarket Tunnel.'

Mac met his old friend in the street. 'Sandy,' he said, 'I wonder if you would oblige me with a cigarette?'

'But I thought you'd stopped smoking?' said Sandy, reluctantly producing his packet.

'Well, I've reached the first stage,' said Mac eagerly. 'I've stopped buying them.'

Highland Corn

Can you take a few pages of corn—the stuff that makes strong men weep? Right—here goes!

Robbie, all the way from Aberdeen, had emigrated to America and applied for a job in the police force. In the course of his examination he was asked, 'What would you do to disperse a crowd?'

'Well,' replied the Aberdonian, 'I don't know what should be done in New York here, but I know what I'd do at home.'

'What's that?'

'I'd pass round the hat.'

A man and his wife were travelling to Perth by train when the wife said, 'I'm not feeling so well, Rab. I think I'm going to be sick.'

'For heaven's sake woman,' said her frugal husband, pointing to the penalty notice in the carriage, 'you can't be sick here; they charge you two pounds just for a spit.'

The worried face of the bridegroom disturbed the best man. Going up the aisle he whispered, 'What's the matter, Jock?' Have you lost the ring?'

'No,' was the unhappy reply, 'it's worse than that; I've lost the willingness.'

A true Scot is a man who never sends his pyjamas to the laundry unless he has a pair of socks stuck in the pocket.

The meanest Scot alive is the one who, on Christmas Eve, went into the garden, fired off his shotgun and then told his children that Father Christmas had committed suicide.

A rare form of the Highland Fling is a drunken Aberdonian throwing money all over the street.

79

An old Scottish minister asked the station-master if a parcel of books he was expecting had arrived.

'Aye,' said the station-master, 'and you'd better take it away soon because it's leaking.'

A farmer's wife who was noted for her niggardly drams was one day treating a Highland shepherd. She filled the glass half full and said it was extra good whisky, being twelve years old.

'Well, well,' said the shepherd, taking the glass in his hand and looking at it ruefully, 'd'ye no' think it's kinda wee for it's age?'

A visitor asked, 'Whose funeral is that?'
'Jock Tamson's.'
'What complaint?'
'Oh, there's no complaint. Everybody's perfectly satisfied.'

Young Rab came rushing home from school one day and said to his father, 'Dad, teacher says that I've to get a new atlas.' To which his father replied, 'Ah weel, ye can just wait till the world's a bit more settled.'

A thirsty Scot went into an English local and ordered a pint of beer. Looking thoughtfully at the generous 'top' he asked, 'D'ye think you could get a nip of whisky into this glass?'
'Certainly sir,' said the barmaid.
'Well, in that case ye'd better fill her up wi' beer.'

'D'ye know, Roddie, I'm the happiest man in the world. I've got the best wife in the country.'
'Who wouldn't be happy with his wife in the country?'

And what about the lad who called on Jones and Jones the well-known solicitors in Cardiff? When he asked to see one of the principals the clerk queried. 'Which Mr Jones do you wish to see? McTavish or McGregor?'

Then there was the Aberdonian who used to run behind the local bus going to work every day. He thought it was a clever way of saving 8d. until his pal pointed out that by running behind a taxi he could save 10s. 'Apart from the 3d. tip,' he added.

. . . or the one about the Scottish baker who tried to economise by making the hole in his doughnuts bigger, only to discover that the bigger the hole the more dough it took to go round them.'

Maggie had put 'Rest in Peace' on the tombstone of her departed husband's grave—but when she discovered that in his will he had left nothing, she hastened to the mason and told him to add the words 'Till I Come'.

Then there was the reunion of old friends. The Englishman brought a crate of beer. The Irishman brought an enormous cooked ham. And the Scotsman brought his brother.

MacPherson, being drunk, fell down a dark staircase from top to bottom. He had a half-bottle of whisky in his hip-pocket and unfortunately it broke. Finding liquid on his hands he muttered: 'I hope to God it's blood.'

Donald: 'I've nae sympathy for the man who gets drunk every Saturday night.'
   Sandy: 'Aye, you're right, Donald—he disnae need it.'

A Scotsman, travelling by train, took a bottle of whisky out of his pocket and began to drink it. A fellow traveller, a teetotaller, began to remonstrate with him, adding, 'D'ye know, I've never touched the stuff in a' my life.'
   'Maybe,' said the other, corking the bottle firmly, 'and you're no' starting noo.'

The oldest inhabitant of a Highland village was often asked the secret of his long life.
   'Moderation in all things,' he said. 'Especially drink. I make two rules for my guidance in this matter. First, never to take whisky without water: the second, never to take water without whisky.'

A minister came upon a member of his flock staggering home and gave him a helping hand. He was pressed to enter the house but demurred. 'Oh, come on man,' he was urged. 'Let the wife see who I've been oot wi' the nicht.'

An elder who had been out collecting money for the church called at the manse on his way home. He was quite tipsy but excused himself on the pleas that his friends had insisted on his taking a dram.

'Dear me,' reproved the minister, 'are there no teetotallers in the congregation?'

'Oh aye,' said the elder, 'quite a few—but you'll no' find me calling on them.'

Angus delighted his wife Jean by giving her a diamond ring.

'Is it real?' asked Jean.

'If it's no',' replied the indignant Angus, 'I've been done for 11/6d.'

Jock was in a quandry. What to do?—marry the wealthy widow that he didn't love, or the poor lassie that he loved over-much?

'Listen to your heart, man,' urged his best friend. 'Marry the one you love.'

'Aye, ye're right as usual, Geordie,' he nodded, 'money's no' everything.'

'In that case, Jock, would you mind giving me the widow's address?'

The old farmer was being reproached by the minister about his absence from his usual place in the kirk.'

'I was at Mr Munn's kirk,' was the defence.

However, the minister was not to be so easily placated. 'I don't care much for this running to strange kirks—even to hear Mr Munn. How would you like it if your sheep strayed into strange pastures?'

'Indeed, sir,' came the caustic reply, 'I wouldn't give it a thought if it was better grass.'

The branch line between St. Andrews and Leuchars was noted for being very slow considering the short distance. It may have been this which caused the traveller to say as he changed trains there, 'Well, that's the worst part of my journey over.'

'Where are you off to?' asked a fellow passenger.

'South Africa.'

Old Mrs MacIntosh had at last consulted her doctor about 'trouble in her stomach'. After a careful examination he assured her that there was nothing to worry about.

'It's just wind,' he diagnosed. But Mrs Mac. was not to be put off so easily, even by her doctor.

'Just wind?' she replied angrily. 'Have you forgotten that it was "just wind" that blew down the Tay Bridge.'

During the First World War a Glasgow man was unfortunate enough to be seconded to a Yorkshire regiment. Sunday morning, during church service, the sergeant caught him bent low, poring over a pack of cards.

He was hauled before the C.O. on the following day. When the charge was read out the old man barked at him, 'And what have you to say for yourself?' The Scot swallowed, 'Well, sir, I was using them in place of the prayer book.'

'How do you mean?'

Warming to his task the Glaswegian went on:

'Sir, the Ace stands for The Eternal One,

'Two is for the Old and New Testament,

'Three is the Holy Trinity,

'Four is for the Evangelists,

'Five—The Wise Virgins Watching
    At The Door,

'In Six days the Earth was Created,

'Seven is for the Lord's Day,

'Eight for the Inmates of the Ark,

'Then we had the Nine Grateful Lepers,

'Ten is for Moses and His Commandments,

'Queen is the The Queen of Sheba,

'King?—that's for the Ruler of The World.'

'Ah!' said the C.O. 'but what about the Knave?'

The Scot gave a sideways jerk of his head—'That's the big b——d that brought me here.'

A Scotsman went into a hardware shop. 'I'm looking for a nice wee pocket knife,' he announced. 'Surely,' said the shopkeeper: 'Here's the very thing; four blades and a corkscrew.'

'Man,' said the Scot, 'have ye no' got one with four corkscrews and a blade?'

Rab was due to speak at a meeting in the village hall and was very anxious to make a good impression. To his horror a few minutes before the meeting opened he broke his artificial teeth.

'Don't worry about that,' said one of the platform party, 'I've got a friend who'll fix you up—no bother.'

Off he went and in a few minutes returned with a choice of dentures for the unfortunate speaker. He was delighted to find a set which fitted so well and saw him through the evening successfully.

'That must be a wonderful dentist friend you have,' he said afterwards, 'to be able to fix me up like that.'

'My friend is no dentist,' came the reply, 'he's an undertaker.'

A miserly old man had a reprobate of a son who took seriously ill. The doctor was sent for and began to examine him. As he was doing so, the old man butted in, 'Now, doctor, before you go any further, if you think he's no' worth repairing don't put out too much expense on him.'

'And where d'ye come from?' said a Scot to a boastful American.

'From God's own country.'

'Man, ye've an awful poor Scots accent.'

On the Old Course at St. Andrews two of the natives had started out nice and early for their round of golf. Later in the morning members at the club-house saw them return—one man carrying his friend over his shoulder. They rushed to help and found that the man was dead.

'Oh, that must have been terrible for you,' they exclaimed.

'It was indeed,' came the reply. 'It wasn't so much having to carry him as having to put him down and pick him up at every stroke.'

The skipper and chief engineer of a Clyde steamer were inclined to underrate each other's job, so one day they agreed to swop for a spell. All went well for a time, then the skipper called up from the engine room to say that he was afraid he had messed things up.

'Don't worry, man,' the engineer replied. 'We're half-way up Sinclair Street in Helen'sburg.'

Mrs MacFarlane rushed into the house shouting, 'Andrew! Andrew! Look—there's a cow in the garden!'

'Well, don't just stand there, get a bucket, woman, and milk the damned thing.'

A canny old Scot lay dying and the minister was at his bedside.

'Tell me, minister,' said the old man, 'do you think if I left all my money to the Free Church I would be sure of getting into Heaven?'

'I couldn't promise,' was the reply, 'but the experiment is certainly worth a try.'

An old Fife miner had lost his wife. A friend called to express his sympathy. As he left the house, the visitor asked about the date for the funeral.

'Oh,' was the reply, 'it'll no' be for a fortnight.'

'A fortnight?' gasped the visitor. 'Man, you can't put it off as long as that!'

'Why no'?' said the old miner. 'All our married life we kept saying as to how we would love a wee quiet fortnight to ourselves— and this is our very first chance.'

A stubborn old Scotsman lay dying. The relatives gathered round his bedside and, as he seemed to be unconscious, they began to discuss his funeral arrangements. But the old man, hearing what was going on, suddenly got up on his elbow and said, 'Mind this— if ye get Alex Fraser to mak' ma coffin, I'll never pit a fit in it.'

There's the story of an elderly couple from the Borders who had taken a seaside holiday where the weather had been exceptionally sunny. On the day after their return the husband fell suddenly ill and died. A few hours later one of his cronies called to pay his last respects. After gazing at the corpse for a few moments he turned to the widow and sniffed, 'Just the same, Mrs Brown,' nodding down at the sunburnt face, 'you must admit that the holiday did him the world of good.'

And what about the three Scotsmen who were found drowned in a loch? Turned out that they had bet each other a shilling as to who could stay under longest—winner take all.

MacTavish was in a London store and having some difficulty in choosing a suit. The assistant had shown him at least a dozen but all he got was a shake of the head.

At last the Scot seemed interested. 'Now we're getting somewhere, young fellow. That's exactly the *opposite* of what I want.'

Sandy had hitched-hiked to Wembley for the International and had thumbed his way back as well.

'Was it a big gate?' asked his pal.

'Aye, the biggest I've ever climbed over,' said Sandy.

Whether it was her smile or the nearness of the collection-bag being shaken in front of his face we'll never know, but whatever the reason McPherson found himself giving a penny to the Salvation Army lass.

He had no sooner turned the corner when he was approached

again. 'No, no,' he explained, 'I've already made my contribution.'

'You can't do a good thing too often,' the girl smiled. 'The Lord will repay you a hundredfold.'

'That might be,' said the Scot, 'but I'll just wait till the first transaction's finished before I start on the second.'

The laird was a catankerous old character and was forever changing his servants. To one young lad he had just hired as a groom he demanded: 'What's your name, boy?'

'Alexander, sir.'

'Far too imposing—from now on it's young Sandy.'

'What might be your name, sir?'

'Nicholas.'

'Well, in that case you'll no' mind if I just call ye Auld Nick.'

Sandy, up in Edinburgh for the day, ran into an old pal whom he hadn't seen in almost three years. Naturally, the two Scots made for the nearest pub.

Having ordered their favourite tipple and dutifully admired each other at arm's length, Sandy enquired, 'Well, and how's the wife?'

'Och, man,' was the reply, 'we broke up about a year ago.' With a shake of the head he added, 'I never liked her much anyway.'

'But, man,' said Sandy, 'you were married nigh on 15 years.'

'Aye, that's so,' his friend sighed, 'I suppose she must have wanted me worse than I didnae want her.'

Heard in the bus queue: 'And how's your man keeping, Mrs Brown?'

'Ach, pour soul, he's back in the pits and it's fair killing him—but thank goodness it's permanent.'

Then there was the one about the old Scot who had died. One of the neighbours had called to pay her respects. She looked at the still, quiet face.

'My, but it's terrible!' she wept, 'And he's that happy-looking.'

'Aye,' sniffed the widow, 'but John was always a bit slow on the uptake.'

Wee Johnnie: 'Why did you pick the man with the patched knees to work for you, Dad?'

Willie: 'Did ye no' see the other man had a patch on his seat?'

'Would you love my Jeannie as much if she had no money?' asked the canny Scot.

'I would that, sir.' Came the eager reply.

'Then away wi' ye—I don't want another fool in the family.'

The lady had recently lost her husband. One day soon after, she went with some relatives to visit his grave.

'Aye,' she said wistfully looking at the corner of the cemetery where he lay, 'there they are! At the left, Professor Murdo and his wife; and here's Dr Cameron; and there's ma James—jist the auld whist party.'

A drunk was helped by his pal to stagger into a temperance hotel in a little town in the Borders.

'You can't bring him in here!' shouted the outraged hotel manager.

'S'alright,' slurred the pal, 'he's too far gone to notice.'

A young Scottish lad was asking an old Scot what were his ideas on the merits of drinking whisky.

'Well,' came the answer, 'one's enough, two's too many, and three not half enough.'

An Aberdeen couple were the only survivors from a shipwreck. By the end of a few weeks on a desert island their clothes were in rags and their provisions finished—the future looked grim indeed.

'Oh my,' sighed the wife, 'things just couldn't be worse.'

'They could that,' answered the husband. 'Ah might have bought return tickets.'

During the war a Scotswoman, one of the canny country type, went to buy some candles and was surprised how much they had risen in price. The assistant told her that it was due to the war.

'Dear me, man,' she sighed, 'd'ye mean to tell me that they're fighting by candlelight?'

Or what about the typical Scottish story?—the kind that's expected of us. The three ex-army pals met up with each other in a London pub. The Englishman stood a round—the Jew stood around—and the Scot stood 6 ft. 2 in.

The commercial travellers' meeting had been organised to propose a league for the abolition of tipping. Hamish, sitting in the front row, showed no great enthusiasm. Looking down the Chairman addressed him personally—'But surely, Mr McMurdo, you'll join?

After all, it's only a matter of a shilling a year subscription.' 'A shilling a year?' was Hamish's rejoinder, 'at that rate it'll pay me to keep on tipping.'

Of course we've all heard the one about the Scot who found a half-empty bottle of cough mixture and sent his children out to play in their bare feet one wintry night so that it wouldn't go to waste.

Then there was the Aberdeen taxi involved in an accident in Bon-Accord Street. The *Press and Journal* reported that two passengers had been detained in hospital but that the other nine had been allowed to go home.

A Scot, in a big London store, was approached by the floor manager.
'Looking for something in men's clothing, sir?' he asked.
'No,' came the reply, 'something in women's clothing—I've just lost the wife.'

The Scottish angler died and made his way to heaven. He was stopped at the gate by St. Peter who said, 'You've told too many lies to get in here.'
Slightly taken aback, but quick to recover, the angler replied, 'Have a heart man, you were a fisherman once yourself.'

A Bannockburn blacksmith who had shown some English visitors over the battlefield and who, for his services and graphic descriptions of the events of that great day, had been offered a tip.
'Na, na, keep your money,' he said with great self-denial. 'This affair has cost ye enough already.'

A commercial traveller, caught up by foul weather in the Orkneys, wired his firm in Aberdeen: 'Marooned here by snow-storm. Send instructions.'
The reply came: 'Start summer holidays as from yesterday.'

A true Scot is one who opens a bottle of whisky and throws the cork in the fire.

'Well Robert,' said Donald, 'and how do you like married life?'
'No' bad,' replied Robert, 'but she's always ask, ask, asking for money.'
'And how much have you given her?'
'Oh, nothin' yet.'

An old lady lay dying and the parish minister called to offer consolation.

'Oh sir,' she said, 'it's a great relief to think I'll soon be lying on Beelzebub's bosom.'

'Abraham's, surely, Jean?' corrected the minister.

''Deed sir,' came the reply, 'when you've been a widow woman like me for thirty years, you don't care much what the gentleman's name is.'

A farmer, wishing to improve his men's minds and to amuse them, left some books in their bothy. Some time later he found the books obviously untouched and unread, so he took them away.

Said one ploughman to another, 'Does the idiot think we'll do his work and read his books for the same money?'

It was a cold, frosty morning. Rab met one of his cronies.

'It's a bit raw, Tam,' says he.

'Aye, 'tis that,' was the reply, 'there's a nip in the air—but I suppose that's the length it'll get.'

'And how is your new minster getting on?' the villager was asked.

'Oh fine, I think,' was the reply, 'but he's hardly settled down yet.'

'But I hear he's one o' the kind that doesn't believe in Hell.'

'Well,' came the grim rejoinder, 'he'll no' be long here before he changes his mind.'

Gordon had played truant from the kirk one Sunday and later ran into Davie who had dutifully attended.

'Was the minister's sermon good today?' he asked.

'Well, his text was from the Proverbs about the snares of deceitful women. He went on like that for quite a bit and from there wandered on to fornication,' explained Davie.

'Did he really? And what sort of treatment did he give it?'

'To be honest,' said Davie, 'he really shook me. D'ye know—he was dead against it.'

As was the custom in the old days a Turiff merchant, having done a lot of business with the railway company, received two first-class return tickets to London as a present.

Presenting himself at the booking-office he demanded the difference in cash between first- and third-class fares, 'You know fine that I never travel first-class,' he added.

The booking-clerk explained that it was no concern of theirs which class he chose to travel by—if he preferred third then that was up to him.

However, the merchant argued that if he and his wife were content to go the cheaper way surely they were fully entitled to the difference in money back. It took the stationmaster fully twenty minutes to convince him that, come what may, no money could be refunded if no money was paid.

At last the merchant gave up and, with a shrug, said, 'Well, I suppose we'll just *have* to go first-class; but to me it's nothing but sheer extravagance.'

Two Scots lasses were discussing the local 'talent'.

'Don't have anything to do with that Duncan Lang,' said Jean.

'Why not?' queried her friend.

'He knows an awful lot of dirty songs,' was the reply.

'Surely he doesn't sing them in front of you?' asked the horrified girl.

'No—but he whistles them.'

The Rev McKnight came upon one of his flock swearing wildly at his car because it wouldn't start.

'No need for that kind of language,' he remonstrated, 'why not try a prayer instead?'

After a bit more handle-cranking the car-owner looked up contemptuously. 'Right, then—pray, and see if you can get it started.'

The minister could do nothing but accept the challenge so, getting down on his knees, he piously touched fingertips and bowed his head. Suddenly the engine roared into life. He looked up in amazement—'Well, I'll be damned.'

He hadn't been feeling up to the mark and at last had paid a visit to Dr MacNab. After giving him a complete check-up the doctor shook his head dolefully.

'You're in a bit of a mess, lad, he said. 'I don't like your chances at all.'

Donald looked at him, 'How long have I got, doctor?'

'Well—it's hard to say. Maybe I could put it this way. Don't waste your money buying any long-playing records.'

Professor McQuirter, a famous Scottish surgeon, was a man of very few words. One day a woman called at his office—her hand badly swollen and bruised. The following conversation, opened by the professor, took place:

'Burn it?'

'Bruised it.'

'Poultice.'
The next day:
'Better?'
'Worse!'
'More poultice.'
Two days later:
'Better?'
'Aye! Fee?'
'Nothing—you're the most sensible woman I've ever met.'

A Sassenach on his way up to Ross and Cromarty pulled up at Perth for lunch. Later in the day he was walking along Kinnoull Street when he saw a wedding-party leaving the church.

There was such a crowd of onlookers that he felt it must be someone of importance. 'Who is it?' he nudged his neighbour. 'Dinnae ken,' was the terse reply.

Finding Perth such a beautiful city he spent quite a few hours wandering around the Inches on the banks of the Tay and was hurrying back to his car when he saw a lengthy funeral procession coming towards him.

He stood reverently with bowed head until it had passed, then, turning to an old man at his side, he asked, 'Who was it?'

'Dinnae ken,' was the quiet answer.

'My gosh! He didn't last long, did he?'

BEST
Jewish
JOKES

Compiled by

S. LEVIN

'Yes,' said Abe to his friend Issy, 'I'm afraid mit mine son it's turned out to be a great disappointment. You know how ve struggled to give him an education vot ve never had; I sent him to de finest business school in de country, and now vot happens? If he rolls up at my dress factory at 10 in de morning; is 11 o'clock he dawdles over tea; tvelve o'clock he's off for lunch; he's not beck till two, end from 2 till 4 he fools around mit de models; vot a rubbish he's turned out to be!'

'Abe,' replied Issy, 'vot troubles you've got is nutting; mine is a tousand times verse. You know how ve struggled to give mine son an education vot ve never had; I sent him to de best business school in de country, and now vot happens? Is he rolls up at my factory at 10 in de morning; is 11 o'clock he dawdles over tea; tvelve o'clock he's off for lunch; he's not beck till two, and from 2 till 4 he fools round mit de models; vot a rubbish he's turned out.'

'But, Issy, since ven is dat a tousand times verse dan me? It's de same story vot you've told me.'

'Abe, you forget vun ting: I'm in men's clothing.'

So this guy phoned Cohen & Goldberg, wholesalers.

'Put me through to Mr Cohen, please.'

'I'm afraid Mr Cohen has gone out, sir,' said the switchboard girl.

'Then get me Mr Goldberg.'

'I'm afraid Mr Goldberg is tied up at present, sir.'

'O.K. I'll phone back later.'

Ten minutes later. 'Mr Goldberg, please.'

'I'm afraid Mr Goldberg is still tied up, sir.'

'I'll phone back.'

Half-an-hour later: 'Get me Mr Goldberg!'

'I'm terribly sorry, sir, but Mr Goldberg is still tied up.'

'I'll phone back.'

Another half-an-hour later: 'Goldberg!'

'I have dreadful news for you, sir. Mr Goldberg is still tied up.'

'But look, this is ridiculous. How can you run a business like that? The one partner's out all morning and the other's tied up for hours on end. What's going on there?'

'Well you see, sir, whenever Mr Cohen goes out he ties up Mr Goldberg.'

Abe was perhaps nine or ten years old, and for the first time in his life he went to Habonim, the Zionist cultural group. As it happened it was Passover time and the Madrich, or leader, told them the story of the Exodus. When he returned home his mother asked him, 'Well, Abe, how did it go? What did you do? What were you told?'

'Ma, we were told about a guy called Moses.'

'And what were you told about Moses?'

'Well, you see, ma, this here guy Moses was a general in the Israelite army you see, and he did sabotage work behind the Egyptian lines, and by a clever military outflanking movement he managed to get the Israelites out of Egypt, and when they got to the Red Sea he called on his engineers to build pontoon bridges over the sea, and when they got to the other side Moses saw the Egyptian tanks coming in the distance so he radioed headquarters on his walkie-talkie and asked them to send over bombers to blow up the bridges . . .'

At which point his horrified mother interrupted with, 'But really, Abe, is that what you were really told?'

'Well, not exactly, ma, but if I had to repeat it the way I heard it, you'd never believe it.'

Abe and Issy were being shown around the ancient sites and ruins of Europe. They were enjoying their tour immensely. In Rome the guide indicated to them the Colosseum.

'Abe,' said Issy, 'dis illustrates vot I've told you not vunce but a hundred times; ven you heven't got sufficient capital, you don't start to build.'

Abe arrived at Issy's house distraught, wringing his hands.

'It's too terrible, too terrible what's happened. I took my son off the El Al plane this morning. A mere ten months he spent in Israel and the first thing he says when he gets off the plane is "Dad" he says, "I'm converted, I'm a Christian." Oh my God, what should I do, Issy, what should I do?'

'End me,' says Issy, 'heven't I a disaster like you? Vosn't I also dis morning at de airport? Seven months mine son spent in Israel and de first ting he says ven he gets off de plane is "Dad" he says, "I've got news for you. I'm a yok (gentile). I've been converted." Oh dat I should live to see such a day. Es a metter of fact you caught me on my vay out to de rabbi. Perheps he could help me, maybe.'

So both of them go along to the local rabbi, who listens gravely to their tale.

'Gentlemen, I don't know who is running the missionary societies in Israel these days, but it is too terrible and too tragic. As a matter of fact, you might have observed that I was also this morning at the airport. Yes, it is true; my own son, my only son; a mere five months he spent in Israel and the missionaries had got hold of him. As a matter of fact, you caught me on my way out. I was on my way to shul to ask the Ribbono Shel Olam (*King of the Universe, God.*) what should be done about it.'

So all three hurried over to shul and prayed like they never prayed before. They poured out their very hearts, and finally a voice was heard, a voice from heaven:

'Gentlemen! You know vot? I've had de same trouble myself.'

The Cohens were busy being divorced in court. The case had been heard, the judge had granted the divorce. They were divided, all was complete and it only remained for the judge to deal with the matter of alimony.

'This court,' he said, 'this court grants Mrs Cohen £50 a month maintenance.'

'Judge,' interjected Cohen, 'dat's very generous of you; and to tell you de truth, ven business gets better I'll maybe also help out a little.'

Mrs Cohen unexpectedly bumped into Mrs Levy.

'Shhhhh,' said Mrs Levy, 'don't tell anybody; I'm having an affair.'

'Oh,' said Mrs Cohen, 'and who is doing the catering?'

A curious custom attends the coronation of a pope, a custom that has gone on for untold centuries. Whenever a new pope is crowned, diplomatic heads and the heads of any religious denominations in Rome at that time proffer their congratulations. Of course, the chief rabbi of Rome would also extend this courtesy to the pontiff. But there was an extra bit, the origin of which was lost in the mists of time. The rabbi had in his possession a message in an envelope, and he would give this envelope to the pope, who would solemnly refuse it and the rabbi would then take it away again.

So when Pope Paul was crowned, the chief rabbi congratulated him and offered him the letter, which the Pope predictably declined.

Later that night the Pope phoned the rabbi.

'Look here, rabbi. About this custom of ours. What is it all about? How does it start?'

'Well, Pontiff, I don't know. I got this envelope from the chief rabbi before me, and he from the one before him, and the Lord knows how many generations it goes back. All I know is that I have to offer it to you and you have to refuse it.'

'Well then, shouldn't you open it and see what it says?'

'Yes, I suppose I should.' So the rabbi opened the envelope and found inside a bill for the catering for the Last Supper.

Noah was the first businessman in the Bible; he floated a company at a time when the rest of the world was under liquidation.

Adam was the first book-keeper; he turned over a leaf and made an entry.

'Are you the defendant?' asked the judge of Abe Cohen, who had been arraigned in the dock on a charge of stealing a car.

'No, no, no,' said Abe, 'I have a lawyer to do the defending; I'm the one who stole the car.'

The Negro preacher was introducing a white minister to the Sunday congregation:

'And brudders and sisters, this morning we have Brudder Smith to give de sermon; I must tell you that though his face be white, his heart is as black as ours.'

The Cohens were trying to impress the rabbi visiting their house. They bragged about the intelligence of their four-year-old David. The rabbi turned to the lad:

'Tell me, David, can you count?'

'Oh, yes; One, two, three, four, five, six, seven, eight, nine, ten, jack, queen, king.'

> Roses are reddish, violets are bluish,
> If it wasn't for Jesus, we'd all be Jewish.

Abe and Issy were on safari when all of a sudden Abe felt something spring onto his back. Terrified, he shouted:

"Issy, what's that thing on my back?'

Issy peered this way and that way beyond Abe's shoulders and then shrugged his own. Abe was frantic:

'Issy, for Peter's sake, what's that thing on my back?'

Once again Issy squinted to the left and to the right and again shrugged his shoulders. Abe panicked:

'Issy, please, what's that thing on my back?'

Again Issy looked, shrugged his shoulders and said:

'How should I know, am I a furrier?'

Abe was astonished; four months after beginning university she arrived home unexpectedly. To his quizzical gaze she replied:

'I'm afraid I can't continue with my studies any longer, Dad.'

'Vy?'

'Well, Dad, I don't know how to approach this, but I'm pregnant.'

'Vot?'

'It's a fact, Dad, I'm pregnant. These things happen.'

'But how could you do a ting like dis? Don't you know how ve struggled to give you an education vot ve never had? And now you come back and say, "I'm pregnant".'

'It's just one of those things, Dad. You read about it all the time. It's happened to me.'

'But dis is terrible. Who's de father?'

'Well, as a matter of fact, Dad, it's difficult to say. I can't pinpoint the father.'

'Vot do you mean you don't know de father? Me and your mudder are simple people, but you I sent to university. Ve ar plain people, but you are educated; ve don't know de proper way to be introduced, but you don't know how to ask, "Mit whom am I having de pleasure?" '

Mrs Cohen and Mrs Levy were talking in the hotel lobby and were introduced briefly to Mrs Rabinowitz. Mrs Cohen continued her chatter:

'Like I vos saying, mine husband goes to his business vot he owns mit de Rolls-Royce, and at de house we have a Rover and to run around mit is de Buick.'

'Yes,' says Mrs Levy, 'mine husband also goes to his clothing factory vot he owns mit a Jaguar, and at home is de Bentley, and to run around mit is de Alfa Romeo.'

Mrs Rabinowitz interjected:

'We aren't so fortunate. We have a small dry cleaning business and a little van which has to serve for the family as well.' And presently she left.

When she was gone, Mrs Cohen whispered to Mrs Levy:

'Tell me, dat Mrs Rabinowitz, dat's an English name?'

Three Jews met in Europe.

'Ver are you from?' asked one of the second.

'I'm from Pinsk.'

'Really, is it a big place?'

'No, it's a small place, a very small place; has maybe a tousand population.'

'And how many Jews are der?'

'Vell, must be of de tousand is seven hundred, eight hundred, maybe nine hundred Jews.'

'So vot do de others do?'

'Vell, you know, der's a fire brigade and a police station and a civil service and dis and dat; der's enough vork for everybody. And ver are you from?' he asks his questioner:

'I'm from Novgorod.'

'Really, is it a big place?'

'No, it's a small place; has maybe a two tousand population.'

'And how many Jews are der?'

'Vell, must be seventeen-hundred, eighteen-hundred, maybe nineteen-hundred is Jews.'

'So vot do de others do?'

'Vell, you know, der is a fire brigade and dis and dat; der's enough vork for everybody. And ver are you from?' He turned to the third Jew.

'Ahm from Noo Yark Cidy.'
'Really, is it a big place?'
'Sure, ten million pahpulation.'
'And how many Jews are der?'
'Why Ah guess there must be five million Jews.'
'Oi, oi, oi, vot a fire brigade dey must have.'

Mr Goldberg had become wealthy and decided to decorate his bachelor flat with good works of art. He approached the curator of the local museum:

'I vont for mine flat I hev heard is a good painter Piccaso. Money is no object.'

'Well, Mr Goldberg, we do have a Piccaso, as a matter of fact, but it's rather expensive: ten thousand pounds.'

'O.K. Wrap it up; de money is available.'

Three years passed and the curator noticed what he thought was a familiar face approaching the museum. Yes, there was no doubt about it; he remembered him:

'Ah, Mr Goldberg, how nice to see you back. As I recall you purchased a Piccaso. What can I do for you now?'

'Pardon me, the name is Gold, and I want a Goya.' (*In Yiddish, goya means a gentile woman.*)

Myers was the firm's finest export salesman. No one could touch him. Wherever he went in every country of the world he came back with magnificent orders and a growing reputation as one of the world's greatest linguists.

Large companies in forty countries did business with him and at trade fairs everyone greeted him like a long-lost friend. The chairman of the board invited him up to congratulate him on his success. 'But tell me, Myers,' he said, 'how is it that you are able to speak to all these people without an interpreter?'

Myers looked at him and said, 'Well, sir, I will tell you my secret. In each delegation I look for a well-dressed man waving his arms about and then I go up to him and we do all our business in Yiddish.'

Two young friends were breaking into society and young Cohen had high hopes of marrying an heiress. To give him moral support he took young Levy along with him to meet the girl's parents. The parents smiled at young Cohen and said, 'I understand you are in the clothing business.'

Cohen nodded nervously and said, 'Yes, in a small way.'

Levy slapped him on the back and said, 'He is so modest, so modest. He has 27 shops and is negotiating for more.'

The parents said, 'I understand you have an apartment.'

Cohen smiled, 'Yes, a modest couple of rooms.'

Young Levy started laughing, 'Modesty, modesty! He has a penthouse in Park Lane.'

The parents continued, 'And you have a car?'

'Yes,' said Cohen, 'quite a nice one.'

'Quite nice nothing!' interjected Levy. 'He has three Rolls-Royces and that's only for town use.'

Cohen sneezed.

'Do you have a cold?' asked the anxious parents.

'Yes, just a slight one,' replied Cohen.

'Slight, nothing!' yelled Levy. 'Tuberculosis!'

Abe Cohen left on a trip, omitting to tell his friends that he was going away for a short while. While he was gone, there was a terrible car accident in Golders Green. The man was so badly mutilated that at the mortuary they could not even identify the body. Eventually it was decided that it must have been Abe Cohen because he wasn't at home, didn't answer his phone and his car was not outside his flat. So they buried him as Abe Cohen.

The next day Abe returned to town, and, idly paging through *The Times*, came to the obituary column and was convulsed with laughter, for there, unmistakably, he saw his name, killed tragically on the 15th, and mourned by all his relatives and friends. Barely able to suppress his guffaws, he phoned another friend, Benny:

'Benny, have you got today's *Times?*'

'Yes, why?'

'Look up the obituary column.'

Benny looks and turns cold. No doubt about it; here he has been talking to Abe Cohen on the phone and yet, here in the paper, in black and white, he is dead, killed tragically and mourned by all his relatives and friends. Shaking, he returns to the phone and whispers,

'Abe, tell me, from where are you speaking?'

Nowadays the young girls are out all night sowing their wild oats and in the morning you find them in church praying for a crop failure.

Who is the chief rabbi of the Eskimoes?

Eskimoses.

What is the difference between a choir boy and a queer boy? The difference is in how they say A-men.

Mrs Cohen had come into some money and asked an interior decorator to re-do her house, Mr Jones said:

'Certainly, Mrs Cohen, I'll be glad to help. Can you give me some ideas of your tastes? Do you like modern decor?'

'Noh.'

'Swedish style?'

'Noh.'

'Italian provincial?'

'Noh,'

'Moorish, Spanish?'

'Noh,'

'Well you know, Mrs Cohen, you really must give me some idea of your tastes otherwise I will not even be able to get started. What is it exactly that you had in mind?'

'Decor, shmecor, vot I vant is dat ven my friends come to visit, dey vill take one look and drop dead.'

During the war a ship was sailing to England. On board Cohen, a merchant, introduced himself to another who looked Jewish. Sure enough, his name was Levy.

'I'm a merchant on de vay to England for vital materials for South Africa. And vot do you do?'

'I'm a professional magician.'

'Takeh, really?'

'Yes, really.'

'But vot is it ectually vot you do?'

'Well, you know, I make things appear out of a hat, and disappear, and so on, the usual.'

'Takeh? Can you really make tings disappear?'

'Oh yes, as a matter of fact, if I wanted to I could snap my fingers and make the whole ship disappear.'

And he snapped his fingers to emphasise the point. Just at that moment a German submarine shot a torpedo at the ship and the next thing they knew was that they were in the water, each holding on to a piece of wood. Cohen turned ruefully to Levy: 'Some trick!'

Day or night Abe always greeted his mother-in-law with 'Good evening.' His friend could not understand it:

'Why do you always say good evening? I notice that even in broad daylight you say good evening. What gives?'

'It's because whenever I see my mother-in-law vert es finster in di aygen.' *(it gets dark in the eyes)*.

'It is true, Abe, that your mother-in-law is ill?'

'Yes.'

'In fact, I hear she is in hospital?'

'Yes.'

'How long has she been in hospital?'

'In three weeks time, please God, it will be a month.'

The bank manager phoned Abe:

'Mr Cohen, I regret to inform you that you have overdrawn your account some £100.'

'Is dat so? Den tell me, mister manager, vot vos my bank balance two months ago?'

The pages of the ledger rustled over the telephone and presently the manager's voice was heard again:

'Two months ago, Mr Cohen, there stood to your credit the sum of £300.'

'Vell den tell me, mister manager, ven dat vos de situation, did I phone you?'

'I'm getting so much pleasure from mine son lately,' said Mrs Cohen to her friend.

'But how can that be? Everybody knows he is a homosexual.'

'Ah, but you don't understand; lately he is going out with such a nice Jewish doctor.'

'Mine son-in-law,' bragged Mrs Cohen, 'he is a scientist.'

'Vy, vot does he do?'

'He vorks in a place, Sasol, vere dey from coal make gas.'

'In dat case is mine aydem also a scientist.'

'And vot did your son-in-law done, Mrs Levy?'

'He made from ten tousand pound ash mit blotah' *(dust and ashes)*.

The Cohens were very wealthy and went down to London on holiday, Mrs Cohen driving their Daimler. She parked outside a de luxe hotel and snapped her fingers. The porters came running.

'Carry my luggage in,' she commanded imperiously

They did. She snapped her fingers again. Mystified, they came running again. What does she want this time?

'Carry Mr Cohen in!'

O.K., if she wants it, Cohen will be carried in. So two porters picked him up and deposited him in a chair in the lounge.

When Mrs Cohen came in, the manager, who had watched all this, said:

'Mrs Cohen, I'm so sorry to see about your husband, that he is sick, and can't walk.'

'Can't walk nothing, but thank God we are in a position where he doesn't have to.'

Cohen was killed in an accident and Levy was deputed to break the news as tactfully as possible to his wife. He knocked on her door and she came out.

'Pardon me, are you the widow Cohen?'

'Certainly not.'

'Want a bet?'

King David and King Solomon led merry merry lives,
With many many lady friends and many many wives:
But when old age crept over them, with many many qualms,
King Solomon wrote the Proverbs and King David wrote The Psalms.

Why were there two tablets?

It appears that when God had completed his Ten Command-ments he approached all the peoples of the earth and asked if they wanted his commandments. He asked the French:

'Would you like my Ten Commandments?'

'What is written there?' they wanted to know.

'Thou shalt not commit adultery.'

'No thanks, we don't think it is suitable for us.'

He approached the Germans:

'Would you like my Ten Commandments?'

'What do they say?'

'Thou shalt not kill.'

'No thanks.'

The Arabs. 'What do they say?'

'Thou shalt not steal.'

'But we earn our living by plundering caravans.'

And so God received rejections, with thanks, from all nations. Finally, in desperation, he approached the Jews: 'Would you like my Ten Commandments?'

'How much do they cost?'

'They don't cost anything.'

'In that case we'll take two.'

Abe viewed the slice of ham in the butcher shop with approval.

'How much is that slice of ham?' he asked.

Just then there was a terrific flash of lightning and a great rolling of thunder.

'It's O.K., God, I was only asking.'

Cohen was desperate. He finally plucked up enough courage and went to see a psychiatrist in London.

'Mr Cohen, your trouble is that you are an introvert. You can't face the world. The treatment is long and expensive. But between you and me, I think that psychoanalysis is not needed in your case. Don't be shocked at what I am about to tell you, but there is a short cut. What you need to give you sufficient self-confidence is to go to bed with a woman.'

'But, doctor, how can I? Do you realise that I am even ashamed to talk to women, to look them in the face?'

'I know, I know. Don't think that this is the first time I am dealing with such a situation. Indeed I have had several successes in such cases. There is an easy way around your difficulty. Just go along to this address in Shaftesbury Avenue (he hands him a card) and say that Dr Levy sent you. The woman there will make you very comfortable, very comfortable indeed. You will not need to feel the least bit ashamed. She has handled several cases for me, and highly successfully.'

So Cohen went and knocked timidly on the door. A madam opened it a fraction:

'What do you want?'

'Dr Levy sent me,' he stammered.

'Ah, one of Dr Levy's cases? Do come in.'

And she showed him a number of photographs, and he selected that one, and she said 'Room 3 upstairs' and the occupant made him very comfortable, very comfortable indeed. It had been a great success. He dressed, and with shoulders back, he went down the stairs and towards the front door.'

'Just a moment, Mr Cohen,' said the madam. 'Just a moment. That will be £5.'

'Oh, no,' said Cohen, brandishing a card, 'look, I've brought my National Health card.'

The prayer of the Catholic girl:

'O Virgin Mother, who didst conceive without sinning, teach me how to sin without conceiving.'

The Russian Premier was getting sensitive about outside protests against Soviet anti-semitism. He called Moscow's chief rabbi and instructed him to send a letter to Israel's Premier stressing that Russia was a paradise for Jews.

'And I want to see the letter before you send it.'

So the rabbi drew up a glowing account, as instructed, and ended with, 'However, there are shortages: there are no candles and no sugar.'

The Russian was pleased but demurred at the concluding sentence. The rabbi explained that he had to add something negative otherwise the outside world would know that it was simply a propaganda stunt.

'Yes, you are right. Leave it in and send it off.'

In Jerusalem the Premier was puzzled. Quite obviously it was a propaganda stunt, yet equally obviously the rabbi was trying to get some message across.

'Let us get another rabbi to decode it,' said an assistant.

So another rabbi examined the missive:

'Oh yes, it's quite easy. No candles, no sugar—in other words, "es is finster und bitter." ' *(Dark and bitter: it couldn't be worse.)*

In New York, Cohen had won a huge sweepstake.

'Now dat you have come into de money,' said his friend Shapiro, 'you can buy yourself an apartment on Fift Avenue, you can move in de best circles, you can drive a Cadillac, you can lose your accent . . .'

'Stop,' said Cohen, 'not so fast. Ven you say dat I can buy mineself an apartment on Fift Avenue, dat I can do. Move in de best circles, also possible. Drive a Cadillac, certingly; but lose mine accent? Never! Vonce a Yenkee, always a Yenkee.'

The Russian Premier called in his chief security officer:

'We have some garbled information that the Israelis have made some sort of discovery about atomic fission. Send one of our agents over and see what he can dig up.'

So the security chief briefed Ivan Ivanovitch about the matter and suggested that he first go to Tel Aviv where they had a contact man called Cohen at a particular address. The password is 'Volga boatmen.'

Ivan arrives in Tel Aviv, finds a three-storied block of flats, but is aghast to observe among the list of names in the foyer some three Cohens living in that particular apartment block.

So Ivan presses the button on the door of the Cohen on the ground floor. A man comes out:

'Yes?'

'Is your name Cohen?'

'Yes.'

'Volga boatmen.'

'Oh, you want Cohen the spy; third floor.'

Abe had both his legs broken in an accident. The bones mended and Abe sued the responsible company for damages, alleging that he was permanently crippled and would have to remain in a wheelchair all his life. The insurance company employed orthopaedic surgeons to assess the situation. They reported that the bones had healed perfectly, that Cohen was well able to walk and that he was simply malingering. However, when it came to court the judge took pity on the guy in the wheelchair and awarded him £10,000 damages. Abe was later wheeled up to head office to collect his cheque.

'Mr Cohen,' said the manager, 'don't think that you will get away with this. We know that you are malingering. And let me tell you that we are going to keep a huge dossier on you. We are going to watch you night and day. We are going to photograph you, and if we produce evidence that you can walk, not only will you have to repay the damages but you will also be had up for perjury.'

'Mister manager, I am permanently crippled in dis veelchair.'

'Very well, here is the cheque for £10,000. What do you intend to do with it?'

'Vell, mister manager, me and mine vife, we've alvays vanted to travel. So ve are starting out at de top of Norvay, and going tru Scandinavia, den Svitzerland, Italy, Greece—and I don't care vot your agents and spies are following after me; I'm crippled in mine veelchair—necherly ve are going to Israel, den Persia and India and across to Japan and de Phillipines—end I am still in mine veelchair so I don't care about your spies vot are following me mit der cameras—and from dere ve are going all across Australia and den to South America and all de vay up to Mexico and America—and remember dat I am still crippled in mine veelchair, so vot is de use of your spies mit der cameras?—and Canada. From der ve go across to France vere ve are going to visit a place called Lourdes, and dere you'll see a miracle.'

In New York Mrs Cohen's telephone rang.
'Hullo.'
'Hullo, ma, this is your son Abe, from Chicago. I've got news for you.'
'Vot news, mine son?'
'Ma, I've just got married.'
'Mazeltov, but vy didn't you tell me? Vot is de suddenness dat I must find out like dis?'
'Well, ma, you see, there's a little trouble. She's—she's—she's not Jewish.'
'Oi Abe, vot have you done? Terrible, terrible, how could you? Are dere no Jewish girls for you? Vell, I guess you must make de best of it.'
'But ma, you see, there's another little difficulty. She's a few years older than me, and she is pregnant.'
'Abe, mine Abe, vot hev you done to me? Vell, you are mine now flesh and blood so I must still congratulate you and give you mit your vife mine best vishes.'
'Thanks ma, but there is also another little matter. She already has five kids.'
'Oi Abe, must you break your moder's heart like dis? Still, you are mine son and I hope you make de best of it. '
'There is another little trouble, ma. We have nowhere to stay.'
'Don't vorry mine son. You can stay here in mine apartment in New York, you mit your vife mit her children.'
'But ma, then were will you stay?'
'Don't vorry, mine son; ven I'm putting down dis phone I'm dropping dead.'

Cohen arrived from London for a visit to Johannesburg. His cousin Bernstein chauffered him around the city's suburbs. In Houghton Bernstein said:
'And here live de settlers.'
'What?' said Cohen. 'I don't believe it. Settlers don't live in such opulent suburbs.'

'Of course dey do. Take for instance dat house; it belongs to Goldberg; he settled for two bob in the pound.'
'Mr Cohen, I'm sorry to hear about your factory that burned down yesterday.'
'No, no, no, not yesterday; tomorrow.'

'Sarah,' cried Abe, 'call a vet, I'm sick.'
　'I'll call de doctor.'
　'I don't vant de doctor; I vant a vet.'
　'Vy a vet?'
　'I vork like a horse, live like a dog and sleep with a cow.'

'Yes,' said the pet shop owner, 'the finest bird in the city. He can even pray. Watch.'

A yarmelke—the ritual head covering—was put on the parrot's head and he prompted parroted off *'Borchu et adoshem hamevorach . . .'* and the rest of the Friday night prayer.

Cohen was stunned at such virtuosity. He gladly bought the parrot, took him home, said 'Watch' and put a yarmelke on his head. The bird promptly completed the Friday night ritual. The family were amazed.

Friday night Cohen took the bird to shul. No need for a cantor he told the congregants, his bird would do very nicely, thank you. They laughed at him.

'Want a bet?' he said. 'Want a bet my bird can pray the whole of ma'ariv *(the evening service)*?'

So they gave him 10-to-1 that the bird would not say a single word of Hebrew.

A triumphant Cohen places the parrot on the bimah, the cantor's platform, puts a small yarmelke on its head, and says:

'O.K., pray'

The parrot keeps silent.

'Go on, pray, like you did in the shop and at the house.'

The bird keeps silent.

'Pray, you idiot; I know you can. I've got a bet on you.'

The bird doesn't open his beak.

So Cohen is laughed out of the shul. Fuming, he turns to the bird at home:

'So you shame me in front of everybody, eh! So you make me lose a 10-to-1 bet! So you pretend you don't know how to pray! What did you do that for?'

'Don't be a shlemiel,' says the parrot, 'next Friday night you'll get 33-to-1.'

The Cohens were on their way to Scotland on holiday. On the train from London to Edinburgh they got caught in a freak snowstorm.

So severe and so heavy was the snow that the train had to stop, and in no time the whole train was covered in a mountain of snow.

Volunteer organisations arrived to shovel the snow from the coaches.

One couple finally succeeded in freeing the entrance to Cohen's coach, came along the passage and entered Cohen's compartment and introduced themselves: 'We're from the Red Cross.'

'But,' said Cohen, 'but only yesterday in London I gave a donation.'

Issy Goldberg was distraught. Here he was, on the last day of his holiday in Spain, and he had not yet been to see a bullfight. What would his friends in Manchester say? So he went along to the local ring but was disconcerted to find that the fight was booked out for weeks in advance. Moreover, a huge queue blocked any hope of easy entrance. Circling the massive stadium, Issy saw a small stage door guarded by a commissionaire. Presently a strapping young fellow arrived and said, 'Toreador.' The commissionaire let him in. Another young chap came and said, 'Matador,' and the guard motioned, 'Enter.' A third man introduced himself, 'Picador,' and the guard answered, 'Come in.' Issy could contain himself no longer. He approached the guard and whispered, 'Isidor.' The guard answered, 'Kumpt arayn.' *(Come in.)*

Levy was a rotten actor devoid of parts. Eventually he gave it up to become an agent.

For weeks he sat in his bare boarded crummy office with nothing but a silent phone, splintered desk and old packing case to sit on.

Then in strode the famous film star. 'Mr Levy, I've heard good of you and want you to act for me on this million dollar contract—but only for 10 per cent, mind you, no fifteens.'

'Certainly, certainly.'

'And my wife has two similar contracts, will you act for her?'

'Yes, of course, my pleasure.'

'By the way, are you Jewish?'

'—Well, not necessarily.'

Cohen built himself a fine swimming pool. Presently an official from the local council arrived:

'Mr Cohen, we have received a complaint and I see that it is justified. You failed to apply for official permission to build this pool.'

'Really, is dat so? I didn't know dat you had to have permission.'
'Indeed you do. A swimming pool must get official sanction. You can build a decorative pool or a fish pool without permission, but not a swimming pool.'
'Vell, in dat case, dis vot you see is a big fish pool'
'Come, come, Mr Cohen, you're joking surely? Twenty feet by thirty feet, this is no fish pool'
'Yes, it's a fish pool.'
Then the inspector's eyes noticed a filtration plant nearby:
'And if, as you claim, this is a fish pool, then why is there a filter?'
'Because dis is a gefilte fish pool.'

Cohen surprised his wife in bed with his best friend. She saw him burst into the bedroom and exclaimed:
'Oh, my God! There's blabbermouth; now the whole town will know.'

Three types of individual commonly watch indoor games like chess or bridge: kibbitzers, dibbitzers and tsitsibachers. A kibbitzer is a person who tells the player what to play. A dibbitzer is a rather more timid soul who stands behind the kibbitzer and tells him what to tell the player. A tsitsibacher is very rare individual who stands at the edge of a large crowd watching a game of chess or bridge and for perhaps an hour at a time says nothing. Yet he knows where every card is, where every trick is, the potential of the weakest pawn. Yet he says not a single word. However, every so often, at the play of a card, he sadly shakes his head and clicks his tongue 'tsitsitsitsi.'

Cohen was enormously strong. When he applied for a job as a lumberjack in the Canadian north, the foreman viewed his muscular arms with appreciation.
'Still, Mr Cohen, perhaps I had better test you out before signing you on. Here is an axe. An average lumberjack can cut down that 8-inch diameter tree in six or seven minutes. Let's see what you can do.'
In but two minutes the tree falls. The foreman is astonished.
'Mr Cohen, I simply can't believe it. The finest lumberjack in the world could not have done that in less than four minutes 18 seconds. It's simply incredible. Please, just to make sure I'm not dreaming, try again. Here's an 18-inch tree; there's no lumberjack alive who can fell that in less than 18 minutes 26 seconds. Do your best.'
The tree is felled in six minutes 55 seconds. The foreman is stunned:
'Your technique is simply unbelievable. Tell me, Mr Cohen, where did you learn lumberjacking?'
'Vell, as a matter of fact, in de Sahara.'
'In the Sahara? But surely, my good Mr Cohen, there are no trees in the Sahara!'
'Vell, not any more der aren't.'

Cohen was rushed by ambulance from his warehouse to the hospital, deathly ill. When he awoke from his coma he looked round to find himself in a great big oxygen tent, with his solicitous partner Levy sitting anxiously by his side. Panting, puffing, wheezing and coughing, he hissed:

'Levy—cough—I'm dying—wheeze—— My share of the—pant—business, you can—puff—have. My stocks and—cough—shares, you can have. My blocks of flats—wheeze—I'm making over to—pant—you. My investments, fluid assets—puff—all yours. Everything I own you can—cough—have.'

'Cohen,' interrupted Levy, 'don't talk silly. You're not going to die. You're going to be all right. You've got the finest doctors battling for your life. The nurses are fighting for your life and, to tell you the truth, I feel rather at a loss. Here I am sitting at your side and unable to do anything for you. Is there something you would want me to do?'

'Yes—cough—there is—wheeze—take your—pant—foot—puff—off the oxygen pipe.'

The tramp surprised Abe in a restaurant.

'Mister,' he said, 'it's three days that I haven't eaten anything.'

'Vell den force yourself.'

On another occasion he again entreated Abe:

'I haven't eaten anything for three days.'

Abe continued munching away.

'Mister, it's three days that I haven't eaten anything.'

Abe paid no attention.

'Three days that no food has passed my lips.'

Exasperated, Abe put down knife and fork:

'Amazing it is—himself he won't eat, and me he also won't let eat.'

When a bearded Israeli arrived, a local Jew asked:

'Maybe you know my friend in Tel Aviv, Isaac Bernstein?'

'No.'

'But surely you know him; he is a bawuste *(famous)* man. He has unfortunately, a parch *(fungating baldness)* on the head.'

Stroking his beard: 'Isaac Bernstein from Tel Aviv with a parch on his head? No, I don't know him.'

'But you must know him. He had a kilah *(rupture)*.'

'Isaac Bernstein from Tel Aviv, with a parch and a kilah? No, I don't know him.'

'But how is that possible? He also has one eye and a hayker *(a hunch-back)*.'

Stroking his beard: 'Isaac Bernstein from Tel Aviv, a bawuste man, with a parch, a kilah, one eye and a hayker? No I don't know him.'

'But it's impossible. He also has a pock-marked face and an oisgedrayteh foos *(a twisted foot)*.'

Pensively stroking his beard: 'Isaac Bernstein from Tel Aviv, a bawuste man, with a parch, a kilah, one eye, a hayker, a pock-marked face and an osigedrayteh foos? Why yes, of course I know him. A shayner *Yid (A fine Jew)*.'

(Alas, only Jews can understand this story.)

Cohen couldn't take his wife a minute longer. He had to get rid of her. But then murder is illegal, so what to do? he unburdened himself to Levy.

'Cohen, it's no great problem. Vy don't you buy her a car? You know she can't drive. So who knows, maybe she has an accident and gets killed.'

So he buys her a little Ford. They meet a week later:

'Vell, how did it go?'

'A vaste of money. She drives it perfectly.'

'Den take my advice and buy her a Daimler. After all, the Ford is a small car and she can manœuvre it O.K. But a Daimler is a big car vot it's hard to handle and she can't drive, so who knows maybe God vill do a miracle and she vill have a smash and get killed.'

So he bought her a Daimler. They meet a week later:

'Vell, how did it go?'

'A vaste of money. She drives it perfectly.'

'Den take my last advice. Buy her a Jaguar.'

'A Jaguar?'

'Yes, a Jaguar.'

So he bought her a Jaguar. They meet a week later:

'Vell, how did it go?'

'Vunderful, vunderful! Vun bite and she vas finished.'

Six-year-old Abe had been asking awkward questions lately so pa told ma to instruct him in the facts of life. 'You tell him' reacted ma. Eventually they decided that the elder boy David should tell him and they suggested that he should introduce the subject by first broaching the matter of the birds and bees.

That night, in bed, David turns to Abe:

'Look here, Abe, do you know what it is that mommies and daddies do at night in bed?'

'Yes, of course I know.'

'Well, it's exactly the same with the birds and bees.'

'Yes,' said Sarah to her little friend, 'it's such a nice big house we have shifted into. We all have our own bedrooms now, but poor mum, she's still in with dad.'

Somehow Abe got lost on safari. One minute he was following the file through the bush and the next minute they had disappeared. He cried aloud, but none answered. He shouted, and only the echo resounded. Imagine that! Lost in darkest Africa, and it was already getting a little dark. The hyenas had begun to bark. He heard a lion roar. He knew that it was the end.

Suddenly he was in a clearing and he looked around. From nowhere a circle of natives appeared among the trees and bushes and began to inch towards him. Petrified, he watched as a little dark old lady emerged from the circle and walked boldly up to him, looked him in the eye and said,

'Shalom aleichem, ir kukt ois vi a Yid tzu mir.' (*Hello, you look like a Jew to me.*)

Abe was thunderstruck. In darkest Africa somebody, a native of all people, should talk Yiddish to him? Amazing, amazing, and what a relief!

Well, she told him the story of how they were the Black Jews from King Solomon's time and could still speak Yiddish and Hebrew. They chatted at length and the old girl told him how to get back to camp. While talking Abe suddenly notices a curious figure come out of the circle, a figure gesticulating and dancing, and with a mask on his face and tiger skins on his body. As if to introduce him, the old lady turned to Abe and explained:

'Und dos is mine zun, der doctor.' (*And this is my son, the doctor.*)

Abe was in the Israeli navy, on manœuvres in the Mediterranean. He was on deck and his captain down below. Peering through his binoculars, Abe was suddenly electrified. Turning to the speaking tube he shouted:

'Ceptin, on de horizon, a submarine, a enemy, a Egyptian. Fire a torpedo!'

'O.K., Abe, I'll keep a watch on my radar. Relax.'

A few minutes later.

'Ceptin, two hundred yards avay, a submarine, a enemy, a Egyptian. Fire a torpedo!'

'O.K., Abe, I have sighted him on my radar. I know when to act. Relax.'

'Ceptin, a hundred yards avay, a submarine, a Egyptian. Fire a torpedo!'

'Relax, Abe, I know when.'

'Ceptin, fifty yards avay, a submarine, a Egyptian, a enemy. Fire a torpedo; I'll pay for it.'

'You know, doctor,' said old Mrs Cohen in the hospital, 'you don't do tings de right vay. Never you ask me how are you Mrs Cohen. You come like all de oder doctors and push me here and poke me der and nobody asks me how I feel.'

The doctor realised that the criticism was justified so that when he approached her bed the next morning, he inquired, 'Well, how are you today, Mrs Cohen?'

'Oi, doctor, don't ask.'

Wanting to open an undertaking establishment, he went to Smith & Co., carpenters and joiners in this field. On the floor were a number of coffins, made of walnut or some other good wood.

'How much are these coffins?'

'These coffins, sir, are £10 each.'

'What, £10 for such coffins? Outrageous! I won't pay £10 for such bits of wood. I'm going round the corner to Abe Cohen's shop.'

At Abe Cohen's joinery shop there were also coffins on the floor, made of tomato box wood or something.

'How much are these coffins?'

'Dese coffins, sir, are £10 each.'

'What, how dare you? Smith & Co. round the corner charge £10 for their coffins, but those are coffins.'

'Ugh, I know dose coffins; you just do dis (Abe pushes his elbows out from his sides) and dey fall to pieces.'

In pre-war Poland the intelligentsia disdained the Polish patois speaking a cultivated French instead. So did the cultured Jews— like Mrs Cohen, who was in labour with her first pregnancy. In her hospital room she suddenly groaned.

'Ah, mon dieu!'

Outside her door the husband became worried and urged his friend, the doctor, to go to her and deliver the baby.

'No,' he said: 'She is not ready yet.'

Presently again, 'Ah, mon dieu.'

'Go to her, she is in pain.'

'Still lots of time; she's not ready to deliver yet.'

'Ah, mon dieu.'

'Go now.'

'Not ready yet.'

'Oi gottentu!'

'Now,' said the doctor, 'now she's ready.'

The patient was admitted to a fine hospital room and she especially appreciated the wide window and view outside.

After her operation she awoke, and opening a tired eye, the first thing she noticed was that the window was closed and curtained. Turning to the surgeon standing at her bedside, she asked:

'Why have you shut the view from my window?'

'Well, you see, at the moment there is a fire raging outside, and I didn't want you to wake up and think that the operation had been a failure.'

It was Yom Kippur, and while praying the cantor happened to look out of the window and framed in the window of a block of flats he could see a girl undressing.

The rabbi noticed that he was visibly disturbed and saw that his facial appearance was not as sombre as it should be on such a holy day, so, ascending the platform, he whispered:

'Today is Yom Kippur, chazen, and in the heart too it must be Yom Kippur.'

'In the heart it is Yom Kippur, rabbi, but in the pants it is Simchas Torah (*a joyous festival*).'

A whole bus-load of women from various Jewish charitable organizations overturned and were killed. At the reception desk, St. Peter, observing Christian teachings to the letter, assigned them to hell. They had hardly been there a week however when Satan phoned Peter and demanded that he remove the women to heaven. They were disrupting discipline and organization in hell.

'Why, what have they done?' asked Peter.

'They have banded together, collected money, employed engineers and installed a cooling system.'

Abe Cohen departed this life and found himself at the reception desk. A guide was assigned to show him around.

'Let us go downstairs first, Mr Cohen, and show you what we have here.'

So they went down and down and down and Abe was delighted to behold a lovely garden with a primrose path leading to a splendid edifice on which was emblazoned 'Hell' in letters of gold. Inside there were gambling dens, steakhouses, sports activities, klaberjas players, bowls, night clubs, girls galore; just what he needed.

'This will suit me fine.'

'Just a moment, Mr Cohen, surely you also want to see what heaven has to offer?' Come this way.'

So they went up and up and up and up and finally they came to an old dirty building on which was written the word 'Heaven'. Inside Abe saw lots of Jews with beards studying Torah.

'Not for me, thank you; I'll take the other place.'

'Are you sure, Mr Cohen?'

'Quite sure.'

So they went down and down and down and down and Abe again saw the splendid edifice of hell. But this time the guide did not take him to the front entrance but to a side door, and Abe sensed that things were very different here. Inside, he was shocked to experience an unbearable heat and everywhere he saw suffering souls shovelling coal into giant furnaces. Behind them stood hideous devils pushing the souls with evil-looking pitchforks.

'But there must be some mistake,' said Abe, 'I want to go to hell with the klaberjas, the girls, you know.'

'Oh that,' said the guide; 'no, no, that's just for tourists.'

On Friday Kelly sat down in a restaurant and asked the waiter:
'Do you have any whale?'
'No, sir.'
'Shark?'
'No, sir.'
'Then give me steak and chips; God knows I asked for fish.'

So the Reverend Jones departed this life and at the heavenly reception desk the clerk said:
'Ah yes, reverend, we have been expecting you. As a matter of fact, the heavenly court has already sat in judgment and we have decided to reward you with the use of an automobile here in heaven. After all, on earth you had only a bicycle with which to visit the members of your flock, so we have decided that you merit a car here.' And with that the clerk snapped his fingers and lo! there stood a brand new Mini.
So the reverend got in and drove around heaven and met a whole lot of old friends that he used to know on earth. However, one day he was disconcerted to see Father Kelly flash by him, Father Kelly that he used to know down on earth, a Catholic priest, and what was Kelly driving? Why, a brand new Rover.
Piqued, he drives back to Reception:
'Look here, I've just seen Father Kelly flash past me in a Rover. What gives here? Favouritism? Why must I drive a lousy Mini while Kelly enjoys a Rover?'
'Calm yourself, reverend,' said the clerk. 'I think you will agree that the heavenly court has not perpetrated an injustice. After all, you had a bicycle on earth; Kelly had to visit the members of his flock on foot. I think you must agree that his award is fair.'
Mollified, he got into his Mini again, and was astounded to see flashing past him none other than Rabbi Rabinowitz, from down on earth, and what was the rabbi driving? A Silver Wraith Rolls-Royce.
Fuming, he returns to Reception:
'Look here, when you explained why Kelly had a Rover, I accepted that. Fair is fair. But I have just seen Rabbi Rabinowitz in a Silver Wraith Rolls-Royce. So explain that. Everybody knows that Jews look after their clergy. They give them houses and cars and servants and everything; they lack for nothing. So why a Rolls?''
'Shhhhhh,' said the clerk, 'Shhhhhhh, he's a friend of the Boss.'

'Tell me, ver do you Catolics get all de money to build catedrals?'
'Well, Abe, you see, we Catholics have a system called Confession. Whenever anybody does something wrong, he comes to church, confesses his sin, puts a little in the kitty and is forgiven, and in this way we can collect large amounts of cash.'
'Really, vot a vonderful system. Maybe ve could adopt it for use

in our synagogue. Let me go along mit you tonight so I could get a for instance of how you vork.'

'Well, Abe, it's strictly forbidden for me, as a priest, to have you along, but seeing as how you've been such a good friend all these years, I'll permit it just this once.'

That evening they are seated in the confessional box, the priest in front and Abe, all agog, behind. Presently a man's voice is heard from behind the curtain:

'Father, I have sinned grievously.'

'What have you done, my son?'

'Last night I consorted with two women.'

'Well, then, put two pounds in the kitty and your sins will be forgiven.'

Abe is very excited. Presently another man's voice is heard:

'Father, I have sinned grievously.'

'What have you done, my son?'

'Last night I consorted with three women.'

'Well, then put three pounds in the kitty and your sins will be forgiven, my son.'

Abe can contain himself no longer:

'Vot a vay to make money; vot a vunderful system! Do me a favour. Let me do de next vun, just to get some practice.'

'Well, Abe, strictly speaking it's not permitted, but seeing as how you have been such a good friend all these years, I'll permit it just this once.'

So they exchange places and Abe sits in front waiting. Presently a woman's voice is heard:

'Father, I have sinned grievously.'

'Nu, nu, vot is it vot you've done?'

'Last night I consorted with four men.'

'Nu, put five pound in de kitty and I'll give you a credit for vun.'

'Is the world round?' asked the teacher, 'or is it flat?'

'Neither,' said seven-year-old Abe: 'My dad says it's crooked.'

The fat little man stood outside his wholesale in Market Street, under his sign 'Kelly & Cohen'.

Someone came up and said, 'That's a curious combination, Kelly & Cohen.'

'Is dat so? Den I'll tell you something even more curious: I'm Kelly.'

So finally the shadchan—the marriage broker—induced Cohen to meet this girl. After all, she was alleged to be beautiful, talented, educated, young and with pots of money.

Cohen, met her, liked her, married her.

A day later, he finds the shadchan and rages:

'Some dirty trick you played on me eh? She admits herself that she had slept with half the men in Plumstead.'

'So? After all, how big is Plumstead?'

'Abe, I have a wonderful bargain for you. I can get you an elephant for £200.'

'But, Issy, don't be a shlemiel. What am I going to do with an elephant?'

'What am I going to do with an elephant? Don't be a shmo yourself. Think of the bargain. Where can you pick up an elephant for £200? Tell me.'

'But I have an two-roomed flat; where am I going to put an elephant?'

'What is the matter with you? Don't you recognise a bargain when you see one? As a matter of fact, I have even better news for you. If you want I can get you two elephants for £300.'

'Ah, now you're talking!'

So Abe sat down in this restaurant and the waiter comes up:

'Pardon me, sir, are you Jewish?'

'Certingly I'm Jewish.'

'Then I'm afraid I can't serve you, sir.'

'Vy?'

'Well, we don't serve Jews in this restaurant, sir.'

'Vot?'

'It's quite so, sir; we have instructions from the management that we are not to cater for Jews, sir.'

'Is dat so? Ver is de manager?'

'He is in his office round the corner, sir.'

So Abe barges in, sees a figure behind a desk:

'Are you de manager?'

The figure nods his head.

'I'm Abe Cohen and vots dis nonsense you don't serve Jews in dis restaurant?'

'Vell, es a metter of fect, ve don't.'

'But dis is fentestic; you are a Jew yourself; I can hear by your accent.'

'Dat's quite so, Mr Cohen, and de fect of de metter is det ve don't serve Jews here.'

'And vy, tell me vy?'

'Vell, Mr Cohen, tell me, hev you ever *tasted* de food in dis restaurant?'

Abe was a tramp, and he stood outside a very exclusive club in Pall Mall—chewing something and spitting the pips on the floor. The commissionaire came out and said:

'Look here, my man, do go away; you are not permitted to spit pips in front of this club.'

Abe sized him up and down:

'Look here: in de first place, dis is a democratic country and I'll spit pips ver I vant, and secondly, let me tell you, dat's no vay to solicit new members.'

Her car broke down on a lonely country road. It was dusk and drizzling, but seeing a house in the distance, she went towards it for assistance. It began to rain heavily and she ran. When she got near to the house she suddenly became frightened. It was a forbidding, double-storied affair, dilapidated, no lights, broken window panes with a ghostly wind whistling through them, tall unkempt grass—a typically haunted house.

By now the rain was coming down in buckets and she needed shelter rather than assistance, so she pressed on the front door. It creaked open and from nowhere a gust of wind blew it shut. She tried the handle in panic, but it would not open. Turning to survey the room, she was horror-stricken: there on the floor, in front of her, was a coffin, and as she watched, wide-eyed, the lid began to open and an arm inched itself out, and a leg, and a head, the head of a vampire, a dracula. She couldn't even cry, but gathering all her energies she dashed up a nearby staircase, and at the top she couldn't go any farther, for the planks were all rotten and broken.

And just then she heard clomp, the first step of the Frankenstein on the staircase, clomp, the second step. Turning now to face this monstrous apparition coming up after her, she suddenly remembered: there is one thing that stops a vampire: the sign of the cross. So she raised her hand and motioned her finger vertically then horizontally, at which the vampire transfixed her with a baleful glare and said—

'Es if det vill help you.'

After many many years Abe met Issy.

'And how many children have you got?'

'I have three boys; the eldest is a judge, then there is a neurosurgeon, and the youngest is a nuclear physicist. And you?'

'As it happens I also have three sons. The eldest is a champion boxer, the second a first-class wrestler and the baby a karate expert. Why don't you bring your boys over? I'll see that they get a bloody good hiding.'

Mrs Cohen was pregnant and was talking to her husband: will it be a boy, a girl? The maid, who was listening, interjected.

'Medem, it will be a boy.'

'How do you know?'

'For sure, medem, it cannot be a gel.'

'But how can you be so sure?'
'Because no gel would stay nine months with the medem.'

Grandma Cohen was proudly taking her two grandsons for a walk. A friend stopped her and asked after the boys.

'Vell, dis vun, Abe, he is four years, bless him, he's de doctor; and here, bless him is David, he's two, he's de lawyer.'

Two Martians met, shook hands, how-do-you-do, and so forth, and the first introduced himself:

'I'm TK55917.'

'And I'm SW63284.'

'Funny,' said the first, 'you don't look Jewish.'

Greenberg had won £10,000 in a sweepstake but they didn't know how to tell him, for his heart was weak and the shock might kill him. Cohen agreed to break the good news gently. He was as good as his word and with great tact he explained it to Greenberg.

'It's great news, indeed. But tell me why did you beat about the bush for so long.'

'We were afraid that with your heart,' said Cohen, 'it might do you harm.'

'That was very kind of you and I tell you this, Cohen, I'm giving you half the money I won.'

Cohen dropped dead.

Issy had a shilling caught in his throat and his mother ran into the street for help. A man passing by caught the lad firmly and with efficient taps on his back made him cough it up.

'God bless you, sir,' said the grateful mother, 'you're a great doctor.'

'I am not a doctor. I'm a tax collector.'

It was Martha's first dance and her mother gave her a thousand warnings. Even when she was leaving the house she had to listen to the advice all over again.

'It's all right, Mammy, don't worry. I have it in my head.'

'Ah my child. They'll find it wherever you have it.'

The widow had a lot of trouble with undertakers, debtors, relations and many others. When the time came for the insurance cheque to be paid over the agent tried to console her with the thought that the money would make things easier for her.

'To tell you the truth,' she complained. 'I've had so much trouble that sometimes I wish my poor Jacob hadn't fallen into the cement mixer.'

The landlord sent a stiff letter to his tenant: 'My rent is considerably overdue and I must ask you to send on some money.'

The reply was swift: 'I don't see why I should pay your rent—I can't pay my own.'

The Bronovski's won a big prize in a sweepstake and bought a house in the country.

Mrs Bronovski was showing off their estate to a visiting poor relation from the city.

'Mrs Bronovski,' asked the visitor as they looked at the poultry, 'do your hens lay eggs?'

'I believe they do,' said Mrs Bronovski haughtily, 'but they don't have to. We can afford to buy them now.'

Cohen was advising his brother what to see in the zoo.

'There'll be a sign "To the Elephants" and you'll like them; and another "To the Lions" and they're very interesting—but don't bother your head with the sign "To the Exit". They haven't got one. I looked.'

Jakie couldn't sleep. For more than an hour he was tossing and turning in bed, making worried noises.

Rachel couldn't stand it any longer.

'Jakie, go to sleep vy don't you? Tossing end turning end muttering all night. You are ruining all my beauty sleep.'

'Oy, Rachel. I'm vorried. I owe Barney Hyman across the vay three hundred pounds. End I haven't got any money to pay him vith.'

'Is det all?' said Rachel. 'Vy didn't you tell me this before?'

Rachel got out of bed, opened the window and shouted across the street: 'Becky! Becky Hyman! I vant a vord vid you!'

Across the street a window opened. Becky Hyman's sleepy voice answered, 'Yes, Rachel. Vat is it at this time of night?'

'My Jakie owes your Barney three hundred pounds. And he hasn't got any money to pay him vid.'

Rachel closed the window and got back into bed.

'There now, Jakie my love, go to sleep. Let *him* vorry.'

The fast-talking, big-time American businessman was trying to pin down Abie on a deal. But every time he thought he had Abie cornered about the prices and delivery times, Abie wriggled out of it.

At last, exhausted and irritated at not being able to get a straight answer, the American roared at Abie: 'What the hell's the matter with you? Why must you Jews always answer a question with another question?'

'Vell,' said Abie, 'vy not?'

Sammy was about to make his shot on the golf course when a golf ball came streaking over and hit him smack on the back of his head.

'Oy, oy, oy,' said Sammy to his partner, staggering about and clutching his head in agony, 'I'll sue them! I'll sue them for every penny they've got. I'll sue them for one hundred pounds. I'll sue them for three hundred pounds. No I von't, I'll sue them for *six* hundred pounds. . . .'

Just then, somebody in the distance shouted 'Fore!'

'Done!' shouted Sammy—'I'll take it!'

'How do I get to the Albert Hall?' a tourist asks a Jewish musician in Shaftesbury Avenue.

'Practice,' the musician says simply.

'Lend me forty pounds,' the man asks the Jewish businessman.

'Here's twenty.'

'But I wanted forty.'

'So you lose twenty—and I lose twenty!'

'Waiter, I asked for a lobster. How come you bring me a lobster with only one claw?'

'So maybe it was in a fight,' suggested the Jewish waiter.

'So maybe you bring me the winner,' rejoined the customer.

WIFE: 'I want for you to go upstairs to thrash that wicked boy of yours.'

HUSBAND: 'All right, all right, but at least give me a few minutes to hate him.'

Cohen was envious of his friends who could afford overseas holidays. So one day he stocked up with food, locked the front door, closed the curtains in the windows and used no lights for three weeks. Nor did he answer the door or the telephone. During this period he had announced that he would be travelling in Europe.

After three weeks he emerged, phoned all his friends and bubbled over with news about his trip.

'Best of all,' he gushed, 'was Italy; and Rome vos simply fantastic. Es a metter of fact, I even managed to get an audience mit der Pope.'

'Really?' they replied: 'How splendid! And what is he like?'

'Vel, he is a fine man, a gentleman, a king all de vay, but between you and me, I didn't care for his wife.'

Cohen came from a very religous family; his father was a rabbi and so was his father-in-law—so he had to be very careful about observing the sabbath and all the holy days.

Cohen's great love in life was golf, which he played every chance he got. One year, at Yom Kippur, he was alone at home, so he thought that no one would be any the wiser if he played eighteen holes. So he went down to his club, which was pretty empty anyway, and started to go around on his own.

It was a lovely day and he was in great form. Now it happened that God and Moses were having a look for any one not observing the festival, and they saw Cohen, playing away happily. Moses was shocked and thought that they should punish him severely, and God agreed.

When Cohen got to the next hole God made his ball fly straight and fast, right towards the green. Moses said, 'Why are you doing that? He should be punished, not rewarded.'

God just nodded and told Moses to be patient.

Meanwhile the ball was continuing on its flight, and landed fair and square in the hole. Cohen had holed in one! Moses was really angry, and said, 'Here's this Cohen, who should know better, flaunting your holy day—and you reward him with the very thing every golfer dreams of!'

God smiled and said, 'Yes, but who's he going to tell?'

Abe had won his fortune the hard way but at last he wanted to show the world he had everything. He ordered a magnificent mansion and told the architect, 'I vont statchoos in every room.'

'What kind of statues, sir?' asked the architect.

'Vite vons,' demanded Abe.

The day the mansion was finished Abe walked in to be shown around by a proud architect. In every room were beautiful Greek classical statues from the museums of the world.

'Vot are they?' asked Abe.

'Statues, as you ordered, sir,' said the architect.

'No, no, no,' said Abe. 'Not that kind of statchoo. I von't the kind of statchoo where you lift it up, dial a number and say, "Hello, Hymie, isstatchoo?" '

123

Hymie bought a donkey for £10, but it died. Broke and dejected he confided in Lew.

'Don't vorry,' said Lew, 'I have an idea—hold a raffle. Sell eleven tickets at £1 each and you save your £10.'

'I don't get it,' said Hymie. 'The donkey is dead anyway, and why £11 to get £10?'

'Oh, that's simple,' said Lew, 'the winner get his money back.'

Cohen, under-buyer for a clothing store, had foolishly bought for stock a yellow check suit with mauve spots. After a year at looking at the monstrosity the shop owner one day couldn't stand it any longer.

'If you haven't sold that suit before I get back you're fired.'

When he got back Cohen was in a terrible state, suit torn and tattered, with mud, scratches and bites all over him; yet he was smiling happily.

'I sold it!'

'Good, but what on earth happened to you?'

'Nothing, it was just that the customer's guide dog objected.'

The theatre was crowded and the comedian started his patter:

'There were these two Jews. . . .'

A voice yelled from the audience: 'Jews, Jews, vy alvays pick on the Jews?'

The comedian ignored him.

'There were these two Jews. . . .'

Again the voice yelled: 'Let dem alone, pick on somevon else!'

'Oh well,' continued the comedian: 'There were these two China-men, and one said to the other: "Well, Lee, how your son's Bar-mitzvah go off, eh?"'

Levy and Isaacs were business rivals and Levy would go to any length to outdo Isaacs. When Levy painted his shop, Isaacs would have his shop front copper-plated. When Levy bought a small car, Isaacs bought a bigger car. When Levy got a Rolls-Royce, Isaacs got a Rolls-Royce Coupé. When Levy got a radio for his car, Isaacs got a radiogram. Then, to cap it all, Levy determined to do something special, and had a telephone installed in his car. Hearing from a friend that Isaacs had done just the same thing Levy thought he would ring Isaacs from his car.

'Hello, Isaacs, is that you? This is Levy phoning from my car.'

'Oh, hello, Levy,' said Isaacs; 'Just a minute—I have got some-one else ringing on my other line.'

Cohen had three daughters and was desperately looking around for sons-in-law. One such young man came on the horizon and Cohen grabbed him. The three daughters were paraded in front of him after a lavish meal. There was Rachel, the eldest, who was decidedly plain—in fact, she was downright ugly. The second daughter, Esther, was not really bad-looking but was decidedly plump—in fact she was disgustingly fat. The third, Sonia, was a gorgeous, lovely beauty by any standards.

Cohen pulled the young man aside and said, 'Well, what do you think of them? I have got dowries for them—do not worry. £500 for Rachel, £250 for Esther and £3,000 for Sonia.'

The young man was dumbfounded. 'But why, why have you got so much more dowry for the beautiful one?'

Cohen explained, 'Well, it's like this. She's just a teeny-weeny itsy-bitsy little bit pregnant.'

The theatre was crowded; in the interval there was a hubbub of conversation. Suddenly an old lady stood up and shouted at the top of her voice, 'Is there a doctor in the house? Is there a doctor in the house?'

A young man sheepishly stood up. The old lady shouted out, 'Would you like to meet a nice well brought up Jewish girl?'

Abe had reached retirement a very worried man. Most of his life he had enjoyed to the full and his savings left a lot to be desired. On the morning of his retirement he turned to Rachel with a worried frown, 'I don't know how we're going to afford it. I don't know how we can retire.'

Rachel reached for a bottom drawer and pulled out a bank book which showed regular deposits over the last forty years. Not only could they retire—they were rich.

'But how did you do it?' said Abe.

Rachel said shyly, 'Well, every time you made an advance to me in our married life I put ten shillings away and look how it's mounted up.'

Overjoyed, he put his arms round his wife: 'Oy vey, this is wonderful. But, Rachel, why on earth didn't you tell me before? If only I'd known I would have given you all my business.'

Levy was dying and his family were gathering to pay their last respects.

'Are you there, Rose?' he asked his wife.

'Yes, dear,' she whispered.

'Abe?'

'Yes, father.'

'Lew?' he asked weakly.

'Yes, father; I'm here.'

'Albert?' came the faint voice.

'Yes, father, we're all here.'

Levy leapt out of bed with a yell, 'Then who the blazes is looking after the shop?'

Cohen bumped into Isaacs who was looking terribly dejected.

'Vot's de matter?' he asked.

'I'm bankrupt,' said a quiet Isaacs; 'my business failed.'

'Oh, vell,' said Cohen, 'vot about the property in your vifes name?'

'There is no property in my vife's name.'

'Vell then, vot about de property in your children's names?'

'There is no property in my children's names.'

Cohen put his hand on Levy's shoulder, 'Levy, you are very mistaken, you are not bankrupt—you are ruined.'

Bloom went to the back of the bus queue, tapped the shoulder of the man in front of him and said, 'If you had what I've got you would give me your place.'

The man moved up and let him in and Bloom repeated this to the next one in the queue, 'If you had what I've got you would give me your place.' And one by one he edged his way to the front of the queue. The bus came with room for one only and Bloom got on it—but had to stand. Leaning forward he tapped a man on the shoulder and said, 'If you had what I've got you would give me your seat.' The man shamefacedly gave up his seat but a belligerent man sitting opposite leaned forward and said.

'Well, what is it you've got?'

Bloom turned to him and said, 'A terrible load of chutzpah.' *(cheek.)*

An anti-Semite hated *all* Jews, although he didn't know why. All his life he wasted his time and energy just loathing them and trying to find out about them. One day, overcome with his emotion, he broke into the house of a Jew and ran out clutching his Mezuzzah. At last he was going to discover the secrets of the Jews! He rushed home fearfully, looking over his shoulder in case he was being followed. He locked his door, got a knife and broke open the Mezuzzah. Inside was a piece of parchment. With trembling hands he unrolled it and on it was written: 'HELP—am prisoner in Mezuzzah factory.'

Mrs Mizner was a very careful housekeeper. Her loving husband, Abe, handed over his pay packet complete every week. One week she looked and found there was 6d. short.

'Abe,' she said, 'you're 6d. short.'

Abe explained that he had felt very hungry and had bought himself a bar of chocolate.

Next week she looked again and the pay packet was still 6d. short. Abe again explained apologetically that his hunger had got the better of him and he had taken 6d. The third time it happened she could contain herself no longer, 'Abe,' she said; 'Have I not been a good wife to you?'

'Yes, dear, the best.'

'Abe, have I not managed everything for you and seen to all your needs?'

'Yes, dear.'

'Then I think I am entitled to know, who is this other woman?'

The American, the Englishman and the Jew were indulging in a bit of boasting. The American said, 'One of my ancestors signed the Declaration of Independence.'

The Englishman spoke up and said, 'That's nothing—one of my ancestors was present at the signing of Magna Carta.'

The Jew just said, 'You think that something? Remember one of my ancestors drew up the Ten Commandments.'

Comrade Cohen was a member of a Russian trade mission to an English industrial town. One evening the Russians were guests at the local working-men's club. One of the club members was Joe Chubb, an earnest young Socialist, who eventually manœuvred Comrade Cohen into a corner by himself.

'Comrade Cohen,' said young Chubb, 'I understand you are a good Jew; I understand you are a man of integrity; I understand you possess considerable political acumen. Now, because you have all these fine qualities, it would be of great interest to me to have your opinion of the Soviet attitude to the Arab-Israeli conflict—and why the Russians support the Egyptian fascists against the democratic Israelis.'

From Comrade Cohen; silence. Just a slight shrug.

'But, come, Comrade Cohen,' the young man persisted: 'After all, *you* are a Jew. Despite the official attitude of your country, of your party, you must have your own view as to where justice lies— of whose cause is the right one.'

But Comrade Cohen would say nothing: not a word.

Joe Chubb leant nearer. In a tone almost of pleading he urged: 'But surely, Comrade Cohen, you must have an opinion!'

Comrade Cohen stirred in his chair and regarded the young man with a steady gaze. And he broke his silence:

'Comrade Chubb,' he said: 'I have an opinion.' He paused: 'But I do not agree with it.'

The Jewish explorer was crossing a sparsely-inhabited and little-known part of China. For days he had seen no human beings at all. Eventually he came across a beautiful valley and heard the sound of chanting.

'Strange,' he thought, 'that sounds just like a cantor. But it can't be . . . not out here. The loneliness must be affecting my mind.'

He followed the sound, and discovered that it came from a building tucked behind some trees. A notice outside, in Chinese, read: *The Hoi Ping Synagogue.*

The explorer look inside the building. It was, indeed, a service, with the cantor, the rabbi, the men in the body of the synagogue and the women on the balcony. Skull caps, shawls, dark suits. The whole scene was Jewish except for one tiny thing—all the people at the service were Chinese.

When the service was over, the explorer buttonholed the rabbi. 'Excuse me, but I'm interested in the customs and religions of this region. Could you tell me what religion you are?'

'I'm Jewish,' replied the rabbi in Chinese. 'We're all Jewish. And we have been holding a service.'

'But you're all Chinese,' said the traveller.

'That's right,' said the rabbi: 'All Jews are Chinese.'

'But look at me,' said the traveller; 'I'm Jewish.'

'Funny,' said the rabbi. 'You don't look it. . . .'

'Mr Cohen, you had better come over here right away; there has been trouble with your son.'

'Vy, vot's happened?'

'I can't discuss it over the phone; you had better come.'

So Abe arrives at the school.

'Mr Cohen, I'm very sorry to tell you but we are expelling your son; we can't tolerate his sort of behaviour here.'

'But vy, vot's he done?'

'Well, to be quite frank, Mr Cohen, we found him playing with his genitals.'

'But dat's not such a terrible ting, some of my best friends are genitals.'

There are two answers to N.W. Ewer's famous epigram
How odd
Of God
To choose
The Jews.

The one answer is simply explanatory:
Not news,
Not odd:
The Jews
Chose God.

The other is in the same tone as Ewer's:
Not odd
Of God:
The goyim
Annoy him.

BEST
Religious
JOKES

Compiled by

EDWARD PHILLIPS

A country clergyman meeting a neighbour who never came to church, although an old fellow of over 60, gave him some reproof on that account.

'I dare say,' said the parson, 'you don't even know who made you.'

'Not I, in troth,' said the countryman.

A little boy coming by at the same time, 'Who made you, child?' cried the parson.

'God, sir,' answered the boy.

'Why look you there,' quoth the honest clergyman. 'Are you not ashamed to hear a child of five or six years old tell me who made him, when you that are so old a man cannot?'

'Ah,' said the countryman, 'It is no wonder that he should remember, he was made but the other day—it is a great while, master, sin' I were made!'

—JOE MILLER

At an interdenominational school in North London, a little Catholic boy was arguing with a Jewish kid.

'I bet my priest knows a lot more than your rabbi,' he said.

'Well of course he does,' answered the Jewish lad. 'You tell him everything.'

'Don't you find the sound of the cathedral bells inspiring?'

'Pardon?'

'I said don't you find the sound of the cathedral bells inspiring?'

'Would you mind speaking up a bit?'

'THE BELLS—DON'T YOU FIND THEM INSPIRING?'

'Sorry—I can't hear a word you're saying for those damn bells.'

'Oh, I'm sorry, vicar—are you busy?'

'No, do come in—I'm just rehearsing one of my sermons.'

'Ah—practising what you preach.'

The Sunday School teacher had been talking about that part of the Gospel according to St. Matthew which dealt with the subject of repentance.

131

'Now can any of you tell me just what repentance is?' she asked.
'Yes,' said one little boy. 'It's being sorry enough to stop doing it.'

Two Englishmen went on holiday to Ireland. One of them had a reputation for tactlessness, so his friend warned him not to say anything disparaging about the Catholic church during their stay.

One evening they were playing darts in the local pub when news came over the radio that the Pope was ill. Immediately all activity stopped and everyone crowded round the radio to listen.

'Oh, to hell with the Pope,' said the tactless one. 'Let's get on with the game.'

He woke up in hospital to find his friend sitting next to him.

'I warned you not to say anything about their religion,' said his friend.

'Yes, I know,' was the reply. 'But you didn't tell me the Pope was a Catholic.'

A certain notorious liar and cheat went regularly to confession each Sunday and made a clean breast of all his sins.

At least he was honest to God.

A little girl in Sunday School when asked who it was that sat at God's right hand suggested 'Mrs God?'

A gambler sat down at the roulette table one evening. Just as he was about to make his first bet, he heard a ghostly voice whisper in his ear, 'Number Eleven.'

He looked round sharply but there was no-one standing near him. Deciding to play along, he staked a modest sum on Number Eleven —and sure enough it came up.

As he was about to place his second bet, exactly the same thing happened, and once again, Number Eleven won. As the game proceeded, Number Eleven came up eight times in a row, and the excited gambler had by this time won £10,000.

He decided to make one more bet and call it a day—but this time to his surprise the strange voice said, 'Put everything on Number Three!' The gambler obeyed; the wheel was spun; the ball went round—and landed in Number Eleven.

And the mysterious voice in his ear said, 'Damnation.'

A small boy was given twopence and sent off to church one Sunday morning. One penny was to buy himself a packet of bubble-gum, the other was to put in the collection.

On the way to church he tripped over the kerb and one of the pennies rolled down an open drain.

Later in church, when the time came for personal prayer, the boy said, 'Oh Lord, I'm very sorry, but I'm afraid I lost your penny down a drain.'

A Catholic priest and a Protestant minister had a heated discussion over the merits of their respective faiths. Finally they agreed to differ and as they parted the Catholic said, 'Let us go our ways—you continue to worship the Lord in your way and I will continue to worship Him in His.'

'I didn't see you in church on Sunday. I hear you were playing golf instead.'
'That's not true, vicar—and I have the fish to prove it.'

'My boy, don't you know it's wrong to fish on the sabbath?'
'Oh I'm not fishing, vicar—I'm teaching this worm how to swim.'

During a particularly dry summer, the vicar included in his Harvest Festival services a special prayer for rain.
Discussing the service with his wife afterwards, he said, 'I must say the congregation didn't seem to have a great deal of faith in the efficacy of prayer—not one of them had brought an umbrella.'

Two men were walking down the street.
'Good heavens,' said one, pointing across to the opposite pavement, 'there's the Archbishop of Canterbury.'
'Of course it isn't,' said his friend.
'Yes it is,' insisted the first man.
'I'll prove you're wrong,' said the second man. 'I'll go and ask him.'
So he crossed the street and spoke to the stranger. When he returned, his friend asked, 'Well—was it the Archbishop of Canterbury?'
'He didn't say,' said the other. 'He just told me to get lost.'

The impact of the vicar's sermon was being rather spoiled by the crying of a baby at the back of the church. Finally the baby's mother got up and started to leave.
'It's quite all right, madam,' said the vicar. 'He's not disturbing me.'
'Maybe not,' said the woman, 'but *you're* disturbing *him*.'

The vicar who said that every blade of grass is a sermon should remember that grass is best kept short and neat.

Three Scotsmen attended church one morning. When the collection plate was handed round one of them fainted and the other two carried him out.

'Have you ever broken any of the Ten Commandments?'
   'I'm not sure—what's a graven image?'

He's a regular churchgoer—never misses an Easter.

A young minister, officiating at his very first service in a new church, noticed that the old churchwarden taking the collection quietly extracted a half-crown piece before taking the plate into the vestry.
   The minister took the old man aside after the service and gave him a lecture on honesty.
   The old fellow didn't seem to understand at first, but when he realised what the vicar was talking about, he burst out laughing.
   'Oh, don't worry about that, sir,' he said. 'Why, I've been leading off with that very same half-crown for over 30 years.'

'Would you say that the vicar's sermon this morning was inspiring?'
   'Oh yes—when he finished preaching a great awakening came over the congregation.'

Little Jimmy had just returned from his first visit to Sunday School.
   'Well,' said his father, 'how much did you learn?'
   'Not a lot,' said the boy. 'I've got to go back again next week.'

'Father, would you bless my new motor-cycle please?'
   'Certainly, my son—but remember the blessing isn't valid over 50 miles per hour.'

'I hear she had her husband cremated.'
   'Isn't that typical! Some of us can't get a husband for love or money—others have husbands to burn.'

The only times a lot of people step inside a church are when they're born, when they're married, and when they die. It's not surprising when you think that each time they get things thrown at them—water the first time, rice the second time, and dirt the third time.

134

'George,' said a country vicar to one of his oldest parishioners, 'why is it that immediately after evening service every Sunday, you go straight across the village green and into the Rose and Crown?'

'Well, vicar,' said old George, 'I suppose it's what you would call a "thirst after righteousness".'

'Your husband walked out in the middle of my sermon last Sunday, Mrs Jones.'

'It was nothing personal, vicar. He was just sleepwalking.'

On important Jewish holidays in America, it's the custom to charge for seats in the synagogue, the money going to charity. On one of these occasions, a man rushed up to the door of the synagogue where he was stopped and asked for his ticket.

'I have no ticket,' he gasped. 'Our warehouse is on fire, and my partner Goldstein is in there—I must tell him!'

'Well,' said the official doubtfully, 'all right, you can go in and tell him, but remember now—no praying.'

Overheard at a revivalist meeting:

'I understand you're a Christian Scientist?'

'Yes.'

'Well, would you mind changing places with me? I'm sitting in a draught.'

A Catholic girl fell in love with a Jewish boy and decided to try to convert him to her faith. Unfortunately she overdid it. Now he wants to become a priest.

'I shall omit the blessing this Sunday,' said the minister. 'I don't think you need it. The Lord said "Blessed are the Poor", and judging by the size of the collection, that covers all of you.'

A young Irish policeman in New York waved down a car that had just gone through a red light. He walked over prepared to deal severely with the erring driver, but when he came up alongside the car he saw that the man behind the wheel was a Catholic priest.

'Father, you just went through a red light,' he said in a mildly reproving tone. 'I won't say anything about it this time—but be very careful at the next set of lights. The cop on duty there is a Methodist.'

SUNDAY SCHOOL TEACHER: 'When boys and girls do naughty things, do you know where they go?'

SMALL BOY: 'Hampstead Heath if the weather's fine.'

A Scotsman on a visit to the Holy Land took a trip to the Sea of Galilee to see the spot where Our Lord walked upon the waters. He thought he would take a boat trip across the lake, but on hearing that this would cost him 30s. decided against it.

As he made his way back to his hotel he was heard to mutter, '30s. for a wee boat-ride! Och—it's nae wonder He walked.'

Religion is a very positive force which adds purpose to our daily lives.

That's why churches have plus signs on top of their towers.

A famous surgeon died and went to heaven. The angel at the gates said, 'Is there anything you'd like to get off your mind before you come in?'

'Yes,' said the surgeon. 'In my younger days when I was a junior surgeon at St. Bartholomew's, I used to play for the hospital football team. During a closely-fought match against Guy's Hospital, I scored a goal which I thought was offside, but the referee allowed it and it won us the match.'

'That's all right,' said the angel. 'We have a note of that particular incident and you needn't worry about it at all.'

'Well thank you, St. Peter,' said the surgeon. 'You've set my mind at rest.'

'Oh I'm not St. Peter,' said the angel. 'I'm St. Bartholomew.'

A very voluble preacher was working himself into a frenzy during a sermon on hell and damnation. A little four-year-old in the congregation couldn't take her eyes off the wild figure in the pulpit. Finally she whispered to her mother, 'What will we do if he ever gets loose?'

A tribe of cannibals in Africa were converted to Christianity by a Catholic missionary.

Now on Fridays they only eat fishermen.

The Sunday School teacher had been talking to the class about charity, kindness and brotherly love.

'Now, David,' she said to one seven-year-old, 'if somebody gave you a bar of chocolate, would you share it with your brother?'

'Which brother are you talking about?' asked David. 'My big brother or my kid brother?'

A missionary in a native village in Central Africa insisted on performing the full Christian marriage ceremony for all the adults of the tribe.

Later he said to the tribal chief, 'Don't you all feel much better now that you've been through the marriage service?'

'Oh yes—we're all very happy,' chuckled the chief. 'Everybody got new wives.'

'Why is it I never see you in church, Matthew?'

'There are too many hypocrites there, vicar.'

'Don't worry about that—there's always room for one more.'

ST. PETER (*to new applicant at the Pearly Gates*): 'And what good deeds did you do during your lifetime?'

NEW APPLICANT: 'Well, I once gave an old tramp sixpence for a cup of coffee.'

ST. PETER: 'Anything else?'

NEW APPLICANT: 'I'm afraid not.'

ST. PETER: 'Well, here's your tanner back—you can go to Hell.'

Notice over church collection box in the vestibule:
> *Please give generously. Remember—you can't*
> *take it with you—so why not send it on ahead?*

Did you hear about the short-sighted penguin who escaped from the zoo, wandered into a convent by mistake, and had a nervous breakdown? He thought he had shrunk.

'Your suit will be ready in three months, sir.'

'Three months! Why, it only took six days to make the whole world.'

'Yes—and have you noticed the state it's in?'

A woman was talking to the vicar after the service one Sunday morning.

'I enjoyed your sermon very much,' she said, 'but I thought it was rather long.'

Realising her *faux pas*, she tried to correct the situation.

'Well, it wasn't really long, I suppose,' she said. 'It just *seemed* long.'

A man on a train found himself sitting between a rabbi and a priest.

'Ah, the Old and the New Testaments!' he said with a grin.

'Yes,' said the priest, 'and the space between them is usually completely blank.'

'I'm going to play handball with the angels,' said four-year-old Georgie.
'How on earth can you do that?' asked his mother.
'Easy,' said the boy. 'I throw the ball up to them and they throw it back down to me.'

You can't expect to cover up the week's bad habits just by wearing your best clothes to church each Sunday.

'I intend to put together a volume of my collected sermons to be published posthumously.'
'Oh really—I shall look forward to that.'

'Vicar, could I borrow that book of Bible stories again—the one you lent me last week?'
'Why certainly—I'm glad you found it so inspiring.'
'It's not that—it's just that I used my copy coupon as a book-mark and I want to check my football pools.'

A minister was taking a stroll around Leicester Square one Sunday morning when he came across a small crowd listening to a disreputable-looking youth playing a guitar and accompanying himself on the mouth organ.
During a pause in the music, the minister said reprovingly, 'Young man—do you not know the Fourth Commandment?'
'No, I don't,' said the youth. 'Whistle a couple of bars of the melody and I'll pick it up from there.'

A Jew was arguing with a Christian.
'Your whole religion is based on ours anyway,' he said. 'Why, you even took the Ten Commandments from us.'
'We may have taken them,' said the Christian, 'but you certainly can't say we've kept them.'

A little boy returning home from his first church service asked his mother what the preacher had meant by the phrase, 'Dust to dust, ashes to ashes.'
'It means,' answered his mother, 'that we all come from dust and we shall all return to dust.'
That night, mother was startled to hear her son call down to her

from his bedroom, 'Come quick, Mummy—there's someone under the bed either coming or going.'

A Quaker was in bed one night when he heard a burglar ransacking his house. Taking his shotgun from the wall, he crept downstairs and opened the door quietly.

'Friend,' he said, 'I mean thee no harm but thou are standing where I am about to shoot.'

Much-married film star (at her 12th wedding) to short-sighted old minister trying to find the marriage ceremony in the prayer-book: 'Page 37, darling—take it from the top.'

An English tourist went to a wedding service in Scotland and was most surprised when he noticed a collection plate being passed round.

'Is this a Scottish custom?' he whispered to the usher.

'Not usually,' was the reply, 'but on this occasion, the bride's father insisted.'

An old Irishman on his deathbed was asked by the priest if he renounced the Devil.

'Just a moment now, Father,' he replied. 'I don't think this is a good time to be making enemies.'

FIRST VICAR: 'I hear you had a record crowd at your church last Sunday?'

SECOND VICAR: 'Yes. It burnt down.'

Adam was giving the animals their names. 'And that,' he said, 'is a rhinoceros.'

'Why rhinoceros?' asked Eve.

'Because it looks like a rhinoceros, stupid,' said Adam.

From time to time, saints are allowed to visit the earth in disguise. Saint Theresa had long wanted to pay a visit to Hollywood but Gabriel, who was in charge of the roster, thought that even a saint would not be able to come through unscathed after visiting the movie capital.

Eventually, however, Saint Theresa persuaded him that no harm would come to her, and set off on the first available earth-bound cloud.

The weeks stretched into months without any word from earth, so one day a very worried Gabriel put through a telephone call to Los Angeles.

The connection was made, the phone rang, and finally a voice said, 'Terry here—who is this? Gabby—darling! How absolutely marvellous to hear from you . . .'

A Sunday School teacher had just finished explaining about Heaven.

'Now,' she said. 'Hands up all those children who would like to go to heaven.'

All the children put their hands up at once, except one little boy in the front row.

'Don't you want to go to Heaven, Billy?' asked the teacher.

'I can't,' said the youngster tearfully. 'My mum told me to come straight home.'

Two clergymen were talking about a third when the subject of their conversation suddenly appeared round the corner.

'Well, well, talk of the Devil . . .' said one.

'Vicar—I believe the Bible says it's wrong to profit from other people's mistakes?'

'That is substantially correct, yes.'

'In that case, how about refunding the £5 I paid you for marrying us last year?'

A woman noted for her explosive temper and angry outbursts finally died. At the funeral, the coffin was lowered into the grave and the attendants started to shovel in the earth. Just as they were completing the job, a tremendous clap of thunder rent the air.

The woman's husband looked upwards and said, 'Well—it looks like she's arrived.'

A shipwrecked sailor had been drifting in an open boat for a week when one morning he suddenly sighted land. As he came closer to the shore, he saw a group of men on the beach putting up a gallows.

'Thank God!' he cried. 'A Christian country.'

The Archbishop's little boy was asked if he believed in God.

'Oh yes,' he said.

On being asked why, he said, 'Well I suppose you could say it runs in the family.'

'It took me 30 years to discover that I had no talent for preaching.

'So why didn't you give it up?'

'How could I—by that time I had become an archbishop.'

A very fat parson was giving a sermon on the Second Coming. Towards the end of his discourse, he said in a loud voice, 'I shall come down and dwell amongst you,' at the same time striking the pulpit rails to emphasize his point.

Unfortunately, the pulpit gave way under the strain and the whole thing came crashing down on the front row of pews, parson and all.

Picking himself up out of the wreckage, one old parishioner remarked, 'Well—you can't say he didn't warn us.'

The local branch of the Rotarian Club asked the vicar to come along and speak at their monthly meeting. However, the chairman spent over three-quarters of an hour on his introductory remarks, so that when he finally asked the vicar to give his address, the latter got up and said, 'My address is St. Stephen's Vicarage, Cathedral Close, and that's where I'm going now. Good night!'

Many people who call themselves churchgoers only attend once a year—at Easter.

A minister preaching to an unusually large Easter congregation included a sly dig at the once-a-year crowd with these words:

'I'm very pleased to see so many unfamiliar faces here on this Easter Sunday morning and before closing, I'd like to take this opportunity of wishing you all a very Merry Christmas.'

A young preacher was asked to give a sermon at a small country church. He worked hard on the sermon but was disappointed to find when he arrived that there was only one man, an old farmer, in the congregation.

On being asked whether he wished to hear the sermon, the farmer said, 'Well, if I took a bucketful of meal down to the yard and only one chicken showed up, I'd still feed her.'

So the preacher delivered his sermon, which took about an hour and a half. Afterwards he asked the old farmer what he had thought of it.

'Well,' was the reply, 'if I took a bucketful of meal down to the yard and only one chicken showed up, I'd feed her of course—but I'm blowed if I'd give her the whole bucketful.'

Scene: The Pearly Gates. St. Peter is interviewing a new arrival.

ST. PETER: Name?

NEW ARRIVAL: Melvin.

ST. PETER: Did you ever gamble, drink or smoke when you were on earth?

MELVIN: No.

ST. PETER: Did you ever steal, lie, cheat or swear?

MELVIN: No.
ST. PETER: Were you promiscuous?
MELVIN: Oh no.
ST. PETER: Tell me—what kept you so long?

'Why did Mary and Joseph take the infant Jesus to Jerusalem with them?' asked the Sunday School teacher.

'Because they couldn't get a baby-sitter?' suggested one modern miss.

A parson was playing a round of golf with one of his parishioners. At the 8th hole, the parishioner had to make a very difficult putt. As he squared up to the ball, he said jokingly to the parson, 'I think I'll offer up a prayer while I make this stroke.'

After missing the hole by a good eighteen inches, he said, 'Well, that prayer didn't do much good, did it?'

'No,' said the parson, 'but next time, try keeping your head down when you pray.'

Three rather ancient clerics were taking tea together one afternoon, and the conversation turned to their most embarrassing moments.

When it came to the turn of the third member of the group, he explained how his mother had caught him looking through a crack in the bathroom door while the maid was taking a bath. The other two chuckled.

'Yes,' said one, 'we certainly got up to some tricks in our youth.'

'What are you talking about?' said the third cleric. 'This was yesterday.'

One very cold December not long ago, a newspaper reporter attending an ecclesiastical conference found himself staying in the same hotel as most of the delegates.

On the morning of the first day, he came down to breakfast to find most of the assembled clergymen gathered round the blazing log fire in the breakfast room. As he sat shivering in the cold, he suddenly said, 'Last night I dreamed I was in Hell.'

The churchmen looked round with interest.

'Really?' said one. 'What was it like?'

'Not all that different,' was the reply. 'Couldn't get near the fire for clergymen.'

A missionary was captured by cannibals and popped into the pot. Thinking that his last hour had come, he was most surprised to see the cannibal chief suddenly sink to his knees and lift his hands in prayer.

Hopefully he said, 'Am I to understand that you are a practising Christian?'

'Of course I am,' said the chief irritably. 'And please don't interrupt me while I'm saying grace.'

Everyone in the school was very excited over the impending visit of the Archbishop of Canterbury.

'The Archbishop is a man of God,' said the teacher, 'and if he speaks to you, you should address him as My Lord.'

The Archbishop arrived on schedule and the children lined up to meet him. Singling out one little boy, the Archbishop bent down with a smile and asked, 'How old are you my son?'

Completely confused and overawed, the little fellow gasped, 'My God, I'm six.'

WOMAN AT CONFESSION: 'Oh father, I spent an hour this morning looking in the mirror and thinking how beautiful I was. Will I have to do penance?'

PRIEST: 'Not at all, my child. You only have to do penance for a sin, not a mistake.'

An old gentleman who belonged to some of the most exclusive clubs in London eventually died and went to Heaven.

'Come in, sir, come in,' said Saint Peter at the Pearly Gates.

'Thank you, no,' said the old gent. 'I do not wish to join if you accept a complete stranger without even a proposer and seconder.'

A sailor on leave went round with his girl friend to the local padre.

'How soon can you marry us?' he asked.

'Well, we have to allow three weeks to elapse before—'

'Three weeks! But I've only got a 36-hour pass!'

Then, taking the minister to one side he whispered, 'Do you think you could just say a few words to see us over the weekend?'

A young lady was being interviewed for a job at a rather old-fashioned business house which required its employees to be of sober habits and regular churchgoers.

'What is your full name?' asked the interviewer.

'Elizabeth Waters,' said the girl.

'And do you have any denominational preference?' was the next question.

'Oh no,' said the young lady, 'but most people call me Lizzie.'

A little boy opened the large family Bible at the first chapter of Genesis and gazed with awe at the large pressed leaf lying between the pages.

'Oh look,' he said in hushed tones, 'Adam's best suit.'

A priest announced one Sunday that his sermon the following week would be on the subject of lying. During the week, he asked that everyone read the 51st Chapter of Genesis.

The following Sunday he asked everyone who had *not* read the 51st Chapter of Genisis to raise their hand. Not one person in the entire congregation raised his hand.

'In that case,' said the priest, 'my sermon on lying should be most appropriate. There is no 51st Chapter of Genesis.'

'So you're an only child,' said the minister to little Victoria, aged six.

'And does your mummy want you to have any brothers and sisters?'

'Oh no,' said Victoria.

'And how do you know that?'

'Well, I've heard her saying her prayers about it.'

'And what did she say?'

'Thank God there aren't any more of you.'

The following story is credited to Mark Twain:

'I once heard a preacher who was powerful good. I decided to give him every cent I had with me. But he kept at it too long. Ten minutes later I decided to keep the bills and give him my loose change. Another ten minutes and I was darned if I'd give him anything at all. Then when he finally stopped, and the plate came round, I was so exhausted, I extracted two dollars out of it in sheer spite.'

A Methodist minister was asked to resign from the ministry because of his addiction to drink and horses. He wasn't exactly defrocked— it was more a case of his being unsuited.

The lesser of two evils may just be the one you think you'll enjoy more.

'Of course I haven't been going out with another woman!' said Adam. 'You know perfectly well you're the only woman here.'

Eve was still suspicious. That night she sneaked over to where Adam was sleeping and quietly started counting his ribs.

A little girl, rather prone to exaggeration, rushed into the house one morning and said, 'Mummy, mummy, there's a great big bear in the garden!'

Her mother looked out of the window and saw that it was, in fact, just a rather large dog.

'Now you go up to your room this instant,' said the mother, 'and you say a prayer to Our Father in Heaven and ask him to forgive you for telling lies.'

Ten minutes later the little girl came downstairs and said, 'God wasn't cross, mummy. He said He thought it was a bear himself at first.'

'Father, did I understand you to say in your sermon this afternoon that on the Day of Judgement, when Gabriel blows his horn, *everybody* will be there?'

'Yes indeed, my son.'

'Does that include all the Catholics and all the Protestants?'

'Yes.'

'And the Jews too?'

'Yes.'

'And the Baptists and Methodists, the Episcopalians, the Seventh Day Adventists and—'

'Yes, yes, they'll all be there—but why do you ask?'

'I was just thinking—there'll be very little judging done on the first day.'

'I understand that your wife coverted you to religion?'

'Oh yes. I didn't believe in hell until I married her.'

A Scotsman put a half-crown in the collection plate instead of his usual penny.

When the usher refused to let him take it out again, he muttered, 'Och well—I'll be credited for it in Heaven.'

'Oh no ye won't!' the usher muttered back. 'Ye'll be credited for a penny and nothing more.'

An elderly bishop was being interviewed on television on his 90th birthday. In closing, the interviewer said, 'Thank you for coming, My Lord, and perhaps I may have the pleasure of interviewing you on your 100th birthday?'

'No reason why not,' said the bishop. 'You seem in good health.'

'Why did the Children of Israel make a Golden Calf?' asked the Sunday School teacher.

'Because they didn't have enough gold to make a cow?' suggested one little boy.

Two boys were always trading insults at school; when they finally left, one went into the army and one into the church. They both prospered and eventually one reached the rank of Colonel and the other became a bishop.

One day they both found themselves in full regalia on a station platform waiting for the same train. After a moment's scrutiny, the bishop turned to the Colonel and said, 'Excuse me, porter, am I on the right platform for Manchester?'

'Oh yes, madam,' said the Colonel, 'but should you be travelling in your condition?'

The curate of a small parish had been given the opportunity to transfer to a bigger parish with a consequent increase in salary. Unfortunately, his vicar would not give him permission to make the move.

Shortly after the interview, the vicar came across the curate earnestly praying in a quiet corner of the church.

'I see,' he said crossly. 'Going over my head, eh?'

A young lad left the small village where he had been born and went to live in London. After a few weeks he wrote to his old parish priest: 'Dear Vicar, I am living at the Y.M.C.A., and have a job as an invoice clerk in a shipping firm. I work from 8.30 to 6, and I have to be in by 10 p.m. each night. I make £8 10s. od. a week. Do you feel that I can lead a good Christian life under these conditions?'

The vicar replied, 'Dear Arthur, Under those conditions, that's about all you *can* lead.'

WIFE: 'Did you notice that atrocious hat Mrs Connolly was wearing in church this morning?'
HUSBAND: 'I'm afraid I slept through most of the service.'
WIFE: 'Well really! I don't know why you bother to go to church at all.'

An elderly cleric saw a small boy chasing a cat out of his back garden and shouting, 'Get the b—— hell out of it!'

'Now, now,' said the old clergyman. 'There's no need to talk to the poor animal in that way. All you have to say is "Go away, pussy, go away"—and the cat will get the b—— hell out of it just the same.'

The pilot of a new high-altitude jet fighter took the plane up on a test flight one sunny morning.

The plane climbed easily to 50,000 feet and the pilot was too busy with other controls to glance at the altimeter again until several minutes had elapsed.

When he did have time to check, he saw to his amazement that the needle registered an altitude of 18 miles! Completely startled, he involuntarily said, 'Oh, my God—!' And a voice answered, gently, 'Yes, my son?'

'My wife is an angel.'

'Lucky you—mine's still alive.'

A young minister began his sermon with the words: 'Some of the most enjoyable moments of my life were spent in the arms of another man's wife—my mother.' He then went on to preach about the innocence of childhood.

Another minister happened to be in the congregation and thinking that this was a very arresting way to open a sermon, determined to use it himself.

Unfortunately he had a very bad memory, with the result that on the following Sunday, he started his sermon in this way: 'Some of the most enjoyable moments of my life were spent in the arms of another man's wife—er—now, let me see, what was her name again?'

'Tell me about this young lady you want to marry.'

'Well, vicar, she's only a farmer's daughter but she——'

'How dare you! And anyway, I've heard that one before.'

'I didn't sing with the choir last Sunday for the first time for eight months.'

'Oh, is that what it was? I thought they'd had the organ repaired.'

A little boy was taken by his mother to a seance, and on being asked by the medium if there was anyone he would like to speak to, said 'My grandpa.'

Shortly afterwards the medium went into a suitable trance and sure enough, a spooky voice came floating through the air saying, 'This is Grandpa speaking from Heaven—what is it you would like to know, my boy?'

'Hello Grandpa,' said the boy. 'What are you doing in Heaven—you're not even dead yet!'

When a minister is preaching, nothing is more off-putting than seeing someone look at his watch. Except seeing someone shake his watch and hold it up to his ear.

The first thing today's motorist prays for when he gets to church on Sunday morning is a place to park the car.

A Methodist minister, a Catholic priest and a Jewish rabbi were talking.

'One of my ancestors wrote over 150 hymns,' said the Methodist.

'One of my ancestors wrote a revised version of the Bible,' said the Catholic.

'One of my ancestors wrote the Ten Commandments,' said the Jew.

147

Many people have nothing but praise for the Church, especially when the collection plate is handed round.

A group of children were asked to draw their impression of The Flight into Egypt. One little boy produced a drawing of an aeroplane with three figures seated inside.

On being asked who the figures represented he said, 'This is Mary, this is Joseph, and this one is Pontius the Pilot.'

It is not generally known that British Railways is mentioned in Genesis where it is clearly stated that the Lord made every creeping thing. . . .

'What do we know about the Phoenicians?' asked the religious instructor of his class.

'Weren't they the people who invented blinds?' said a voice from the back.

The vicar's wife was entertaining one or two small children to tea. Turning to one little girl she said, 'I understand God has sent you a little baby brother.'

'Yes,' said the little girl. 'And He knows where the extra money's coming from too. I heard Daddy say so.'

Is it true that when the Ark landed on Mount Ararat and Noah told the animals to: 'Go forth and multiply,' the two snakes stayed behind because they were only adders?

One Sunday afternoon, Murphy was taking a walk when he met his old friend Flanagan.

'Flanagan,' he said, 'people are saying that you don't go to church any more, and you don't believe in God. Is that true?'

Flanagan glanced round furtively and walked away without answering.

The next day, Murphy met Flanagan again.

'Look,' said Murphy, 'I must know. Do you or don't you believe in God?'

'No I don't,' said Flanagan.

'Well why couldn't you have said so yesterday?' asked Murphy.

'God forbid—on a Sunday?' said Flanagan.

It has been said that a good sermon should be like a woman's skirt—short enough to retain the interest but long enough to cover the essentials.

A clergyman was asked to officiate at the Mothers' Union Bible class but instead of discussing matters theological, the ladies spent most of the time chattering about their aches and pains, their children's tonsils and adenoids, and their husbands' slipped discs and dicky hearts.

On returning home, the clergyman's wife asked him how he had enjoyed the evening.

'Well,' said the minister, 'it was not so much a Bible Class, more an Organ Recital.'

'Nice to see you're attending church again,' said the vicar, meeting a parishioner in the street. 'Is it because of my sermons?'

'Not yours,' was the reply. 'My wife's.'

A vicar was shaking hands with members of the congregation at the church door after service. He was highly delighted when one parishioner remarked that his sermon had been like the peace and mercy of God.

On returning to the vicarage however, he was not quite so pleased when he referred to his Concordance and found the words 'The peace of God passeth all understanding and his mercy endureth for ever.'

Have you ever wondered where people in Hell tell each other to go?

'Did Moses ever get better in the end?' asked a little girl home from Sunday School.

'Why, whatever makes you think he was ill?' asked her mother.

'Well, he must have been,' was the reply. 'Didn't God tell him to take the tablets?'

A mother discovered her two small children on their knees in the garden; the older boy, six-year-old Billy, was solemnly saying grace.

'What are you doing?' she asked. 'You only say grace when you eat.'

'I know,' said Billy, pointing to his younger brother. 'Johnny's just swallowed a worm.'

Twelve wives arrived in Purgatory.

'Now ladies,' said the officiating angel. 'How many of you have been unfaithful to your husbands?'

Eleven ladies blushingly put up their hands.

'OK,' sighed the angel, picking up the telephone. 'Hello—is that Hell? Have you got room for twelve unfaithful wives—one of them stone deaf?'

A lady attended a seance to get in touch with her deceased husband who had been a waiter at a big restaurant. After the lights had been dimmed, the medium went into a trance and suddenly the table began to move.

'Joe—is that you?' cried the wife. 'Speak to me, speak to me!'

'I can't,' came a muffled voice from afar. 'It's not my table.'

A very conscientious young parson was walking through his parish one morning when he chanced to meet an attractive young lady who was known to be very free with her favours.

'I prayed for you last night,' he said reprovingly.

'Silly—you should have given me a ring,' she replied. 'I wasn't doing anything all evening.'

Everybody ought to have a religion of one kind or another. You owe it to yourself to know what church you're staying away from.

An old Irishman was attempting to smuggle a jar of whiskey across the border between Eire and Ireland. When asked what the jar contained, he said, 'Holy Water.'

The Customs officer insisted on opening it and taking a sniff.

'Good God, man, this is whiskey!' he said.

'Saints be praised!' cried the old man. 'A miracle!'

A shapely young lady was leaving a revivalist meeting one evening when she slipped and fell, landing in a most embarrassing position with her skirt around her waist.

To save her confusion, the preacher shouted out, 'Anyone who does not avert his eyes will be struck blind!'

One old fellow turned to his friend and muttered, 'I think I'll risk one eye.'

A rather elderly minister nodded off during the sermon. When the time came for him to begin the Creed, he was fast asleep, so his young curate nudged him gently and whispered, 'I believe in God the Father.'

'Of course, of course,' said the minister, waking with a start. 'We all do—that's why we're here.'

An interviewer from the B.B.C. was sent to interview a Roman Catholic priest for a religious programme. When he arrived at the church, the priest was taking confession so the B.B.C. man thought it would be a good idea to interview him at the confessional grille.

Accordingly he waited until the last of the penitents had gone, then went up to the confession box and said, 'May I speak to you for a moment, father? I work for the B.B.C.'

The priest replied, 'I'm glad you came to me, my son. It must have taken courage to make a confession like that.'

The Sunday School teacher asked the young members of her class to look up an appropriate text and read it out as they were putting their pennies in the collection box on the following Sunday.

A week later, the first little boy came up with, 'It is more blessed to give than to receive,' as he dropped his penny in the box.

The second child's quotation was, 'The Lord loveth a cheerful giver,' and this too was well received. And so on down the line to little Billy.

As he grudgingly made his contribution, he mumbled, 'A fool and his money are soon parted.'

An old parishioner was talking to the vicar's wife, a lady noted for her good works.

'I believe there is a special place in heaven for the wives of clergymen,' he said at length.

'Oh, I'd much rather stay with my husband,' she replied.

Did you hear about the vicar who decided to brighten up Sunday School activities and give them more appeal for modern youth? He installed a juke-box, a coffee-bar and a discotheque, booked pop groups, let the boys and girls mix freely together, allowed them to smoke, and encouraged them to talk freely about their sexual problems. Attendance dropped to nil. Parents claimed that Sunday School was no fit place to send their children.

St. Peter challenged the Archangel Gabriel to a game of golf.

St. Peter's first drive resulted in a hole in one. Gabriel's first drive produced the same result.

St. Peter looked at Gabriel thoughtfully and said, 'What do you say we cut out the miracles and play some golf?'

Many people spend a lot of time in church praying that the parson didn't notice that this is the first time they've attended since Easter.

'Where in Hell have you been?' as the sorcerer's apprentice said after waiting three hours for the Devil to appear.

Many people aren't interested in religion because they can't see what earthly use it is to anybody.

The vicar of a small country parish was offered the chance of a very much more lucrative living in a large city diocese. He was very well-liked in the parish, and so he had something of a struggle with his conscience over whether or not to take the new offer.

When a delegation of the local villagers came round to find out what he had decided to do the maid informed them that the good man was at that moment in his study praying to God for guidance.

'Perhaps we might speak to the vicar's wife for a moment then,' said the leader of the delegation.

'All right, I'll call her,' said the maid. 'She's upstairs packing.'

A man called Agnew was posted to Central Africa. On arriving at his new post, he sent a telegram to his wife in London. Unfortunately it was delivered to another Mrs Agnew by mistake.

Her husband had just died the day before so you can imagine her feeling when she received a wire reading, 'Arrived safely this morning. The heat is awful.'

The minister was baptising the sixteenth child of a local family.
'Name?' he asked.

'Er—Alfred,' said the harassed-looking husband.

'Oh for heaven's sake!' said the wife irritably. 'We've got an Alfred already.'

The scene is the Ark. Sailing has been delayed for 24 hours because of a spell of good weather. Mr and Mrs Noah are checking off the animals.

NOAH: Elephants.
MRS NOAH: Two.
NOAH: Camels.
MRS NOAH: Two.
NOAH: Sheep.
MRS NOAH: Two.
NOAH: Rabbits.
MRS NOAH: A hundred and ninety three . . .

'Do you go to church on Sunday mornings or do you sleep late?'
'Both.'

A schoolboy once described a monastery as a sort of hotel with cold and cold water in every room.

A Sunday School teacher was very keen on religious ceremonial and had spent an entire session talking to the class about the correct way to pray.

'Now,' she said finally, 'suppose we want to pray to God for forgiveness. What must we do first of all?.

'Sin?' suggested one little boy.

Judging by the inscriptions on the tombstones in most cemeteries, all the sinners must have been cremated.

If you think you are indispensable, take a walk round the local cemetery one afternoon.

THINGS THAT COULD HAVE BEEN BETTER PHRASED:
A missionary lecturing on the years he had spent in Africa said, 'For 18 months I lived and worked in a little village on the Upper Zambesi which was completely cut off from the outside world. Just how unpleasant and trying an experience it was may be judged by the fact that during the whole of that time, the only white person I spoke to was my wife.'

A man had been married about twelve months when he happened to meet the vicar who had officiated at the ceremony.

'Here,' he said, 'I thought you told me when you married us that I was at the end of my troubles!'

'Yes, I did,' said the vicar, 'but if you think back you'll recall that I didn't specify which end.'

The sermon was on the subject of the Ten Commandments. When the minister got to the Commandment, 'Thou shalt not steal,' a meek-looking gentleman in the front row began to look decidedly uneasy.

Later on, however, when he reached the Commandment, 'Thou shalt not commit adultery,' the man smiled and gave a little sigh of relief.

The vicar had noticed his behaviour and asked him afterwards why the Commandments had affected him in this way.

'Well,' explained the man, 'when you came to the one about "Thou shalt not steal", I noticed that my umbrella was missing. But when you came to the one about "Thou shalt not commit adultery", I suddenly remembered where I had left it.'

A church organist sent the following note round to his vicar: 'I am sorry to say that my wife died last night. Could you please find a substitute for me for the next few weeks?'

A parson found himself sitting next to a rather belligerent drunk on a bus. The drunk stared rudely for a few moments and then said loudly, 'I don't want to go to Heaven!'

The minister ignored him.

'I don't want to go to Heaven!' the drunk shouted, more loudly than before.

Still the minister said nothing.

At last the drunk stood up and shouted, 'I SAID I DON'T WANT TO GO TO HEAVEN!'

'Well, go to Hell then,' said the parson, 'but for God's sake don't make so much noise about it.'

A couple of astronauts knocked at the Pearly Gates.

'Come in, come in,' said St. Peter.

'Oh, we don't want to come in,' said one.

'What do you want, then?' asked St. Peter.

'We just came to ask if we could have our capsule back please?' said the astronaut.

'Actually, there's a lot to be said for sin, you know,' said one clergy man to another. 'After all, if it didn't exist, we'd be out of a job.'

'You're lucky you don't have to get up and go to church on these dark Sunday mornings.'

'No—I'm an atheist—thank God.'

An atheist is a man who goes to a Celtic v. Rangers match and doesn't care who wins.

TIRESOME PARISHIONER: 'Vicar—do you believe in the existence of Hell?'

BUSY PARSON: 'Certainly, madam, but I'm afraid I can't go into it with you just now.'

A little boy was taken to church for the very first time. When he returned home, his father asked him what he had thought of the service.

'Well,' he said, 'I suppose it wasn't a bad show for a penny.'

'What are you giving up for Lent?'
  'Smoking, drinking and chasing women. What are you giving up?'
  'Telling lies.'

Two small children were studying their old grandmother who was sitting in her favourite armchair reading the Good Book.
  'Why does Granny spend so much time reading the Bible?' asked one.
  'I think she's studying for her final exams,' said the other.

An itinerant preacher arrived at a small country town and asked a young urchin to direct him to the Church Hall where he was due to preach that evening.
  After receiving directions, he said, 'Don't forget to come along and bring all your friends.'
  'What for?' said the small boy.
  'Because I'm going to tell you how to get to Heaven.'
  'You must be joking,' said the kid. 'Why you didn't even know how to get to the Church Hall.'

The Hyde Park Corner preacher was getting quite worked up.
  'And on the Day of Judgement, my friends,' he shouted, 'there will be weeping, wailing and gnashing of teeth!'
  A very old lady in the front of the crowd shouted out, 'I'm all right then—I 'aven't got any teeth!'
  As the crowd started to laugh, the preacher pointed a stern finger at the old lady and said, 'Madam, that has been taken care of. Teeth will be provided.'

A young curate was talking to his vicar, who was shortly leaving to take up duties in another parish.
  'You have certainly been a great inspiration to everyone in the parish,' said the curate. 'I think I can honestly say that we didn't know what sin was until you came.'

A Catholic priest found himself standing next to a Jewish rabbi by the buffet table at a garden fête.
  As he selected some of the cooked meats he said jokingly, 'I wonder if I shall ever see you helping yourself to a plate of cold ham?'
  'I expect you will—at your wedding,' said the Rabbi.

People today hate to think they're missing out on anything. A recent bulletin issued by the Vatican mentioned in passing that there are now 143 officially recognised sins; since when have they had thousands of letters from all over the world, asking for a copy of the complete list.

'Ah, Frederick—I was very glad to see you at my temperance lecture on Saturday night.'
'Oh, so that's where I was.'

Item from the small-ad section of a local newspaper:
> *For Sale cheap—slightly used tombstone— would make ideal present for someone named George Albert Jenkins. Box 83.*

An inexperienced young curate rushed into the vicarage one weekday morning and said, 'Excuse me, vicar, but there's a rather strange, bearded figure sitting in church all alone, and he says he's God! What shall I do?'
The old parson was equally at a loss.
'Well, you'd better not leave him there alone. Go back and keep an eye on him. And try to look busy.'

'Some of those girls in your Bible class look rather grown up,' said one young curate to the other, 'How do you manage?'
'Well, you know what they say,' said the other. 'There's safety in Numbers.'
'I think I'd put my faith in Exodus,' replied the first.

In a certain religious order, at mealtimes each monk attends to the needs of his neighbour, but is not allowed to serve himself.
One day at dinner, a monk noticed a dead beetle on his plate and he looked up hopefully at his neighbour, expecting him to remove it. Unfortunately, the brother next to him did not notice.
Finally, the monk had an idea. Turning to the Abbot at the head of the table, he said, 'Father, I believe my neighbour does not have a beetle with his dinner.'

MEDIUM AT A SEANCE: 'I believe this is your late wife knocking.'
HUSBAND: 'Ah—she hasn't changed a bit.'

Four men of religion in a confidential mood were discussing their own secret vices.
'I'm very partial to ham sandwiches,' said the Jewish Rabbi.

'I get through a bottle of whisky a day,' said the Protestant minister.

'I have a girl friend on the side,' said the Catholic priest.

Then they turned to the Baptist minister and said, 'What about you—surely you have a secret vice?'

'Yes,' he said, 'I like to gossip.'

A little boy was watching his father making notes for his sermon for the coming Sunday.

'How do you know what to say, Daddy?' he asked.

'Why, God tells me,' said his father.

'Well then, why do you keep crossing bits out?' asked the boy.

A preacher had been talking for an hour and a half on the subject of brotherly love.

'And now, dear friends, what more can I say?' he said at last.

'How about Amen?' said a voice from the back.

Little Arthur, four years old, was attending Sunday School for the very first time.

At the end of the proceedings, the teacher said, 'And now children we will all kneel down and say our prayers.'

'Please miss, I can't,' said Arthur. 'I didn't bring my pyjamas.'

It has been said that motorists should always leave plenty of room for lady drivers and clergymen, the former for the usual reason and the latter because faith in everlasting life is supposed to apply to tyres, brake linings and steering mechanisms.

A Catholic and a Protestant family went on holiday to the South of France. As the weather was warm and the beach secluded, the parents let their little Catholic boy and Protestant girl, both aged 5, go swimming without any costumes.

When they came out of the water some time later, they both looked very pleased with themselves.

On being asked why, the little boy said, 'Well, at last we know the difference between a Catholic and a Protestant.'

DID YOU HEAR THE ONE ABOUT . . .

——the two angels who were having a heated discussion on whether there was life in the herebefore?

——the Methodist minister who found too much lipstick distasteful?

——the young lady who was so naïve, she thought Winchester Cathedral was where they held the shotgun weddings?

——the missionary who gave a tribe of Congo cannibals their first taste of Christianity?

——the missionary that a tribe of cannibals tried unsuccessfully to boil? He was a friar.

——the monks who decided to open a fish and chip shop but went broke in a week? They couldn't find a qualified friar.

——the local publican who acted as usher at a funeral and asked the mourners to pass round the bier.

——the educated chimpanzee who read Darwin's *Origin of Species* and said, 'Good gracious—I am my keeper's brother.'

——the doubting vicar who insured himself against Acts of God?

——the church that was so full it only allowed one prayer per person?

——the elderly bishop who dreamed he was preaching a sermon and when he woke up, he was?

——the man who believed so strongly in reincarnation that he made a will leaving everything to himself?

——the reformed Jewish church that was so progressive, it was closed on Saturdays?

——the two newly-ordained priests who went out on the town to celibate?

——the man who thought VAT 69 was the Pope's personal telephone number?

——the old verger ringing the bells one Sunday morning who got caught up in his work, dropped a clanger and tolled himself off?

——the go-ahead laundryman who called at the local monastery to see if the monks had any dirty habits?

——the nun who had a wooden leg? The other sisters called her Hopalong Chastity.

——the ambitious undertaker whose wife divorced him because he kept bringing work home with him?

——the vicar who bought a second-hand car and found he didn't have the vocabulary to run it?

——the comedian who was booked to appear at the Vatican, then found he was expected to do his whole act in Latin?

——the ministers who formed a bowling team and called themselves the Holy Rollers?

——the man who was caught kissing a nun, and explained that he was merely embracing Mother Church?

——the conscientious parents who practised on their baby with a watering can for two weeks before it was baptized?

——the crematorium that was bottling the ashes and exporting them to New Guinea as 'Instant People?'

——the efficiency expert who popped his head out of his coffin and said, 'If you were to put this thing on wheels, you'd only need one man instead of eight?'

——the ostentatious bishop who had his car fitted with stained glass windows?

159

EPITAPHS

Some appropriate inscriptions seen on tombstones:

A hippie: Don't dig me, man, I'm real gone.

A waiter: God caught his eye at last.

A pin-table addict: Please don't tilt.

A cowboy: He called Billy the Kid a coward.

An old maid: And they say you can't take it with you.

A lawyer: The prosecution rests.

A gentleman: Excuse me for not rising.

A husband (from Rest in peace.
   his wife):   Until we meet again.

SOME INTERESTING SIGNS SEEN OUTSIDE CHURCHES

'Just What Are You Doing For Heaven's Sake?'

'The preacher for next Sunday will be found pinned up in the side porch.'

'Men and women wanted to form congregation—no experience necessary.'

'Sunday next: 6 p.m.—Farewell Sermon by the Reverend Sinclair.
                6.30 p.m.—Hymn No. 14—'O Come Let Us Rejoice.'

Sign on the front door of a church undergoing extensive repairs:
    'This Is The Gate To Paradise.'
    (Will all visitors please go round and use the back entrance.)

'The lesson next Sunday will be the 20th Chapter of Exodus—the Ten Commandments. You saw the film—now come and hear the book.'

CHILDREN AT PRAYER

Little boy about to tell God what he wants for Christmas:
'And now, God, stand by for the commercial.'

BOAC pilot's son:
'God bless Mummy, and God bless Daddy, and God bless me. Roger and out.'

Disc-jockey's son:
'That is the end of my prayers for tonight. Tune in again on this wavelength at the same time tomorrow night.'

And we mustn't forget:
—the little boy who got into bed without saying his prayers, and explained to his mother that he didn't need anything that night.

—the child who finished his prayers one night with the words: 'And I'm afraid this is goodbye God—tomorrow we're moving to Liverpool.'

—and the young fellow who, when his mother complained that she couldn't hear what he was praying answered, 'I'm not speaking to you.'

AMEN

✳

A to Z of *Bible Characters*

Adam: inventor of the looseleaf system.

Ariel: patron saint of TV.

Balaam: a sacrificial sheep.

Bathsheba: inscription on the door of the Queen of Sheba's private ablutions.

Caesar: name given to all Roman Emperors to distinguish one from the other.

Caesarea: interrogative form of the above as in the question 'Is Caesarea?'

Cain: wanted to be as popular as his brother, but turned violent when he found he wasn't able.

Dan and Beersheba: famous husband and wife team.

Daniel: wrote the book of the same name—the first author in history to be lionised.

Delilah: ran one of the earliest men's hairdressing salons—inventor of the 'short back and sides'.

Eve: the first woman to persuade her husband to turn over a new leaf.

Gabriel: patron saint of Louis Armstrong.

Gideon: wrote a special version of the Bible for use in hotel rooms.

Goliath: a big man with no head for drink; David gave him a small shot and he got stoned.

Ham: son of Noah—was in charge of the canteen on the Ark. Also patron saint of actors.

Jonah: a character who was down in the mouth but he came out all right in the end.

Levi: inventor of jeans.

Lot's wife: one of the earliest known acrobats—on one occasion she looked back and turned a somersault.

Martyr: sister of Mary.

Matthew, Mark, Luke and John: patron saints of beds.

Salome: danced naked in front of Harrods.

Samson: an early strong man act—brought the house down on one occasion.

Solomon: a much-married king who was also a great animal-lover —kept 300 wives and 700 porcupines.

A GLOSSARY OF RELIGIOUS TERMS

Apocalyptic: a kind of fit or seizure.

Apostle: a letter: e.g. St. Paul's Apostles to the Corinthians (an early Rugby team). When St. Paul stopped writing these letters the Corinthians were said to be excommunicated.

Atheist: a teenager who doesn't believe in the Beatles.

Archangel: a crafty angel.

Banns: words spoken in church which prevent two people from getting married. Usually happens on three consecutive Sundays.

Beatitude: a Biblical cliché.

Benefit of clergy: a special concert held to raise funds for a vicar who is retiring.

Book of Numbers: Telephone directory mentioned in the Old Testament.

Burnt offering: a sacrificial meal that was overcooked.

Canon: a very small noise in the church hierarchy.

163

Canonised: when a canon is fired.

Cassock: what the congregation kneels on to pray.

Catacombs: used by the early Christians to groom their pets.

Censer: man who checks sermons and prayers for blasphemies, obscenities, etc.

Circumcision: that which cuts off the Jews from the Gentiles.

Convocation: having a strong sense of calling for a life of crime.

Deacon: stands on top of a hill and gets lit up at times of danger.

Epistle: a disciple—one of a wandering band of variety entertainers. The Acts of the Epistles were performed at various places including the Colosseum. Top of the bill was the singing team of David and Jonathan. David later became Jonathan's road manager and the latter was known as the Star of David. Other acts included the St. Vitus Dancers, Daniel and his Lions, the Gaza Strip, Sodom and Gomorrah, etc. Material used in the show was known as Corn of Egypt.

Faith: something that makes you believe what you know isn't true.

Holy orders: for example: 'Let us pray.'

Handmaiden: girl employed in early Christian barber-shops, generally as a manicurist.

Incense: spices and gums burned in High Church rituals—the smell is said to make Low churchmen very angry—hence the term 'incensed'.

Intone: used to describe a method of singing when the whole choir manages to keep time together and in harmony. Also known as Evensong; when the choir sings in unison, it is known as Plainsong.

Jacob's well: used by early Christian straightman—comedian replies, 'I didn't know he'd been sick.' (See Acts of the Epistles).

Missal: any object thrown at the preacher during a bad sermon.

Mitre: a small martyr.

Mothering Sunday: nine months after Father's Day.

Original sin: there is no such thing as original sin but it is possible to use your imagination on some of the old ones.

Palm Sunday: the ceremony of the laying on of the hands.

Parable: a heavenly story with no earthly meaning.

Psalmist: Old Testament fortune-teller.

Psalter: early form of cruet, used on the Psabbath Day by the Psamaritans and the Psadducees.

Redemption: the ceremony of exchanging Green Stamps for gifts.

Sexton: church official employed to explain the facts of life to young children.

Stained glass: one of the hazards facing old churches with bats in the belfry.

Suffragan Bishop: Churchman who believes in equal rights for women.

Surplice: a garment worn by the priest, over and above his minimum requirements.

Usher: church official employed to keep an unruly congregation quiet.

Vestibule: garment worn by the priest under his chasuble.

Vestry: boutique specialising in clerical underwear.

Walls of Jericho: early example of jerry-building.

BEST
Army
JOKES

Compiled by

EDWARD PHILLIPS

A young officer cadet, on his first day at training school, was taking a squad for drill. Everything went fairly smoothly at first, but when the time came to give the squad the order to mark time, he realised that he had completely forgotten the correct word of command.

Conscious of the fact that the eyes of the drill sergeant instructor were on him, he stammered desperately, 'Er—men—er—quick march—but don't go anywhere.'

A young soldier was posted to Malaya. He wrote home to his mother as follows: '*I think the public should be told just how bad things really are here in Malaya. Nobody does any work, bribery and corruption are everywhere, most of the day seems to be spent in drinking, gambling and sex. Now, as to the natives . . .*'

The cavalry major was in a towering rage.

'Trooper Collins!' he thundered: 'I thought I told you to collect my horse from the stables and have it shod!'

'Shod?' said the trooper, turning white. 'Blimey, I thought you said shot.'

The orderly officer put his head round the cookhouse door.

'Oh, Staff Sergeant,' he said to the chief cook on duty, 'there's a party of 50 gunners coming through in transit in half an hour. They'll be eating in the main dining-room with the rest of the battalion.'

'Very good, sir,' said the staff sergeant. As the officer disappeared, he turned to his assistants and said, 'Well, you heard the captain. Throw four more buckets of water in the Irish stew.'

During the days of conscription, a young lad received notification to go along for his medical.

When the doctor asked him for a sample of his water, he pretended to be unable to provide this, and was told to go home and bring back a sample the next morning. To fool the doctor, the young fellow got his dog to provide the sample. The medical officer took it and disappeared into a back room to carry out his analysis. After about 15 minutes he returned with a puzzled frown on his face.

'I think you're in trouble,' he said. 'Not only do you have rabies—I think you're pregnant as well.'

A private was driving a young officer along Piccadilly in a staff car one morning. While the car was held up at traffic lights, a very beautiful blonde in the briefest of mini-skirts walked past.

As the lights changed, the officer said, 'Quick—catch up with that girl.'

However, the driver was unable to get the car started for several minutes and by the time they were moving again, the girl had disappeared.

'I must say,' said the officer in disgust, 'you wouldn't be much good in an emergency!'

'Oh, I don't know, sir,' said the private. 'That was my fiancée.'

Three generals, one French, one American and one British, were attending NATO manoeuvres in Germany when the talk turned to the subject of courage.

'I will show you what I mean by courage,' said the French general. Calling over a private in a French combat company, he said, 'I want you to go through that minefield there, turn around and come back through it again, and report to me here.'

Without a word, the French soldier carried out the order. The French general said, 'That is what I call courage, gentlemen.'

The American general then called over a soldier from a Texas infantry regiment and said, 'Soldier, I want you to run through that minefield, double back through that valley where the tank battle is going on, along that river-bed which is being shot up by rocket-carrying aircraft, and report back to me here.'

Twenty minutes later, the soldier arrived back breathless, having carried out the general's orders to the letter. 'And that,' said the general, 'is what I call courage!'

Then the British general called over a private in the uniform of a cook's assistant, a lad about 18 years old.

'Did you see what that American soldier just did?' he asked. 'Well, I want you to do the same, but in half the time, and carrying this case of live ammunition.'

'Blimey,' said the soldier, 'you must be off your chump, mate! You ruddy-well do it yourself—you could do with the exercise by the looks of you!'

'And *that*, gentlemen,' said the British general turning to the others, 'is what *I* call courage.'

The commanding officer of a Highland Regiment had a certain Private Crawford brought up before him on a charge of using obscene language and fighting. Giving evidence was the Mess

Sergeant who said, 'It was at breakfast yesterday morning, sir. Private Crawford came in late, pulled Private Dunfie's chair out from under him, picked up Private Campbell's chair with Private Campbell still in it and threw it across the dining-hall. Then when Privates Kyle and McBain protested, he banged their heads together and said, "Shut your ******* mouths, you ***** *******'s and get on with your ******* breakfast!" '

'Well,' said the CO, turning to Private Crawford, who stood six feet four in his kilt, 'what have you to say for yourself?'

'Sir,' said the soldier, 'it's a pretty poor show if I'm not to be allowed to greet my comrades at breakfast.'

A young soldier was up before his commanding officer on a charge of assaulting his wife. After hearing all the evidence, the CO awarded him 14 days confined to barracks.

'I suppose you realise,' said the soldier, 'that this is going to ruin our honeymoon.'

'Do you have any physical disabilities?' asked the medical officer at the army examination centre.

'As a matter of fact I have,' said the young man hopefully. 'One of my legs is shorter than the other.'

'Oh, don't worry about that,' said the officer. 'We'll make sure that you're stationed in hilly country.'

'How did you get on with your date last night?' asked one soldier of another at breakfast.

'Just great,' was the reply. 'I finally persuaded her to say yes.'

'Oh, congratulations! When's the wedding to be?'

'Wedding? What wedding?'

A girlie show was touring army camps in Cyprus. After giving several performances at a remote army camp, arrangement were being made for the girls to have a meal before leaving.

'Now then,' said the officer in charge, 'would you like to mess with the officers?'

'All right, dear,' said the leading 'lady', 'but we must have something to eat first.'

The General Officer Commanding, Southern Command, was once making a tour of inspection round a large camp in Borden, Hants. As he passed the back door of the cookhouse, accompanied by the commanding officer of the camp, and the usual retiune of lesser ranks, two privates emerged from the door, carrying a large, steaming soup cauldron.

'Aha,' said the general, 'so this is what the lads are having for lunch today is it?' 'Well, sir . . .' said one of the privates.

'Let's have a taste then,' said the general.

'But sir . . .' said the other private.

'Stop arguing,' shouted the commanding officer. 'Let the general taste the soup!'

Obediently, one of the privates handed the General a large spoon. The General dipped this into the cauldron and took a long swallow of the steaming mixture; his face immediately turned red and it was at least five minutes before he could stop coughing and spluttering.

'Why that's not soup!' he shouted at last. 'It tastes like dirty washing-up water!'

'That's what we've been trying to tell you,' said one of the privates. 'It *is* dirty washing-up water.'

During the Suez crisis in 1956, a reservist was called up. When he reported to the formation unit, he demanded an interview with the commanding officer. On appearing before the CO, he said, 'Violence is against my principles. You can't make me fight if I don't want to.'

'No, we can't,' replied the officer, 'but I'll tell you what we'll do. We'll take you to where the fighting is and let you use your own discretion.'

INSTRUCTOR *to new recruit on the rifle range:* 'None of your shots seem to be hitting the target! Have you any idea where they're going?'

NEW RECRUIT: 'No, sergeant. All I know is they're leaving this end all right.'

The drill sergeant stopped the squad of officer cadets and walked over to a tall, thin young second lieutenant in the front rank.

'Excuse me—sir!' he said sarcastically. 'Everybody seems to be out of step except yourself. I just don't know what to do about it!'

'Well,' said the young man, 'I really think you ought to tell them, sergeant. After all, you are in charge.'

During the Zulu Wars in South Africa, a small patrol was heading south through a mountain pass when the sergeant-major, who had been scouting up front, rode back with the news that a large war-party of Zulus was waiting in ambush about a mile ahead.

'How many would you say there are, sergeant-major?' asked the commanding officer.

'About six thousand, sir,' was the reply.

'And what is our strength?'

'Including yourself, sir—ten.'

'Ah', said the officer, 'should be quite a decent show then.'

Did you hear about the soldier who was so absent-minded that one night on guard duty he forgot the password? Had to shoot himself, of course.

FIRST ARMY WIFE: 'I understand your husband is a second lieutenant?'
   SECOND ARMY WIFE: 'That's right.'
   FIRST ARMY WIFE: 'What happened to the first one?'
   SECOND ARMY WIFE: 'He got away.'

A soldier stationed in Germany received a photograph from his girl-friend taken at a party. The photo showed the party in full swing with couples dancing and necking everywhere, but his girl-friend was sitting alone on a sofa nursing a drink. He was very pleased to think she was behaving herself until the thought occurred to him that somebody must have taken the picture.

During the six-day war between Israel and Egypt, an Egyptian regiment was in full retreat. A private chose this moment to put in for a fortnight's leave.
   His commanding officer said, 'What do you mean—leave? Don't you know there's a war on? Absolutely impossible—but I tell you what I'll do, Abdul. I'll try to retreat through your home town.'

The scene was the selection board at a military training camp somewhere in the south of England. Each trainee was brought in before the assembled officers and asked what trade or branch of the service he would like to join. Next in was a pimply-faced youth with glasses.
   'Now my man,' said the officer in charge, 'what would you like to be?'
   'A brigadier general,' said the youth.
   The officer exploded with rage. 'Are you crazy?' he shouted.
   'Sorry,' said the youth. 'I didn't know that was a necessary qualification.'

Did you hear about the stork who threw an entire WRAC barracks into confusion by circling overhead for a whole afternoon? He wasn't delivering—it was just his idea of a joke.

OFFICER (*pointing to cigarette end on parade ground*): 'Is that yours soldier?'
   PRIVATE: 'That's all right sir—you saw it first.'

A new recruit, on sentry duty for the first time, had not quite got the hang of army rules and regulations. When the commanding officer appeared in plain clothes, returning from a visit to town, our friend was sitting in front of the sentry box, eating a sandwich.

'Don't you know who I am?' roared the officer.

'Not until you tell me,' said the rookie good-naturedly.

'I'm your commanding officer!' shouted the CO.

'Oh my goodness,' said the soldier, scrambling to his feet. 'Hold my sandwich a minute, will you, while I present arms?'

It was probably the same soldier who was on sentry duty the following evening. This time he was determined to do everything correctly and practised what to say all day.

However, he became confused when an officer approached and, stepping out in front of him, cried, 'Halt! Look who's here.'

PRIVATE ON SICK PARADE: 'I have a pain in my abdomen, sir.'

MEDICAL OFFICER: 'Listen soldier—officers have abdomens, NCO's have stomachs. What you've got is a pain in your belly.'

Did you hear about the private in the Signals who crossed a carrier pigeon with a parrot so that it could deliver messages verbally? The first day he tried it out, it turned up three hours late.

'What kept you?' asked the soldier.

'It was such a lovely day, I decided to walk,' said the bird.

'Now then,' said the sergeant, 'I want this barrack room swept out thoroughly, I want the windows cleaned inside and out, and I want all your equipment polished and laid out on your beds for inspection.'

As he turned to go, a soldier muttered, 'I know what he wants!'

Quick as a flash, the sergeant spun round and snapped, 'Oh yes? And what do I want?'

Swallowing hastily, the soldier said, 'You want this barrack room swept out thoroughly, and you want the windows cleaned and . . .'

Private Potter had only been in the army a few weeks when he began to act very strangely. Every time he saw a sheet of paper, he would study it closely and then toss it aside saying, 'That's not it! That's not it!'

This happened not only in the company office where he worked, but whenever he passed a notice board or a dustbin which contained pieces of paper; even if he saw a sheet of paper blowing across the parade ground he would chase after it, look at it carefully, then throw it aside saying, 'That's not it!'

His obsession eventually grew to the extent that he was unable to perform his duties satisfactorily, so his company commander had him remanded for psychiatric examination. On entering the psychiatrist's office, he immediately started grabbing the papers on that officer's desk, and tossing them aside, muttering, 'That's not it! That's not it!'

It was obvious that he was not in full possession of his faculties and, within a week, his discharge came through.

On the morning his Discharge Certificate was handed to him, he took one look at it and went bounding out of the gates of the camp shouting. 'This is it! This is it!'

SENTRY: 'Halt! Who goes there?'
 OFFICER: 'Orderly Officer.'
 SENTRY: 'Halt! Who goes there?'
 OFFICER: 'I've just told you! Orderly Officer.'
 SENTRY: 'Halt! Who goes there?'
 OFFICER: 'What's the matter with you, soldier? Are you deaf or just stupid!'
 SENTRY: 'I'm sorry, sir. The sergeant said if anyone came up that I didn't recognise, I was to shout "Halt! Who goes there?" three times, and then fire.'

A soldier in charge of a string of pack mules carrying supplies during the Burma Campaign, was several hours late in arriving in camp with the week's provisions.

'Why are you so late?' demanded his sergeant.

'Well,' replied the soldier, 'on the way here, I met the regimental chaplain and offered him a ride back to camp. And from then on, those mules didn't understand a word I said.'

Did you hear about the short-sighted tortoise who fell in love with a soldier's steel helmet?

Towards the end of the last war, the chauffeur to the Chief of Staff was continually being asked by his fellow-soldiers if he'd heard any news about when the war was going to end. He promised to tell them the minute he had anything to report.

One day he came into the mess-hall and said, 'Well, lads, the Chief of Staff spoke to me this morning.'

After the excitement had died down, a corporal said, 'What did he say?'

'Well,' said the driver, 'he said, "Tell me Private Hoskins—when do *you* think this war is going to end?" '

The Gurkhas had a great reputation for toughness during the last war and the story is told of two who joined a parachute regiment. During their first week of training, they were told that they were going to make a practice jump from 1,000 feet.

'We'd rather start from 100 feet,' said one doubtfully.

'That's quite impossible,' said the instructor. 'From that height your parachutes wouldn't have time to open properly.'

'Oh I see,' said the Gurkha, looking relieved. 'We get parachutes do we?'

A soldier once bet his comrades a week's pay that he could fire 25 shots from a rifle, from a distance of 500 yards, and call every shot correctly. The rest of his platoon eagerly took him up on the offer and they all trouped down to the rifle range. The young soldier settled down comfortably, took aim, fired his first shot, and said, 'Miss!'

Sure enough, the marker at the butts signalled a miss.

The soldier then fired a second time and again said, 'Miss!'—and again, he had missed.

This happened several times in a row until at last one of his friends said, 'Just a minute—you're not even trying to hit the target!'

'Of course I'm not,' was the reply, 'but I'm calling the shots correctly.'

The sergeant-major, the sergeant and the corporal were arguing about the ratio of work to pleasure involved in making love. The sergeant-major was of the opinion that making love was half work and half pleasure. The sergeant, however, thought that making love was about 25% work and 75% pleasure; while the corporal was of the opinion that it was 10% work and 90% pleasure.

To settle the argument, they called over a private who was sweeping the floor of the mess-hall.

'Well,' said the latter, when the problem was put to him, 'I would say that making love was 100% pleasure—if it involved any work at all, you blighters would have had me doing it.'

'Did you ever hear the case of the girl who passed herself off as a man and joined an infantry regiment during the war?' asked one old soldier of another during one of the annual Burma Campaign reunion dinners.

'Hear of her?' said the other. 'Why she was in my regiment! She was just one of the lads—ate with us, marched with us, slept with us, took showers with us, the lot! Not bad looking either!'

'But how on earth did she get away with it?' asked his friend incredulously.

'You don't think any of us were going to give her away do you?' was the reply.

'Excuse me, sir, we're out of ammunition,' said the private in the Irish infantry regiment to his CO during a fierce battle.

176

'We mustn't let the enemy know,' said the officer. 'Whatever you do, keep firing.'

Three young girls were on a hiking holiday and were crossing Salisbury Plain on a very hot day. They came to a shady pool surrounded by trees and bushes, and as there was nobody in sight, they took off their clothes and jumped in. They splashed around happily for about an hour, then got out and lay in the sun to dry off.

After they had dressed and were about to move off, an army truck drove up and stopped. An officer leaned out and shouted, 'Camouflage Company—fall out!'—and all the trees ran over to the truck and climbed in.

A new recruit was being interviewed by a medical officer.

'Tell me,' said the MO, 'are you ever troubled by sexual fantasies?'

'Oh no,' said the young man, 'I quite enjoy them.'

CAVALRY OFFICER *to new recruit on horse:* 'Trooper Simmonds, you've only got one spur on!'

NEW RECRUIT: 'Yes, sir. If I get one side of the horse to go, I expect the other side will go as well.'

A young subaltern in a jeep had become separated from his battalion during military exercises in a remote part of Wales, and was completely lost. There was no sign of habitation anywhere nor were there any signposts; so he was quite relieved when he saw a farmer driving a small flock of sheep along the road ahead of him. Pulling up alongside he said, 'Pardon me, but could you tell me where this road leads?'

'To my farm,' replied the countryman.

'Oh,' said the officer. 'And where does it lead to in the other direction?'

'Away from my farm,' replied the old man.

A young private, obviously new to the service, walked into the Army Recruiting Office off Whitehall and said to the sergeant behind the desk, 'Oh, sergeant—do you remember my coming in here a few weeks ago and asking you about life in the army?'

'Yes,' said the NCO.

'And do you remember you told me what a great life it was, and how you got a chance to travel and learn a trade, and how there were opportunities for sports, and for promotion?'

'Yes.'

'Well would you mind telling me again?—I'm getting a little discouraged.'

Did you hear about the new recruit who, on his first day, was issued with battledress, beret, underwear, socks, boots and walking-out uniform, all of which fitted him perfectly?

They discharged him, of course—the army can't use you if you're deformed.

Another new recruit, just out from the quartermaster's stores, walked straight past his commanding officer without saluting.

The officer called him back and said, 'I'm sure you didn't recognise me, son, but just take a look at this uniform I'm wearing, will you?'

The soldier examined the officer's uniform carefully and said, 'Blimey, you've done all right there, mate! Look at the load of old rubbish they palmed off on me.'

A young second lieutenant, fresh from Sandhurst, was posted to a barracks in Colchester. He was met at the station by another officer, and as the barracks was quite close, they decided to walk.

As it was Saturday afternoon, they passed quite a number of soldiers each of whom naturally saluted as he passed. The older officer, being the senior, returned the salutes, and each time he did so, he muttered under his breath, 'And the same to you, mate!'

Eventually, the young lieutenant could contain himself no longer and said, 'Why on earth do you say "And the same to you, mate!" every time you salute?'

'Well,' replied the other, 'I was in the ranks myself once and I know just what they're thinking.'

During a particularly fierce battle shortly after the Normandy landings, a young and inexperienced artillery officer was called upon to provide covering fire for an infantry advance.

His orders to his battery resulted in their firing in the wrong direction so that most of the shells landed on brigade headquarters to the rear. When the shelling had stopped, an orderly ran into the battery headquarters with a message from the brigadier.

The young officer, full of his own importance said, 'Read it out, will you?'

The orderly opened the message and read out in a loud voice, 'You are the most inefficient, stupid, bungling, incompetent in the whole of my Brigade.'

The officer glanced round at the headquarters staff who had heard every word of this, and said hastily, 'Er, yes, well—have that decoded at once, will you.'

At an army camp in the remote islands of the north the visiting general was surprised to see pin ups of incredibly ugly women dressed in full length slacks.

The CO explained.

'We make them standard issue, sir, and when we see any man looking lovingly at one of them we know it is time to send him on leave.'

'Yes,' said the club bore, 'my great-grandfather fought with Wellington in 1810, my grandfather fought with Redvers Buller in 1870, my father fought with Kitchener in 1916, and I fought with Monty in 1943.'

'Your family doesn't seem to have been able to get along with anyone does it?' said another member with a yawn.

A soldier wrote home just after the war. He finished up by saying: 'I am not sure whether or not the stupid idiot of a censor still opens our letters, so I don't know whether this will arrive intact!'

When the letter reached its destination, the boy's family found a note from the censor inside saying: 'For your information, the censor does *not* open letters and furthermore I am *not* a stupid idiot.'

An orderly officer was inspecting the cookhouse before the evening meal. He thought he would test the intelligence of the cook on duty.

'Why is it,' he said, pointing to the hot water in the large copper, 'that the water is only boiling round the edges of that copper and not in the middle?'

The cook said, 'Ah well you see, sir, the water round the edges is for the guards' tea; they come in an hour before the others.'

A new recruit was filling up a medical form before being sworn in. The routine questions on name, address, nationality, place of birth, and so on, gave him no difficulty, but when he came to 'Sex' he paused thoughtfully for a few minutes before writing 'About twice a week.'

Did you hear about the hippie in San Francisco who asked for deferment from the army on religious grounds—he was a devout coward?

Then there was the young man whose draft board received a letter from his employers which read: 'We would ask for exemption from call-up on behalf of Mr McGraw. This is a small factory which at one time employed a total of 15 men. All but Mr McGraw have been called up which means that he is now having to carry on with 14 inexperienced women.'

Did you hear about the soldier who was serving 28 days in the glasshouse? It appears that he had been asked to do duty as doorman at a party thrown by his commanding officer. It had been explained to him that all he had to do was stand at the door as the guests came in and call the officers names.

A private on sentry duty was taken ill with stomach trouble and rushed to hospital. He fell into an uneasy sleep but woke suddenly as a nurse approached his bed.

'Halt—who goes there?' he shouted, reacting automatically; 'friend or enema?'

Hitler was reviewing a regiment of crack troops during the war when he heard someone sneeze.

'Who sneezed?' he shouted.

Nobody replied, so Hitler ordered the entire front rank to be shot.

When this was done, he asked again, 'Who sneezed?'

Again there was no reply so he ordered the whole of the second rank to be shot.

Once again he shouted, 'Who sneezed?'

Private Muller in the third rank stepped forward, quaking.

'I did, mein Fuhrer!'

'Ah,' said Hitler. 'Gesundheit.'

Soldier's first letter home to his mother: 'Dear Mum: you remember that I always used to love the army because the uniforms and the guns and the barracks were always kept so neat and clean and tidy? It's only since I joined up that I realised who it is that keeps them so neat and clean and tidy.'

Shortly after the outbreak of the Second World War, a soldier was asked what had made him join up.

'There were several reasons,' he replied. 'I wanted to serve my country; I wanted to fight fascism; I wanted to build a brave new world fit for heroes. But the main reason was that they came and got me.'

We were the best drilled regiment in the army,' said one Chelsea pensioner to another. 'Why when we presented arms on parade, all you could hear was "Slap-2-3-slap-2-3-slap!" '

'We were pretty good on drill too,' said his friend. 'But of course we were mainly a fighting unit. When we presented arms, all you could hear was "Slap-2-3-slap-2-3-slap-2-3-jingle!" '

'Jingle?' said the first old sweat. 'What was that?'

'Medals!' said his friend.

'Procedure for cleaning the rifle—rule number one?' snapped the sergeant, pointing to a new recruit.

'Check the serial number,' answered the rookie.

'What's that got to do with it?' yelled the sergeant.

'To make sure I'm not cleaning someone else's rifle.'

A soldier took his girl-friend for a walk in the woods and although up to then she had resisted all his advances, this time she succumbed. Afterwards she burst into tears.

'How can I face my parents now?' she sobbed, 'after I've been naughty twice in one afternoon?'

'Twice?' said the soldier, puzzled.

'Well you're going to do it again, aren't you?' said the girl through her tears.

Two soldiers were sitting together one morning on the deck of an army transport ship heading for the Far East. One turned to the other and said, 'Could I borrow your pen a moment?'

'Yes—here you are,' said the other.

'Thanks. You wouldn't have a piece of scrap paper, would you?'

'Will this do? Or you can have this envelope if you like—I haven't used it.'

'Oh thanks—I'll take both.'

The first soldier then settled down to write a letter on the piece of scrap paper; when he had finished, he folded it, put it in the envelope and sealed it.

'You wouldn't happen to have a stamp would you?' he asked.

'Yes, here you are,' said his friend resignedly.

Licking the proffered stamp, the first soldier said as he stuck it on the envelope, 'Would you mind posting this as you go past the Post Room?'

'Certainly,' said his friend. 'And is there anything else you'd like?'

'Yes,' said the first man as he prepared to fill in the envelope. 'What's your girl's address?'

It was At Home Day at the local army camp. A very attractive young lady was amongst the crowd at the rifle range. Suddenly a volley of shots rang out without warning; the young lady gave a small scream of surprise and involuntarily clutched the arm of a young second lieutenant standing next to her.

'Oh I do beg your pardon,' she said. 'I was startled by the noise.'

'That's quite all right,' the young officer answered. 'Let's get out of here and take a walk down to the artillery range.'

A very large and hairy private in an Irish regiment rushed into a pub in Camden Town and said, 'Quick—gimme a treble whiskey and two pints of best bitter! Oi must have a drink before the trouble starts!'

The startled barman hastily poured the drinks which the Irishman downed in a trice.

'Now then,' said the barman, 'what's all this about? When's the trouble going to start?'

'Right now!' answered the Irish soldier. 'Oi can't pay for me drinks.'

The new recruits marched onto the rifle range and took up their positions at a range of 1,000 yards from the targets. On the command, they loaded, took aim, and fired. After a few minutes the results came through from the markers. Not one of them had hit the target.

The sergeant instructor moved them up to 500 yards. They fired again; and again, not one single hit was registered.

He took them to 300 yards, then to 100 yards and then to 50 yards. The result was the same—every single bullet missed the target.

Finally he said, 'All right you lot—fix bayonets! It's our only chance.'

A soldier was posted overseas and as he kissed his girl-friend good-bye before embarking, he said, 'You will wait for me, won't you darling?'

'Oh yes,' she replied. 'I'll wait.'

The soldier completed his three-year tour of duty but liked the station so much that he signed on for another three years.

At the end of the six years, he wrote to his girl-friend saying that he was thinking of signing on for another year.

A few weeks later he received a telegram which read: 'Couldn't wait any longer so have married your father. Love and best wishes, Mother.'

Two young WRAC typists at the Ministry of Defence were discussing the handsome young captain for whom they both worked.

'He's very good-looking,' said one.

'Yes—and have you seen him out of uniform?' said the other.

'You bet,' said the first girl with a smile.

'No, you don't understand,' said her friend. 'What I mean is—he dresses so well.'

'Yes, and so quickly too,' said the other.

Two troopers in the Horse Guards staggered back to barracks after a particularly hectic night on the town. They didn't feel in the least bit tired, so they decided to go down to the stables and take out a couple of horses for a ride round the park. They managed to reach the stables without being seen and the first one in grabbed hold of a saddle and threw it over the nearest horse.

'Hey—jush a minute!' said his friend. 'You've put tha' saddle on the horse backwards!'

'Is that so!' said the first soldier. 'And jush how do you know which way I'm going to go?'

An orderly room clerk had to work late one evening to clear up a backlog of filing. By the time he had finished it, the office clock stood at 9.35 p.m. and he realised that he had missed his evening meal. Just as he was about to lock up, the telephone rang.

Angrily, the soldier grabbed the receiver and said, 'What the hell do you want at this time of night? Don't you know what time it is?'

'Do you know who I am?' said the voice at the other end.

'No,' said the clerk. 'Go on—surprise me!'

'I am Colonel Bull, the camp commandant!'

'And do you know who I am?' asked the clerk, after a brief pause.

'No, I don't.'

'Thank God for that.'

A soldier on leave took his girl-friend round to see the vicar and asked him to marry them.

'I'll be glad to,' said the minister, 'but as you know, the banns have to be read on three separate Sundays and . . .'

'But I've only got a 48-hour pass,' said the soldier, 'and . . . well . . . you know . . .'

'I'm afraid there's nothing I can do,' said the vicar.

'Well,' said the lad in desperation, 'couldn't you say a few words just to tide us over the weekend?'

When the time came for young Joe to join the army, his mother was very upset—Joe had never been away from home before, not even for one night.

'Well, goodbye, son,' said his mother at last. 'Be sure to get up early in the mornings so as not to keep the other soldiers waiting at breakfast.'

The pilot of an army reconnaissance plane persuaded his friend to come up for a spin one Saturday afternoon. Showing off, the pilot put the plane into a steep dive, only pulling out at the last moment, some 50 feet from the ground.

'Did you see them scatter?' he yelled to his companion. 'Half of them down there thought we were going to have an accident!'

'Half of them up here thought so too!' gasped his friend.

183

A retired army officer placed an advertisement in *The Times* for a valet, and was surprised to receive a letter from his former batman, also now retired. He arranged an interview and when the two had finished talking about old times, the ex-officer said, 'Well, Farrell, I don't think I need look any further—the job's yours if you want it. Your duties will be exactly the same as they were when we were both serving overseas together.'

The ex-soldier accepted the job and arranged to start work the following morning. He went home for his things and got up early next day to be round at his boss's house before anyone was up.

He went straight to the kitchen and prepared breakfast; then he tiptoed into the main bedroom, placed the tray on the table next to the sleeping colonel, went round to the other side of the bed, slapped the officer's wife on the bottom and said, 'Come on sweet-heart—time to get back to the village.'

Two old soldiers were sitting in the park one sunny lunchtime. The park was full of gorgeous mini-skirted typists taking an al fresco lunch in the sun. After a while, one old veteran turned to the other and said, 'Albert—you remember that stuff they used to put in our tea back in 1914? I think it's beginning to work.'

During the latter part of the Second World War, two soldiers were queueing up for the evening meal in a mess-hall at a camp some-where in southern England. The camp was not noted for its culinary delights and the meal that evening was particularly drab and un-appetising.

'Blimey, look at it!' said one soldier, as the food was dished out. 'I can't even tell what it's supposed to be!'

'Now look here,' said the cook who was doing the serving 'food could win the war you know.'

'It could I suppose,' said the second soldier, 'but how would you ever get the Germans to eat here?'

The sun beat down in the parade ground where the First Battalion, the Coldstream Guards were drawn up in all their glory.

The regimental sergeant major walked along the ranks making a preliminary check before the main inspection started. Suddenly he stopped before a new recruit and stared pointedly at the top button of the man's battledress blouse which was undone.

Finally he looked up and said, 'Sunbathing, eh.'

During a particularly fierce battle in North Africa in World War II, a private decided that discretion was the better part of valour, and set off for the rear. He had been travelling for several hours when a jeep came towards him along the road; it stopped alongside him and an officer stood up and shouted, 'Hey, you, soldier—where do you think you're going?'

'There's a ruddy great battle going on up there,' said the private, 'and I'm trying to get as far away from it as possible.'

'Do you know who I am?' said the officer. 'I am your commanding officer!'

'Blimey, I didn't realise I'd got as far to the rear as that!' said the soldier.

NEW RECRUIT *at medical examination:* 'You can't take me—I'm short-sighted.'

MEDICAL OFFICER: 'That's all right, son. We'll put you right up in the front line—you won't miss a thing.'

'I don't think I'd like to be anything higher than a corporal,' said one private to another. 'I would like to have *some* friends left.'

The Royal Corps of Signals are now working on a very advanced project. They're trying to cross a carrier-pigeon with a woodpecker so that it can knock on the door before delivering the message.

A despatch rider was crossing Salisbury Plain on his motor-cycle one afternoon, when a sudden storm blew up. He found that he was being gradually soaked by the rain and frozen to death by the wind, so he stopped his bike, took off his leather jacket and put it on again backwards, to form some protection against the wind.

The storm got worse, and on a particularly sharp bend, his machine skidded and crashed into a tree, knocking him unconscious.

At the inquest, the truck driver who found him said, 'I can't understand it at all, sir. He was OK until I turned his head the right way round.'

'So you want to come and work in the quartermaster's stores, eh?' said the QM. 'Do you think you're intelligent enough?'

'I don't rightly know, sir,' said the rather dimwitted private.

'Well, I'll ask you a few questions to test your intelligence,' said the officer. 'Now what is it that has two soles, two heels and 24 lace-holes?'

'I don't know sir,' said the soldier after thinking hard for five minutes.

'A pair of boots, of course,' said the officer. 'Now here's another question. What is it that has four soles, four heels and 48 lace-holes?'

'It's a bit hard, isn't it sir?' said the soldier vaguely. 'Er—I don't think I . . .'

'Why, man, two pairs of boots of course!' said the officer.

185

'Now I'll give you one last chance. What is it that has four legs, two horns and flies in summer?'

'Ah yes sir, I think I've got it!' said the lad with a smile. '*Three* pairs of boots sir.'

A sergeant walked into the barrack-room one morning and was horrified to see that every window boasted a neat little pair of chintz curtains. Turning to the corporal in charge, he bellowed. 'Who the devil had the idea of putting those things up?'

'I did, sergeant,' said the adjutant, suddenly appearing through the barrack-room door.

'What a lovely colour scheme, sir!' said the sergeant.

'Hello,' said one gay young recruit to another. 'My serial number is 19114582 but you can call me 19.'

Question in examination paper on military matters: 'What is a lieutenant commander?'

Answer given by one examinee: 'A lieutenant commander is the wife of a lieutenant.'

The plain daughter of a field marshal was engaged to be married to a young officer on her father's staff.

'Couldn't you do something for Frank now that he's asked me to marry him?' she asked her father one day.

'There's not much I can do really,' replied the field marshal, 'except get him a medal for gallantry.'

'I think you're the most beautiful girl in the world!'

'Oh don't be silly! You're only saying that because I've just come back from the beauty parlour!'

'No—I'm only saying that because I've just come back from Borneo.'

A snooty young officer was trying to make a telephone call from one of the boxes on Piccadilly underground station.

He stopped a passing private and said, 'Have you got sixpence for two threepenny bits?'

'Hang on a sec,' said the soldier. 'I'll have a shufti.'

'Don't you know the correct way to address an officer?' said the lieutenant. 'I'll ask you again—have you got a sixpence for two threepenny bits?'

'No, sir,' answered the private.

'Do you know why they didn't bury the Duke of Wellington with full military honours in 1850?'

'No—why?'

'He didn't die until 1852.'

The officer was visiting the new conscripts after their first week of service.

'Are you happy in the army?' he asked one bespectacled youth.

'As happy as one can be expected I suppose,' was the reply.

'And what were you before you were called up?'

'A lot happier.'

Two young WRAC privates were sneaking into camp through a hole in the perimeter fence, several hours after lights-out, when they bumped into a young corporal sneaking out of camp.

'Sssshh!' said one of the girls. 'We've been out after hours!'

'That's OK,' said the corporal. 'I won't say anything. I'm just going out after mine.'

Did you hear about the WRAC hospital orderly whose statistics were 39–25–36? She was never able to make the bed without disturbing the patient.

'Now, gentlemen,' said the general, briefing his officers before the battle, 'it is vitally important that we hold on to this section of the front for as long as humanly possible. I want you to fight to the last round of ammunition; and when you've done that, retreat in an orderly fashion to positions along this river, fifteen miles to the rear. As I am lame in one leg,' he added, folding up his maps, 'I shall start now.'

The English soldier abroad has always had great confidence in his ability to make himself understood to the natives. Just after the end of the war, a young soldier in a small French village approached a seasoned campaigner and asked him if he spoke French.

'Like a native,' said the old sweat. 'Why—what's up?'

'Well,' said the youngster, 'I've just bought a bottle of wine in that shop and I can't make the chap understand that he's given me the wrong change.'

'I'll soon put that right,' said the old soldier and together they went into the shop.

'Parlez-vous français?' said the old sweat.

'Mais, oui, monsieur,' the Frenchman answered.

'Well, then, you dummkopf, can't vous comprenny that vous avez given this squaddie le wrong change?'

An officer was giving his men a pep-talk just before they embarked for service overseas.

'Now men,' he said, 'I know it's not easy to leave your girl-friends behind alone . . .'

A simple rule-of-thumb for new recruits in the army: 'If it moves, salute it; if it doesn't move, pick it up; if it's too big to pick up, paint it.'

Two privates were put on fatigues and were given the task of peeling what looked like a ton of potatoes. As they settled down to it, one said to the other, 'You know, I feel like telling that sergeant major where to get off again!'

'What do you mean "again"?' said his mate.

'Well, I felt like it yesterday too.'

An officer of the guard, making his rounds with the corporal on duty, noticed a light on in one of the huts, although it was long past lights-out. Glancing through the window he saw a card school in progress.

'Corporal,' he said, 'go in there and break up that poker game.' The corporal disappeared inside the hut and the officer returned to the guard-house. Three hours later, the corporal returned.

'Surely it couldn't have taken you three hours to break up a card-school!' said the officer.

'Sorry, sir,' said the corporal, 'I only had sixpence on me to start with.'

The pilot of an army helicopter arranged unofficially to take his girl-friend up for a short trip one Saturday afternoon. He put the machine through its paces and pulled every trick in the book to impress his girl.

When they eventually landed, she said, 'Well, thank you for both of those rides!'

'What do you mean "both"?' said the soldier. 'There was only one.'

'I made it two,' said his girl. 'My first and my last.'

An Irish sergeant was drilling a squad of new recruits. He was teaching them how to mark time and was having a great deal of difficulty in getting them to keep in step.

Deciding to start right back at the beginning, he said, 'Now when I give the command "One", I want you all to raise your right legs, knees bent, in the air and hold them there. Squad—One!'

The whole platoon obediently raised their right legs in the air, except for one young fellow who raised his left leg by mistake.

Glancing down the front rank, the sergeant bellowed, 'And who's the idiot with both legs in the air?'

A very green young officer cadet was drilling a squad under the eye of a seasoned drill sergeant. His squad was marching away from him towards the edge of the parade-ground and, to his horror, he found that he couldn't remember the command either to halt them or to turn them about.

As he stood there, speechless, while his squad disappeared towards the gates of the camp, the sergeant turned to him and bellowed, 'For God's sake say something, sir—even if it's only goodbye.'

A new recruit on his first day in the army walked blithely past his commanding officer without saluting him. The colonel called him back and said, 'Do you know who I am?'

'No—who are you?' said the soldier.

Controlling himself with difficulty, the CO said, 'I am the officer in charge of this camp. I am a full colonel, and I have 1,240 men under me.'

'Well you've got a bloody good job there mate—I should hang on to it if I were you,' said the private, walking off with his hands in his pockets.

A soldier who returned home after the Battle of Cassino, was describing in great detail to his friends the withering machine-gun fire which his regiment had suffered at the hands of the German defenders.

'Why didn't you get behind a tree?' asked one.

'Behind a tree?' laughed the soldier. 'There weren't even enough trees for the officers.'

It was VE-Day; the war was over and the thoughts of most soldiers turned to demobilisation and civvy street. A group of squaddies on the way home for discharge were talking about what they were going to do once they were out of uniform.

'Well,' said one, 'I'll tell you the very first thing I'm going to do. I'm going to go up to our sergeant major and spit in his eye!'

'Oh no you're not!' said the corporal. 'You're going to line up in order of seniority and take your turn like the rest of us.'

FIRST PRIVATE: 'What does a soldier have to be, to be buried with full military honours?'

SECOND PRIVATE: 'Dead.'

189

My brother-in-law had a very impressive military record. He blew up three ammunition dumps, destroyed a tank, and knocked out an anti-aircraft gun single-handed. And that was *before* they sent him overseas.

A rookie ran into the guardroom and said to the guard sergeant, 'Quick—lock me up at once! I just punched the sergeant major in the nose!'

'Did you kill him?' asked the sergeant.

'No—that's why I want you to lock me up.'

A number of Scottish soldiers were court martialled for wrecking a public-house and one of their number was asked to explain to the court how the trouble had begun.

'Well, sir, there wasn't much to it really. It all started when Private MacKechnie called Private McNeill a liar, and Private McNeill hit him over the head with a chair. Private Fraser pulled out his dirk and cut a slice out of Private McNeill's leg. Two or three of Private McNeill's friends piled on to Private Fraser, and a couple of others started throwing glasses and tables around. One thing led to another and then the fighting started.'

'Let me have a look at that signal you've drafted,' said the captain to the signaller. After glancing through it he said, 'This is no good—I can't understand half of it! You must draft your signals so that even the most ignorant fool can understand them!'

'Yes sir,' said the signaller. 'Which are the bits you can't understand?'

During the war, a soldier from the special section of military intelligence concerned with propaganda was sent over Germany to supervise a propaganda leaflet raid. He didn't return to his unit until seven weeks later, and received a severe ticking-off from his commanding officer.

'You're not going to tell me it took you seven weeks to drop one batch of leaflets over Hamburg?' said the officer.

'Drop them?' said the soldier. 'Blimey I thought I was supposed to push one under every front-door.'

The scene was a court-martial. The platoon sergeant was giving evidence against a private who was accused of calling a lieutenant an idiot.

'Now sergeant,' said the president of the court, 'how can you be sure that the accused was in fact referring to Lieutenant Jones when he called him an idiot?'

Sergeant Cox replied, 'Well sir—Lieutenant Jones was the only idiot there at the time.'

Military experts tell us that if World War III were to break out at 9 o'clock one morning, it would be over by teatime. At least that will leave us the evening free.

'Do you call this a straight line?' yelled the Irish drill sergeant to the squad of awkward new recruits. 'Just fall out and take a look at it.'

The company was on a route march; they had been marching all morning and were now some 25 miles away from their barracks. The officer in charge halted his men and stood them at ease. Then he addressed them: 'We are now going to fall out for half an hour during which you will have your midday meal. Several trucks will then arrive to take you back to camp, but I would prefer that this squad creates a good impression by marching back to camp. Will all those men who are too tired to march the 25 miles back to barracks take two paces forward.'

Every man in the company stepped forward, except one solitary soldier in the rear rank.

'Congratulations,' said the officer. 'You are the only man in the entire company who is not too tired to march back to camp.'

'It's not that, sir,' said the soldier. 'I'm too tired to take the two paces forward.'

If conscription ever comes back, there's one sure way of staying out of the Army. Join the Air Force.

At a remote army camp in North Wales, two soldiers were on guard duty at the main gate when a small boy came past leading a donkey.

'Hey sonny,' said one soldier. 'Why does your brother have to have a rope around his neck when he goes out for a walk?'

'In case he tries to join the army,' answered the boy.

There was once an army camp in Yorkshire which had a large river about a quarter of a mile away, a favourite haunt of fishermen. One evening, after duty, a soldier who was a keen fisherman in his spare time was quietly fishing on the river bank when a small frog jumped up beside him.

'Hello!' said the frog. The soldier was so startled that he almost dropped his rod.

'Hello,' he answered. 'I've never met a frog who could speak before!'

'Oh I'm not really a frog,' said the frog. 'I'm a beautiful princess who's been turned into a frog by a wicked, spiteful old witch. The only way to break the spell is for me to spend the night on the pillow of a handsome young man—such as yourself,' she added slyly.

Of course, the young soldier took the frog home and it spent the night on his pillow, and the next morning, there was a beautiful young woman in his bed!

At least, that was the story he told at his court-martial.

PARADE, MEDALS, GOOD-CONDUCT, FOR THE AWARD OF:

The under-mentioned personnel will parade outside Company HQ at 1400 hours today for award of good-conduct medals. Disciplinary action will be taken against any personnel late on parade.

SMITH: 'I was in the regular army for seven and a half years.'
JONES: 'Did you get a commission?'
SMITH: 'No—just a straight salary.'

A young second lieutenant was posted to a remote camp in the Highlands of Scotland. He was met at the station by a private with a jeep and they set off up into the mountains.

After they had travelled a couple of miles, the driver stopped the jeep, took out a large tin of white powder, and sprinkled it liberally on the road around the vehicle. Then without a word, he got in and drove off. During the course of the journey, this happened time and time again until eventually the officer could contain his curiosity no longer.

'What on earth is that powder for?' he asked.

'It's anti-elephant powder, sir,' answered the driver. 'Keeps elephants away.'

'Elephants!' said the officer. 'Don't be ridiculous! This is the north of Scotland—there are no elephants around here!'

'I know,' answered the private. 'Effective isn't it.'

Just after the end of the last war, a soldier was posted to the Far East. He wrote home regularly during the voyage but because of censorship regulations, he was unable to tell his mother exactly where he was.

His first letter read as follows: 'Dear Mother, I cannot tell you exactly where I am at the moment, but we had shore leave yesterday and I went hunting and shot an elephant!'

His next letter read, 'Dear Mother, I still cannot tell you where I am, but yesterday we went ashore again and I danced with a geisha girl.'

His third letter started off like this: 'Dear Mother, I still **cannot** tell you where we are but yesterday the medical officer told me it would have been better if I had danced with the elephant and shot the geisha girl . . .'

Did you hear about the army mule that died suddenly after establishing an all-time record by kicking one general, five staff officers, 18 NCO's, 26 privates and a hand-grenade?

Legend has it that Diogenes spent years searching for an honest man. One day he met an ex-soldier just returned from the wars.
'What were you?' asked Diogenes.
'A private,' said the man.
And Diogenes gave up his search and went home.

SERGEANT: 'The trouble with you is you're too fond of the bottle. You'll never become a sergeant like me.'
PRIVATE: 'Why should I want to? When I'm drunk, I'm a field-marshal.'

Two privates in a Welsh regiment were sent overseas for the first time, and on the first day out, when the coastline had receded out of sight, they were both leaning over the rail gazing with rapt attention out to sea.
'Well did you ever see so much water before together all in one place?' asked one.
'No I didn't!' said his friend. 'And do you realise Dai—that's just the top of it.'

A candidate for an officer's training school was being given a general oral examination before a board of senior officers.
'Now then,' said the president of the board, a brigadier, 'who, in your opinion, are the three greatest names in the British Army in the last fifty years?'
'Wavell,' said the candidate, 'Montgomery, and . . . I'm sorry, sir, I didn't quite catch your name.'

A soldier retired from the army after serving for over 40 years without ever rising above the rank of corporal, mainly because of his fondness for the bottle. He had however been able to save quite a considerable amount (through working mostly in the stores) and with this and his gratuity, he bought a small pub in a Worcestershire village.
On the first day of his tenancy, the locals came round at opening-time as usual, only to find the front door securely locked and

bolted, and all windows tightly shuttered. They hammered on the front door for a full ten minutes before an upstairs window opened and the ex-soldier stuck his head out.

'What do you want?' he called down.

'When are you going to open up?' shouted one of the villagers.

'Open up?' came the reply. 'You must be mad! I bought this place for myself.'

The new recruit came back from the rifle range with the lowest score ever recorded in the history of the regiment.

'I don't know what to say!' he said to his platoon sergeant. 'I feel like going off into a quiet corner and shooting myself!'

'Well, you'd better take plenty of bullets,' said the sergeant.

During the Suez crisis, a reservist was undergoing a medical examination to determine his fitness for recall to the army. The medical officer was testing his eyes and pointing to a wall-chart said, 'Read the top line of letters please.'

'What top line?' asked the reservist.

'On the chart,' said the MO.

'What chart?' asked the man.

'The chart on the wall,' said the officer.

'What wall?' asked the man.

In the end he managed to convince the medical officer that his eyesight was much too bad for him to be considered for active service, and he was sent home.

That evening he decided to visit a cinema to celebrate. As the lights went up during the interval, he happened to glance at the man sitting next to him, and was shocked to see that it was the very same medical officer who had examined him that morning. Quick as a flash he said, 'Excuse me—could you tell me if this bus goes to Walthamstow?'

A private in a north country regiment had a habit of putting in for leave on all sorts of pretexts. One day he approached his commanding officer with a request for a 48-hour pass as his wife was having a baby.

'This time you've gone too far,' said the CO. 'I happen to have received a letter from your wife warning me that you might try this trick and saying that she is *not* expecting a baby and does *not* want you home this weekend as she is in the middle of spring-cleaning.'

'Well, sir,' said the soldier, 'it looks as though this regiment now has *two* first-class liars. I'm not married.'

FIRST WRAC: 'I'm afraid I've got to go into hospital for an operation.'
SECOND WRAC: 'Major?'
FIRST WRAC: 'No—lance-corporal.'

194

A certain Corporal Henderson of the Pioneer Corps in Malaya was mentioned in despatches for saving two women.

He saved one for himself and one for his commanding officer.

The drill-sergeant had been drilling the new recruits for about three-quarters of an hour and had just about come to the end of his patience.

'Stand at ease, stand easy,' he said at last. 'I want to tell you all a little story. When I was a lad, I had a box of wooden soldiers, and I used to play with them every day. Then we moved house, and during the move, my box of soldiers was lost! Well, I cried and I cried and I cried, but my mother said to me, "Don't cry, son—one day you'll find your little wooden soldiers again!" And she was right, you 'orrible lot—she was right.'

'Now then,' said the major to the corporal newly posted to his command, 'I hear you're a great gambler. Well, I don't want any gambling in my camp, is that understood?'

'Yes, sir,' said the corporal, 'but the thing is, sir, I can't help myself. For instance, I'll bet you a week's pay you're wearing a string vest at this moment.'

'Right,' said the major, 'I'll teach you a lesson my lad.'

And he promptly stripped off his jacket, shirt and tie, proving without a shadow of a doubt that not only was he not wearing a string vest, but in fact was not wearing a vest at all.

'Let that be a lesson to you,' he said with a smile as the corporal handed over his week's pay.

That evening in the mess, the major told the story to the adjutant. The adjutant was horrified.

'My God!' he said. 'I met the corporal when he first reported to camp—and he bet me a month's pay that he would get you to strip to the waist within five minutes of meeting you.'

Inter-service rivalry is still very keen. Now that the RAF has planes that will travel faster than sound, the army is working on plans for a sound that will travel faster than planes!

The nearest they've come to it so far is a regimental sergeant major spotting a private with one button undone, three hundred yards away across the parade ground.

'And what do you think you're doing?' asked the sergeant of the guard to the sentry.

'I'm writing a letter to my mother,' replied the soldier.

'Oh yes? I thought you told me you couldn't write?' said the sergeant suspiciously.

'That doesn't matter,' was the reply. 'My mother can't read.'

A new recruit to the cavalry was having a great deal of difficulty with his mount, partly because his stirrups were far too long. Every time the horse started to trot, one of its back hoofs caught in the stirrup. Finally the soldier pulled the horse up and dismounted.

'And where do you think you're going?' asked the officer in charge.

'Well, sir,' replied the lad, 'I thought if the horse was going to get on too, I'd rather get off and walk.'

A very young looking American soldier had rows and rows of medal ribbons, medals for shooting, swimming and service for short periods in many places. He was explaining each one to the new recruits.

'And what is that one for?' one asked of a particularly bright ribbon.

'I saved two women from attack.'

'How?'

'I changed my mind.'

'What's for pudding tonight?' said one army cook to his mate. 'I've got to make out the menu.'

'It's rice again,' said his friend, 'but let's call it something different for a change.'

'OK,' said the first man 'How do you spell semolina?'

'S-E-M-L-E-, no, just a minute—it's S-E-M-M-E-R- . . .'

'Oh, never mind,' said the man writing the menu. 'How do you spell tapioca?'

'Er—T-A-P-E-R-, no, T-A-C- . . .'

The pudding that night was rice as usual.

A soldier with a three-day pass turned up at the local railway station.

'Where to, soldier?' asked the clerk.

'Back here, of course!' said the squaddie.

A forward unit of infantry in the Malayan jungle once sent a signal back to base saying, 'WE HAVE ONE CASE OF BERI-BERI. PLEASE ADVISE DISPOSAL.'

The reply signal read: 'HAND OVER TO OFFICERS MESS STEWARD—ISSUE ON SCALE OF ONE BOTTLE PER OFFICER.'

During the First World War, a journalist was visiting the front line and a captain was assigned to show him around. From base head-quarters, they trudged up to the trenches in silence and as they ducked down into the dugout, the captain whispered, 'This is the forward line of trenches.'

'How far are we from the enemy?' whispered the journalist.

'About a mile and a half,' the captain whispered in return.

'A mile and a half?' said the journalist, 'then what are we whispering for?'

'I don't know about you,' replied the officer, 'but I've got laryngitis.'

A private and a WRAC were court-martialled for running naked across the parade ground at midnight. They were both acquitted however, when defending counsel drew attention to that section of the Army Manual which states that the wearing of uniform by other ranks when off-duty is not compulsory, so long as they are appropriately dressed for whatever sport or activity they are engaged in.

Landmarks in the desert are few and far between and it is often necessary to work out one's exact position by compass readings.

During the North Africa campaign, a patrol had been crossing the desert for several days and had got lost. The officer in charge detailed a young second lieutenant to work out their exact position—unfortunately, the lieutenant was hopeless at taking readings of this kind.

Not wishing to be shown up, he went ahead and took the reading, handing the map reference to his CO when he had finished.

The senior officer studied it carefully for a few minutes and then said, 'Thank you lieutenant. I suggest we remove our helmets—according to your calculations, we are now standing in the middle of St Paul's cathedral.'

The scene was an officer's mess in India. The evening meal was over and the officers were sitting around chatting and reading their newspapers. Suddenly one officer turned to another and said, 'Good heavens! Do you remember old Carstairs—used to be adjutant here—disappeared about eight months ago. Well it says here that he's been found. Apparently he's been living in the jungle with a monkey!'

'Good lord!' said the second officer. 'Was it a male monkey or a female monkey?'

'Female monkey, of course,' said the first. 'Nothing strange about old Carstairs.'

A new recruit was being given a psychiatric examination.

'Now tell me,' said the medical officer, 'do you ever hear voices when you're alone in a room?'

'Oh yes, frequently,' said the young fellow.

'Oh,' said the officer with interest. 'And exactly when does this happen?'

'Whenever I answer the telephone,' was the reply.

A hundred and fifty years ago, illiteracy was quite common. One day a sergeant was questioning a young fellow from the country who had come up to London to volunteer.

'I can write,' said the lad, in answer to the sergeant's question, 'but I can't read.'

'All right,' answered the sergeant, 'write your name on that piece of paper.'

The young fellow obediently scrawled a completely illegible signature on the proffered piece of paper and handed it back to the NCO.

'What on earth is that supposed to be?' asked the sergeant.

'I don't know,' answered the youngster. 'I told you—I can write but I can't read.'

Did you hear about the army guard dog who wasn't happy with his post?

At a re-union dinner to commemorate VE-Day, an ex-GI got talking to a retired British army officer who was accompanied by his father, a rather deaf old gentleman, also ex-army. When the ex-GI mentioned the name of the village at which he had been stationed during the latter part of the war, it turned out to be that this was where the father and son had their home.

'Well I'll be darned!' said the American. 'What a small world! Wonder why I didn't run into you two? Guess you must have been away at the time. Why I had the time of my life there! I was stationed at that large house on the hill—somebody's stately home I guess—they were all away except the lady of the house—what a doll she was—and generous too, you know what I mean! Wow—what a time I had!'

The older man leaned forward and said to his son, 'What did he say?'

The younger man leaned across and said, 'It seems he met mother during the war.'

A soldier on a weekend pass had nowhere to be alone with his girl-friend. They tried the park, and the bus shelter, and the public library, but wherever they went, as soon as they started kissing, everyone stopped and stared and giggled.

Finally they had a brainwave. They went down to the local rail-way station. They thought they wouldn't be noticed there as the place was full of couples kissing each other goodbye. Accordingly they went over to a platform from which a train was about to leave, and hugged and kissed unnoticed until the train pulled out. Then they repeated the process at another platform until the train had departed, and so on and so on. After they had done this about five or six times, an old porter who had been watching them came up and said, ''Ere—why don't you try the Underground—there's a train every four minutes down there.'

A sergeant on guard duty decided to slip home to the married quarters for a few hours sleep, although this was strictly against the regulations. He tiptoed into his bedroom, undressed in the dark and got into bed.

'Is that you dear?' asked his wife, who seemed strangely ill at ease.

'Yes, of course it's me,' said the sergeant.

He set the alarm a few hours ahead and dropped off almost immediately. Four hours later, the alarm sounded. He struggled into his clothes in the dark, kissed his wife goodbye and left. When he got back to the guard-room, he was conscious of curious stares from the rest of the detail.

Finally, the guard corporal said, 'Excuse me, sergeant, but why are you wearing a private's uniform?'

Two paratroopers were sitting in a plane heading for the dropping zone.

'Are you nervous?' asked one.

'I'm not nervous about jumping,' said the other. 'I'm nervous about flying.'

'You shouldn't be,' answered his friend. 'Look at it this way— when your number's up, there's nothing you can do.'

'Yes, but supposing the pilot's number comes up while we're in his plane?'

The inspecting officer was very angry indeed.

'Sergeant!' he bellowed. 'Do you know that there are several articles of women's underwear hanging all over the washroom?'

'Yes sir,' answered the sergeant. 'It was the married men's idea, sir. Some of them are getting a little homesick.'

'Soldier—what the hell do you think you're doing?'

'Procrastinating, sergeant.'

'OK—just don't let me catch you loafing around, that's all.'

'Do you love me?' whispered the girl to the soldier.

'Of course I do,' he whispered back.

'Will you marry me then?' she asked.

'Let's not change the subject,' he said.

A young soldier was on a map-reading course. He wrote home to his mother saying that he was being taught how to use his sextant.

'Good heavens!' said his mother. 'This permissive society is really going too far.'

A private was giving evidence against a sergeant at the latter's court martial. The sergeant was accused of being drunk and disorderly after lights-out.

'What evidence can give support to your statement that the sergeant was drunk?' asked defending counsel.

'Well he told me to be sure and call him early,' answered the private.

'But surely there was nothing unusual about that! Did he say why he wanted to be called early?'

'Yes, sir. He was going to be Queen of the May.'

An extremely thin and emaciated young man was being examined by a panel of army doctors before being accepted into the service. After the examination had been completed, the doctors went into a huddle in the corner of the room. After a while, the draftee went over to find out what was going on.

'Well, gents,' he said. 'Let's have it—how do I stand?'

'That's what we're trying to work out!' said one of the doctors.

A man was explaining to his small son exactly what he had done in the War. The recital took about three hours, ending up with VE-Day and the return of the hero.

'And there you have it son,' said the father. 'Any questions?'

'Just one, Dad,' said the boy. 'What did they need all those other soldiers for?'

Did you hear about the soldier who was decorated for saving the lives of a whole company during the invasion of Normandy? He shot the cook.

'Having a bit of a lie-in are you, Eugene?' said the sergeant. 'Now don't tell me you didn't hear reveille being sounded?'

'Was that what it was?' answered the soldier from his bed. 'Silly me! I can't tell one tune from another.'

A few months after the end of hostilities, the commanding officer of a holding unit in France was ordered to withdraw to Calais for embarkation. The unit had been concerned with civilian administration in the area and had accumulated a large number of documents, most of which were now out of date and useless. The officer requested permission from HQ to destroy all but essential papers.

'Documents may be destroyed as requested,' HQ signalled back, 'but please make copies before burning.'

'And what were you in civilian life?' asked the sergeant of the rather effeminate-looking young man, newly drafted to the regiment.

'I was an interior decorator for a while,' he replied with a charming smile, 'and then I became a ladies' hairdresser.'

'Oh, really,' said the sergeant sarcastically. 'And do you think you could kill a man?'

'Oh I expect so,' was the reply, 'eventually . . .'

An army parachutist was asked on a TV quiz show when he decided to become a parachute jumper.

'The day my plane caught fire,' he replied.

Two American soldiers were the sole survivors of a troopship torpedoed in the Pacific during World War II. They managed to survive for five years on a deserted island and then one day they saw a large object drifting ashore. It turned out to be a giant Pepsi-Cola bottle used for advertisement purposes.

'My God!' said one soldier to another. 'We must have shrunk.'

'Look here—why didn't you salute me?' asked the young second lieutenant.

'I'm sorry sir—I didn't see you,' answered the private.

'Oh, that's all right then,' replied the officer. 'I thought for a moment you were cross with me.'

A journalist was interviewing the commanding officer of an American base in England. Suddenly a corporal put his head round the door of the office without knocking and said, 'Hey Mac—OK if I borrow the staff car for the weekend?'

'Yeah—go ahead,' said the colonel.

'Was that normal procedure?' asked the journalist, surprised by this lack of discipline.

'Heck, no,' said the officer. 'He doesn't usually bother to ask.'

The rookie was up on company orders.

'Now the sergeant tells me that you refused to stand at attention on parade this morning,' said the officer in charge. 'Is that true?'

'No sir,' said the wretched soldier. 'I was at attention all the time —it was my uniform that was at ease.'

Towards the end of 1942, a young man approaching military age confessed to his friend that he would do anything to avoid being called up.

'It's really very simple,' said his friend. 'Do what I did. Buy yourself a truss and say you've been wearing it for years. They won't call you up then.'

So the young man did just that and when he presented himself for medical examination the officer said, 'How long have you been wearing that?'

'Oh, for several years,' he answered.

'OK,' said the officer, 'I'll put you down for the Camel Corps. If you've been wearing a truss upside-down for years, you shouldn't have too much difficulty in riding a camel.'

A bandsman from a northern regiment was having a medical examination before being discharged from the service. After he had stripped off, the medical officer remarked on the great size of his navel.

'Well you see,' said the soldier, 'I always used to lead the parades.'

'What on earth has that got to do with the size of your navel?' asked the doctor.

'I used to carry the flag,' replied the soldier.

A young lady had been flirting quite openly at a party at one of England's stately homes. Towards the end of the festivities, she went over to the host in tears and complained that the hostess had called her a common tart.

'Oh, don't worry about that,' said the host gaily. 'Why I've been retired from the army now for over fifteen years but she still calls me Major.'

For many centuries it used to be the custom in North Africa for women to walk behind their menfolk. Since World War II, however, they have walked a few paces ahead of them. There are still, you see, lots of unexploded mines about.

'Is there any reason why the board should not draft you into the army?'

'Yes. I have defective eyesight.'

'Are you able to substantiate that claim?'

'Well—here's a photograph of my wife.'

Did you hear about the travelling salesman who joined the army because he heard you got plenty of orders there?

The potential conscript stood before the medical officer. Without looking up, the MO said, 'Strip to the waist and sit in that chair.'

The man did so, and the MO looked up and said, 'All right, you're in. Get dressed again.'

'But you haven't even examined me!' protested the man.

'I don't need to,' came the reply. 'You heard what I said so your ears are OK. You saw the chair so your eyes are OK. You were physically capable of taking your clothes off and sitting down; and you had sufficient intelligence to understand and carry out my orders. Next please.'

'Yes—my worst ordeal was during the war in the Pacific,' said the club bore. 'I was on a troopship which was torpedoed and I had to live for two weeks on a tin of beans.'

'Good heavens!' said one of his listeners. 'How did you manage to stay on?'

A sweet young thing was introduced to a much-beribboned elderly general at a party. Thinking to make conversation, she asked, 'Were you in the war, General?'

The regiment had a new officer—Second Lieutenant Green who, as his name suggested, was very young and very inexperienced. At parade that morning, the commanding officer announced a route march for the following day, to be led by the new officer himself. A voice from the rear, said 'And a little child shall lead them!' When the laughter had died down, the parade was dismissed.

That evening the orders were confirmed on the bulletin board as follows: 'ROUTE MARCH. Assemble 0600 hrs. on the parade ground—full marching order. And a little child shall lead them— riding a great big horse. Signed: 2/Lt Green.'

'My God,' said the old Colonel, 'war was won in those days. why I remember the second Ashanti campaign when the regiment faced an attack from 6,000 armed with 10-foot spears! By the time that battle was over I had six of the damn things sticking in me!'

'Did it hurt?' asked a listener.

'Only when I laughed,' said the old boy.

The candidate for officer school was undergoing a psychiatric examination.

'Now let me ask you this,' said the medical officer. 'Do you have any difficulty in making decisions?'

'Well . . . yes and no,' said the recruit.

A high-ranking officer driving out of camp was stopped at the gate by an enthusiastic sentry.

'Drive on, drive on!' said the officer impatiently to his chauffeur.

'Just a minute, sir,' said the sentry. 'Before you go, could you tell me whether I'm supposed to shoot you or the driver?'

Two British soldiers on their way to the Far East attended a mission service at a small church in India, where the service was conducted entirely in the local language. As they didn't understand a word of this, they simply followed the lead of the man sitting in front of them, rising, sitting and kneeling when he did.

Towards the end of the service, the officiating minister made an announcement and the man in front of the two soldiers rose to his feet whereupon they did the same. The rest of the congregation roared with laughter and the soldiers saw that the three of them were the only ones standing.

Afterwards they found out that the minister had announced a baptism for the following Sunday; and had asked the father of the child to stand.

A soldier was driving an army chaplain into town one morning when his engine stalled. All attempts to start it failed and in exasperation, the soldier suddenly let out a stream of invective.

'Well, that certainly isn't going to start the car,' said the shocked padre. 'Perhaps a little prayer would produce the desired result.'

'Why not? I've tried everything else,' said the soldier; so they bent their heads and sent up a short prayer.

Then the driver tried again and this time the car started right away. 'Well I'm damned!' said the padre. 'It ******-well worked.'

The soldier serving in Hong Kong was annoyed and upset when his girl wrote breaking their engagement and asking for her photograph back. He went out and collected from his friends all the unwanted photographs of women that he could find, bundled them all together and set them back with a note saying, 'Regret cannot remember which one is you—please keep your photo and return the remainder.'

During a skirmish in the Middle East, an Egyptian unit lost all its tanks and guns.

'Oh well, never mind,' said the commanding officer, 'they weren't paid for.'

'Halt! Who goes there?' yelled the nervous sentry as something loomed up before him in the fog.

'Nobody,' said a voice.
The sentry gulped. 'Is there anybody with you?'

The son of a field marshal joined the army. On his first day he said, 'Now I don't want the fact that I am the son of a field marshal to make any difference—you must treat me just as you would treat anyone else on his first day in the service. Is that quite clear?'
'Yes, major,' everybody answered.

A soldier stationed in a very remote outpost in Malaya had a parrot for a pet and, over the months, he taught it how to talk. One day the parrot flew into camp excitedly and said, 'A woman! A woman!', and flew off into the jungle.
Eagerly the soldier followed it, and crashing through the undergrowth, he managed with great difficulty to keep up with the parrot which flew overhead with cries of 'What a figure! What a figure!'
After a good half hour, as the soldier was almost on the point of collapse, they burst into a clearing, and there ahead, the exhausted man saw . . . another parrot.

During the war, some of the military camps in remote areas of the country covered several square miles. At one of these, a soldier once put in for weekend leave to visit his girl-friend.
When he went to collect his pass, the officer said, 'I'm afraid you can't be spared for the weekend, but I have been able to get you an eight-hour pass.
'Eight hours!' said the soldier. 'Blimey! I'll just have time to get to the gates and back.

During the Arab-Israeli war, an Israeli soldier captured an Arab tank and was awarded a weekend pass. Pleased with this, he did the same thing the following week, and indeed every week for the next three months. Finally, his commanding officer asked him how he managed to capture an Arab tank every week.
'Well,' replied the soldier, 'I just drive out in one of our tanks until I meet an Arab in one of their tanks and then I say to him "How would you like a weekend pass?" '

The camp medical officer was driving out to town in his car when the vehicle stalled just outside the canteen. A crowd of onlookers soon gathered, with smiles on their faces, and one of them said, 'What's the matter, sir—won't it go?'
'Of course it won't go,' said the officer. 'Do any of you have any suggestions?'
'Yes,' said another voice. 'Give it an aspirin and mark it "Fit for duty".'

A gushing American lady stopped to take a photograph of a Chelsea pensioner.

'Were you ever wounded?' she asked.

'Yes lady,' replied the old boy. 'I was wounded by a shell in the First World War.'

'My goodness!' exclaimed the matron. 'Did it explode?'

'No,' replied the old sweat. 'It crept up behind and bit me.'

A typist once turned up to work wearing a brooch made from three officer's shoulder pips.

'I suppose that means you have a captain for a boyfriend?' said her boss.

'No,' she replied. 'Three second lieutenants.'

A soldier returned home unexpectedly on leave from the Far East during 1943. That night he was in bed with his wife, when an air-raid warden knocked on the door.

'Good God!' he said, jumping out of bed, 'it's your husband!'

'Don't be silly,' said his wife, 'my husband's in Singapore.'

When the Suez crisis exploded in 1956 a very concientious young man went straight down to his local recruiting office and offered to join. They turned him down. They had enough staff at the recruiting office already.

Four private soldiers were up before a court martial on a charge of gambling. The first soldier said, 'I wasn't gambling—I had just dropped in for a chat with my friends.' He was acquitted through lack of evidence.

The second soldier said, 'I wasn't gambling—I was waiting to sweep up and turn the lights out before going to bed.' He was acquitted through lack of evidence.

The third soldier said, 'I wasn't gambling—I saw the light on and looked in to see what was going on.' He was acquitted through lack of evidence.

The fourth soldier was in a more difficult position as he had been caught with the actual cards and chips on his person.

'Now don't tell me *you* weren't playing cards for money!' said the prosecuting counsel.

'Me playing cards!' said the fourth soldier. 'Who with?'

A squad of soldiers was out doing field work and the officer asked one of them to see if he could estimate without binoculars how many men there were in a party digging a ditch about half-a-mile away.

'There's twelve men, sir, and one officer,' said the soldier. The officer in charge glanced through his field-glasses and said, 'You're absolutely right—but how did you know that one of the party was an officer?'

'There's one of them not digging, sir,' replied the soldier.

At one time during the war, they would take almost anybody in the army. At the physical examinations, one doctor would look in one ear and another doctor would look in the other ear, and if they couldn't see each other, you were in. If they *could* see each other, they sent you to officers' training school.

BEST
Newlywed
JOKES

Compiled by

COLIN CROMPTON

'Darling,' he whispered to his bride after the last guest had left the wedding reception, 'for the rest of your life you will have to put up with my ugly face.'

'Never mind,' she replied. 'You'll be out at work all day.'

The bride lay in bed on the first night of their honeymoon while her husband stood at the bedroom window, gazing at the stars.

'Come to bed, darling,' she whispered after about half an hour passed.

'Not likely,' replied the husband: 'My mother told me that this would be the best night of my life, and I'm not going to miss a minute of it.'

Tom's wife wasn't very attractive, but he was no oil-painting, either. After the ceremony, Tom asked the vicar how much the cost was.

'Just give me what you think it is worth to have this lady for your wife,' replied the Reverend.

Tom looked at his wife, and handed the vicar 10s.

The vicar looked at Tom's wife and gave him 7s. 6d. change.

Jim and Eileen got married early in December and had invited their parents round to share their first Christmas dinner together.

Christmas Eve arrived and Jim announced his intention of going out for a drink 'with the lads' in order to keep out of his wife's way while she prepared the all-important meal.

'Not that you have much to do,' he said. 'I've plucked and stuffed the turkey. All you have to do is kill it and put it in the oven.'

Mr and Mrs Newlywed were walking down the road when a gorgeous blonde approached them.

'Hello, George darling,' she murmured in a sultry voice as she passed by them.

'Who was that?' demanded his irate wife.

'I wish you wouldn't ask awkward questions,' replied her husband: 'I'll have enough trouble explaining who you are.'

'What did your Auntie Gertie buy us for a wedding-present?' asked George of his wife when they had returned from their honeymoon and were settling in their first home together.

'A tea-service, in potato pattern,' she replied.

'Potato pattern?'

'Yes—the cups are chipped.'

'Will you love me when I'm ugly and wrinkled?' asked Pauline after one week of married bliss.

'Of course I do,' replied her husband from behind the morning paper.

'My mother told me that I should always retain an air of mystery and never let you see me naked,' said Linda to her husband after they had been married a month.

'That explains it,' he replied: 'I was wondering why you always came to bed with your hat on.'

'Please don't tell any of the other guests that we are on our honeymoon,' said the blushing bride to the landlady of the seaside boarding-house.

'Of course I won't,' replied the landlady.

The bride told her husband what she had done, and he congratulated himself for having chosen such a thoughtful wife.

Next morning, as they were having breakfast, they were annoyed to notice that all the other guests were muttering to each other and looking over at them.

The husband cornered the landlady as soon as he could, and said, 'I thought my wife asked you not to tell the other guests that we were on our honeymoon.'

'I didn't,' replied the landlady. 'In fact, I told them that you weren't married.'

'Shall we go to bed now, or do you want to stay up late and watch Coronation Street?' said Steve to his wife on the first night of their honeymoon.

After one month of marriage and a lot of pleading from Tom his wife allowed him to go out for a drink with his bachelor friends.

'Well, what's it like?' they asked him.

'Just like getting into a bath,' he replied. 'Not so hot once you get used to it.'

They had been married three whole weeks and she still made the morning tea in her nightdress. They couldn't afford a tea-pot.

'Darling, I have a confession to make,' said Mrs Newlywed to her slightly dense husband. 'Before I met you, I was engaged to a boy with one leg called Albert.'

'Oh, really,' said her husband. 'What was his other leg called?'

After only one week of marriage, Harold's blonde wife gave definite evidence of being 'dizzy'.

She dropped a lump of sugar down the front of her dress by accident. To prove to Harold that she was a thrifty wife who didn't believe in wastage, she poured a cup of tea down there after it.

The honeymoon was over. After his first day back at work he was wondering what his wife would cook for their first dinner together in their own house.

It turned out to be a piece of plaice, beautifully cooked and with all the trimmings.

He congratulated his wife and remarked that fish was his favourite food.

Anxious to please him, his wife cooked him fish every day for the next three months.

As he sat down to eat a piece of haddock at the beginning of the fourth month, his wife dropped a knife on the floor.

'Darling,' she said as she bent to pick it up, 'that knife falling on the floor is a sign that there is a stranger coming.'

'Good,' remarked her husband. 'I hope it's the butcher.'

'I didn't say that you weren't a good cook,' said Mr Newlywed after suffering his wife's meals for the first month of their marriage: 'I merely enquired why ours was the only dustbin in the street with ulcers.'

'Darling, I hope you don't think that I'm extravagant,' said Mrs Newlywed, 'but once a month I like to take a bath in milk.'

'Oh, really?' said her husband. 'Pasteurised?'

'Don't be silly, darling,' she replied. 'Just up to my neck.'

They were reminiscing on their honeymoon.

'Gladys, do you remember the first time you invited me back to your house two years ago? Your parents went out, we went into the lounge and you put the lights out.'

'I didn't,' she replied.

'I know,' he retorted. 'But you put the lights out.'

'Jonathan darling,' cooed Mrs Newlywed, 'have you got a good memory for faces?'

'Why do you ask a question like that?'

'Because I've just broken your shaving mirror.'

They were honeymooning in the Lake District and had found a small stretch of water rather off the beaten track.

'We must come up here again tomorrow, darling,' said Michael. 'We can bring our costumes and have a swim.'

'But,' said his wife, 'the water isn't deep enough.'

'What makes you say that?' asked Michael.

'Well,' she replied, 'look for yourself—it only comes half way up those ducks.'

A young couple went into the office of a building society and spoke to the clerk.

'I earn £10 a week,' said Mr Newlywed. 'How do we stand for a mortgage?'

Came the curt reply, 'You don't, son—you grovel.'

'Darling, I have a confession to make,' said the shy newlywed to her husband at their first breakfast together. 'It isn't a big thing, but I feel I should have told you before. I suffer from asthma.'

'Thank heavens,' said the groom, smiling. 'Last night, I thought you were hissing me.'

After six months of marriage they were having their first argument. He lost his temper completely, and struck his wife across the face.

The vicar, who happened to be passing the window, saw it happen and rushed into the house.

The man, on seeing the vicar coming in, quickly regained his composure. He gave his wife another smack across the face and shouted, 'Now will you go to church?'

STOP PRESS: Lord Willoughby de Wobberley and his wife, Lady Annabelle (former showgirl Lucy Lastic until her marriage last month) were upstairs last night guarding their jewellery, when thieves broke into the house and watched television.

They were celebrating their first wedding anniversary, and she told her husband that she had visited the doctor during the day.

'Why?' he asked. 'Have you got Asian Flu?'

'No,' came the reply. 'I've got Egyptian Flu.'
'What does that mean?'
'I'm going to be a mummy.'

The lovely girl with the practically new wedding ring was voicing her troubles to a friend in the supermarket: 'I hate being married. Harry hasn't spoken to me for a fortnight.'

'That's terrible,' sympathised her friend. 'Do you think you'll divorce him?'

'I can't,' came the reply. 'I'm not married to Harry.'

After their honeymoon, the young couple were staying with the bride's parents until they could afford a place of their own.

'Don't talk too loudly,' said the bride as they entered their room 'My mother's got very sharp ears.'

'I wondered what those notches were round the keyhole,' he retorted.

The young married couple were window-shopping for furniture for their new house.

'I wish I had enough money to buy an elephant,' said the groom.

'Why on earth do you want an elephant?' asked wifey.

'I don't,' came the reply. 'I just wish I had the money.'

'What a clever husband I've got,' said Mrs Newlywed to her next-door neighbour. 'He waters our lawns with beer so that the grass will come up half cut.'

After six months of married bliss Sue and Fred were sitting quietly in front of the fire when there was a knock at the door.

Fred answered the door and Sue's mother stood there with two suitcases.

'I want to stay here,' she said.

'Well, stay there then,' replied Fred as he slammed the door.

The shy young bride was really upset when she learned that her handsome middle-aged husband had been married twice before.

Through her tears she asked what had become of her two pre-decessors.

'Well I may as well tell you,' said her spouse. 'My first wife died of mushroom poisoning.'

'And your second wife?' she insisted.

'She died of a fractured skull,' he replied. 'It was her own fault—she wouldn't eat the mushrooms.'

A little boy's favourite uncle had just got married, and the boy asked his mother several questions about the wedding.

'Mother,' he said finally, 'during the last three days before the wedding they give them anything they want to eat, don't they?'

BRIDE: 'Can you forgive me when I confess that I have false teeth?'
GROOM: 'Thank goodness. Now I can take off my wig, artificial leg and glass eye, and relax.'

The wedding presents were on view for all to see. Displayed in a prominent position was a cheque for £5,000—a gift from the bride's father.

'Who the dickens is that chap, laughing at your father's cheque?' exclaimed the bridegroom, very much annoyed.

'Oh,' answered the bride, 'that's only Daddy's bank manager.'

WIFEY: 'I saw the cutest little hat in town today, darling.'
HUBBY: 'Well put it on then, and let me see it.'

Mrs Newlywed had always wanted to join the local amateur dramatic society. At long last her ambition had been achieved; she was enrolled and given her first part, during which she had to walk across the stage wearing a bikini.

'Darling,' she said to her husband that evening, 'what would people say if I were to walk across the stage wearing a bikini?'

Her husband frowned. 'They'd say I had married you for your money.'

After only three weeks of marriage Ted's wife informed him that if he didn't give up drinking she would leave him.

'That's going to be pretty hard, isn't it?' said Ted's friend at work, when he was told of the ultimatum.

'Yes,' said Ted. 'I'll miss her.'

OFFICIAL: 'Do you remember the exact date of your marriage?'
APPLICANT: 'Yes I do. It was the fourth of November. I remember it quite well because it was the very next day when the fireworks started.'

The embarrassed groom finally plucked up the courage to ask the hotel clerk for a room for his wife and himself.

The clerk, sensing that they were newlyweds, asked, 'Suite, sir?'

The groom blushed furiously, 'Yes, thank you, she's perfect.'

A small crowd had collected to watch the departure of the bride and groom after the ceremony, when an old villager walking along the road met a friend and asked him what was going on.

By way of reply, he received this bit of philosophy: 'It's a man giving away half his dinner to get the other half cooked.'

GROOM: 'Darling, you are a girl in a thousand.'
BRIDE: (tearfully): 'Have there been that many others?'

Andy and Mary MacTavish had arrived in London on their honeymoon.

'Tell me, Mary,' asked Andy, 'd'ye ken the difference between a taxi and a bus?'

'No,' said Mary.

'Well then,' said Andy, 'we'll take a bus to the hotel.'

On visiting her sick husband in hospital Mrs Newlywed discovered that he was just about to have an operation, and exclaimed loudly, 'Oh, no, he's not! Nobody's going to open my male if I can help it.'

A notice in the bedroom at Honeymoon Hotel said, 'A successful marriage is often based on what a husband and wife don't know about each other.'

'I'm glad we are married,' said the blonde, as she and her husband left for their honeymoon. 'Now I can protect you against two-timing gold-diggers like me.'

WIFE: 'How is it that after only three months of marriage you manage to stay out so late every night?'
HUSBAND: 'It's easy. I got into the habit while we were courting.'

The young married couple were preparing to go out for the evening.

'Shall I wear my woollen dress or my chiffon dress, darling?'

'It doesn't matter, dear. I'll love you through thick and thin.'

The man decided to tease his new wife. On arriving at their new house, the bride found one of the rooms locked.

'What's in there?' she asked.

'Oh, that's full of pots of jam,' he replied. 'You see, every time I went out with a different girl I bought a pot of jam, and I've stacked them all in that room.'

The bride burst out crying.

'What are you crying for?' asked her husband.

'I'm just thinking how silly I have been,' she answered. 'If I'd only collected loaves of bread for all the men I've been out with, we would have enough bread and jam to last us a lifetime.'

A young married man arrived home late after telling his wife that he would be working late at the office. He went straight upstairs and began to undress for bed, but his wife, who had been watching him out of the corner of her eye, suddenly yelled out, 'Edward, where is your vest?'

'Well I'm blowed!' replied her erring husband. 'I've been robbed.'

'The bacon is not too bad, darling,' said the young wife. 'But I'm afraid the eggs have turned out a bit messy. They were frying beautifully when all at once the shells cracked and they spread all over the pan.'

At the end of their first week of marriage the young husband gave his wife all his wages except for five shillings which he kept for himself. At the end of the second week, he reversed the procedure, giving his wife five shillings and putting the rest in his own pocket.

'What good is this to me?' exclaimed his wife. 'How do you think I can manage on five shillings?'

'I don't know darling,' replied the young husband. 'I know that I had an awful job making it go round last week.'

'Well, that's that,' said the bride to her groom as they walked to the vestry to sign the wedding register. 'Now to collect a little bet.'

The following report of their wedding was printed in the local newspaper: *The couple were married on Saturday, thus ending a friendship which began in their schooldays.*

ADVICE TO NEWLYWEDS: No family should have fewer than three children. If there is one genius in the family, then there should be two to support him.

A woman worries about the future until she gets a husband.

A man never worries about the future until he gets a wife.

'May I kiss you darling?' said the groom to his bride when they were finally alone.

'Heavens!' she exclaimed. 'Another amateur.'

They were just about to start on their honeymoon and the groom was nervous to the point of forgetfulness.

'Harry, you've only bought one railway ticket,' reproached the bride.

'Just like me, dear,' stammered Harry. 'Always forgetting myself.'

It was their first quarrel, and he told her that he was sorry he had married her.

'Well,' retorted his wife, 'you can't say that I ran after you.'

'No,' he answered. 'And the trap doesn't run after the mouse, but it catches it just the same.'

MEMO TO BATCHELORS: You don't know what happiness is until you get married. And then it's too late.

He thought that the responsibilities of married life would cure him of his addiction to gambling, but he found that he was unable to break the habit.

After only three weeks of marriage and a disastrous run of bad luck he had no choice but to confess all.

'Darling, I have lost all my money and haven't got a penny in the world.'

'That won't make any difference, dear,' she replied. 'I'll love you just as much—even if I never see you again.'

JEAN: 'Fancy you marrying Charlie Harrison. I must say that I don't think much of him.'

JANE: 'I don't want you to.'

Bachelors know more about women than men who've just got married. If they didn't they'd be married too.

It was one of those rough and ready weddings. The groom was rough . . .

After a week of marriage he came home with his pay packet. What a wonderful moment it was. It wasn't very much, but that didn't matter. The main thing was that it belonged to both of them. No longer were they two separate people. They were two young people with all the future to look forward to. As he clutched the pay packet in his hand, he thrilled with pride. He took her hand and gave it to her. She took out the money, looked up at him with all the world in her eyes, and said, 'Hey—where's the rest of it?'

'I should never have got married,' said Mr Newlywed to his pal at work. 'My wife doesn't like me when I'm drunk, and I can't stand the sight of her when I'm sober.'

MRS NEWLYWED: 'I didn't accept Henry the first time he proposed.
HER EX-SCHOOLFRIEND: 'No, dear. You weren't there.'

DOROTHY: 'I hear that you're going to divorce your husband.'
MARGARET: 'Don't be silly, we've only been married a month—I hardly know him.'

BRIDE: 'I made this pudding all by myself.'
HUBBY: 'There's a clever girl. Who helped you to lift it out of the oven?'

The young bride was asked what she thought of married life.
'Oh, there's not much difference,' she replied. 'I used to wait up half the night for George to go home, and now I wait up half the night for him to come home.'

Mrs Newlywed was paying her first visit to the butcher.
'Can I have a pound of steak, please?'
'Certainly, madam. Will there be anything else?'
'And—and some gravy, please.'

Bill and his young wife had just completed their first quarrel.
'I wish I were dead,' she sobbed.
'I wish I was, too,' he blurted out.
'Then I don't wish I was,' she said.
And the fight continued.

After three weeks of marriage he was fast becoming sorry that he hadn't asked his young wife about her cooking ability before the wedding.
It was the last straw when he arrived home one evening after a

hard day's work and was confronted with a small portion of cheese for his main meal of the day.

'Is this all there is?' he demanded.

'Yes, dear,' replied his wife. 'You see, when the chops caught fire and fell into the dessert, I had to use the soup to put it out.'

They soon discovered that their marriage was even more ideal than they had thought. He snored, and she was deaf.

'Dad,' said Clarence, looking up from his history homework, 'who was it that said, "We haven't started to fight yet"?'

'I suppose it was a bride and groom still on their honeymoon,' growled his dad.

'Darling, we've been married exactly a month today, so I've bought you a beautiful surprise,' said Cynthia to George.

'How thoughtful of you,' replied George. 'I can't wait to see it.'

'Just a minute then, and I'll put it on.'

'We have been married a year and never had a quarrel,' said Mrs Green to Mrs Jones in the supermarket. 'If a difference of opinion arises and I am right, Felix always gives in immediately.'

'And if he is right?' queried Mrs Jones.

'That never occurs,' came the reply.

BRIDE: 'You must not expect me to give up my girlhood ways all at once.'

HUBBY: 'That's all right, little girl. Carry on taking an allowance from your father, just as if nothing had happened.'

The newlyweds had just got off the train.

'John, dear,' said the bride, 'let's try to make people think that we have been married a long time.'

'All right, darling. You carry the suitcases.'

The young couple had left for their honeymoon, and the reception was breaking up.

'I thought the bride looked very tired,' said one departing guest to another.

'No wonder, the way she's been running after him,' came the reply.

A recent society bride had six bridesmaids dressed in hyacinth blue silk, and two page-boys in rich crimson velvet, with gold lace. A pale bridegroom completed the colour scheme.

'What makes this meat taste so queer?' asked Mr Newlywed.
'I can't imagine,' responded the fond bride, 'I burnt it a little, but I put sunburn oil on it at once.'

'Now that we are married,' he said, 'perhaps I can point out a few of your defects.'
'Don't bother, dear,' she replied. 'I know all about them. It's those defects that kept me from getting a better man than you.'

'Yes,' said the young wife proudly, 'my father always gives something expensive when he gives presents.'
'So I discovered when he gave you away,' rejoined the young husband.

'I hear that Mrs Newlywed is very disappointed with her husband,' said one gossip to another.
'Indeed she is,' replied the other. 'She understood he was a home-loving man. But now he wants to tag along with her when she goes out every night.'

'Men are too mean for anything,' said the young bride.
'What's the trouble now?' asked her best friend.
'Why, I asked Jack for the car today, and he said that I must be content with the splendid carriage that nature gave me.'

The young bride was heartbroken.
'What's the matter?' asked a friend.
'Oh, my husband is so absent-minded. After breakfast he left a tip on the table, and when I handed him his hat he gave me another tip.'
'Well, that's nothing to worry about—it's just force of habit.'
'That's what worries me. He kissed me when I gave him his coat.'

MR NEWLYWED: 'Did you sew the button on my shirt, darling?'
MRS NEWLYWED: 'No, love. I couldn't find the button, so I just sewed up the button-hole.'

HUBBY: 'Now that we are married, dear, let us have a clear understanding about our future together. Do you wish to be the Managing Director or the Assistant Managing Director?'

WIFEY: 'Neither. You be both. I'll just be the Treasurer.'

'How many wardrobes are there in the house you have just bought, dear?' asked the sweet young bride.

'Six,' replied the husband.

'But that's not enough, Henry.'

'What do you want with more than six wardrobes? That's enough to hang your clothes in, isn't it?'

'Yes, but you'll want part of one for your clothes, won't you, Henry?'

'What are you cutting out of the paper, darling?' asked the young bride of her husband.

'It's an article about a man securing a divorce because his wife went through his pockets.'

'What are you going to do with it?'

'Put it in my pocket.'

'Darling, I have to go to London on business,' said the young married man, shortly after they had returned from their honeymoon. 'It will only take three or four days and I hope you won't miss me too much when I'm gone, but . . .'

'I won't,' answered his young wife positively, 'because I'm going with you.'

'I wish you could, dear, but it won't be convenient this time. What do you want to go for, anyway? I'm going to be too busy to be with you, and . . .'

'I have to go. I need clothes.'

'But, darling—you can get all the clothes you want right here in Leeds.'

'Thank you. That's all I wanted.'

JEAN: 'So you and Tom are married? I thought it was a mere flirtation.'

JOAN: 'So did Tom.'

'What's wrong, Henry?' asked Mrs Newlywed.

'My razor,' said her spouse from the bathroom. 'It doesn't cut at all.'

'Don't be silly. Your beard can't be tougher than linoleum.'

The bride's father was making a speech at the wedding reception.

'A bride wears white,' he said, 'as a symbol of happiness, for her wedding day is the most joyful in her life.'

'And why do men wear black?' someone asked.

'And remember, my son,' said the father of the groom, 'the early husband gets his own breakfast.'

'My dear,' said Mrs Newlywed, her face flushed with the excitement of her afternoon in the kitchen, 'I want you to be perfectly frank and honest with me. What would you suggest to improve these doughnuts I made today?'

'Well,' replied Mr Newlywed, lifting one with a slight effort, 'I think it might be better if you made the hole bigger.'

An Eskimo bride was talking to her friend. 'I'm furious. Last night he didn't get home till half past January.'

As his bride hadn't seemed to have much idea of the value of money during their courtship, the young husband, thinking to restrain her extravagance, presented her with an account book and gave her £20 after the first week of their married life.

'Write down what I give you on one page,' he explained, 'and on the opposite page write down what happens to it. That will enable you to know how much you have spent at the end of any given time.'

When next her husband asked to see the book, his wife told him eagerly, 'I did just as you told me. See.'

On one page was written: 'Received £20.' On the opposite page was noted: 'Spent it all.'

The newlywed's next-door neighbours were discussing them.

'They seem a most devoted couple, John. He kisses her every time he goes out, and even blows kisses to her from the pavement. Why don't you do that?'

'Good heavens!' replied John. 'I don't even know her yet.'

He had been married a month and was talking to his friend who was a bachelor and wanted to know all about it.

'How did you get to know your wife before you married?' asked the friend.

'I didn't know her before I married,' came the prompt reply.

MRS NEWLYWED: 'Darling, as you have already eaten three helpings of the first pie I've ever cooked for you, I'm going to cook another for you tomorrow. Won't that be lovely? Won't that be—speak to me, darling, speak to me.'

224

The bride of a few weeks noticed that her husband was depressed.

'Gerald, dearest,' she said, 'I know that something is troubling you, and I want you to tell me what it is; your worries are not your worries now, they are our worries, yours and mine equally.'

'Oh, very well,' he said. 'We've just had a letter from a girl, and she's suing us for breach of promise.'

'To think,' exclaimed the enthusiastic young husband, 'that by the time we get all this furniture paid for, we shall have genuine antiques.'

'These spoons which Aunt Jane gave us as a wedding present are not real silver,' announced the bride.

'Do you know anything about silver?' asked the groom.

'No,' replied the bride, 'but I know a lot about Aunt Jane.'

MRS NEWLYWED: 'Why do you tell all your friends that you married me because I'm such a wonderful cook? You know that I can't boil a potato.'

MR NEWLYWED: 'But I have to give them some reason.'

It was their first real quarrel.

'I'm sorry that I ever became your wife,' she said bitterly.

'Well,' he flung back, 'you were no young bird when I married you.'

'No,' she retorted, 'but considering what I got, I was an early bird.'

'Are you sure that it was a marriage licence you gave me last month?'

'Yes, sir. What's the matter?'

'I thought there might be some mistake, seeing that I've lived a dog's life ever since.'

MRS NEWLYWED *to her husband*: 'Darling, will you lend me ten pounds and only give me five of them? Then you'll owe me five, and I'll owe you five, and we'll be straight.'

It was that great occasion that happens to every pair of newly-weds: their first quarrel.

'And you tell me that several men proposed marriage to you?' he said.

'Yes. Several,' the wife replied.

'Well, I wish you had married the first fool who proposed.'

'I did.'

'Does your husband talk in his sleep?' asked Mrs Newlywed's friend.

'No, and it's terribly exasperating. He just grins.'

'I am sorry that I am late for dinner. I got arrested for speeding on the way home,' Lord Newlywed explained rather sheepishly. 'I have to appear in court tomorrow and will have to pay a £10 fine or go to prison for seven days.'

'What a stroke of luck!' exclaimed Lady Newlywed. 'You must take the seven days, Peter. The cook has just left, and it will give me time to get another one.'

'Which of those two men is the bridegroom?'

'The anxious-looking one. The cheerful one is the bride's father.

The young couple, thinking that their parents would oppose their marriage, had eloped to Gretna Green.

After being there for the necessary period they got married and had grown to like the small Scottish town so much that they decided to make their home there permanently.

After three weeks of married bliss, a telegram arrived.

'Oh, darling,' said the young wife, 'it's from Daddy.'

'What does he say?' asked the bridegroom eagerly.

'Do not come home and all will be forgiven.'

The bridegroom was in a poetic mood as he strolled along the sea shore.

'Roll on, thou deep and dark blue ocean, roll on,' he recited to his bride.

'Oh, Percy,' she exclaimed, 'how wonderful you are. *It's doing it.*'

'Darling, you have deceived me,' said the young bride to her husband shortly after they were married.

'But I told you that I was a millionaire, and I am,' said her groom.

'Yes,' retorted the bride. 'But you also told me that you were seventy years of age and in poor health, and now I've discovered that you are only fifty-six and as fit as a fiddle.'

'Do you think that you have as good a sense of judgment as I have?' asked Mrs Newlywed, during their first quarrel.

'Well, no,' replied Mr Newlywed slowly. 'Our choice of partners for life shows that you have better judgment than me.'

226

JOHN: 'If I had known you were so extravagant, I would never have married you.'
JEAN: 'If I hadn't been, father would never have let you.'

'Darling, we have been married only a week and already you want to go out for a night with all your girl friends,' complained Harry to his bride. 'It just isn't right. They'll all think that you are unhappy and not content to stay in with me. In fact, I forbid you to go.'

'I don't care what you forbid,' said his wife. 'I'm going out and that's the end of it.'

'But you promised at the altar to obey me,' said Harry.

'Of course I did,' she retorted. 'I just didn't want to make a scene.'

BOB: 'Was it a big wedding?'
BILL: 'Yes. I got in the queue three times to kiss the bride and nobody noticed it.'

They had been married a month when she informed her husband that her mother was coming to stay with them for a few days.

'Oh no, she's not,' said the groom emphatically.

'But before we were married, you said that Mother could stay with us whenever she pleased,' said the young bride.

'Yes, but she hasn't pleased yet,' came the reply.

The young bride was telling her mother how wonderful marriage was.

'Do you know, Mummy,' she said, 'Alan gives me everything I ask for.'

'Which merely shows,' replied her mother, 'that you are not asking for enough.'

The young wife was in tears when she opened the door for her husband on his return from work. 'I've been insulted,' she sobbed. 'Your mother insulted me.'

'My mother!' he exclaimed. 'But she's a hundred miles away!'

'I know,' she replied, 'but a letter came for you from her this morning and I opened it.'

He looked stern. 'I see, but where does the insult come in?'

'In the postscript,' she answered. 'It said: "Dear Alice, don't forget to give this letter to George".'

YOUNG WIFE: 'Oh, I'm so miserable. My husband has been out all evening, and I haven't the faintest idea where he is.'
EXPERIENCED FRIEND: 'My dear, you mustn't worry. You would probably be twice as miserable if you did know.'

A minister of the church was visiting a prison when he came across a prisoner whose features were familiar to him.

'What brought you here, my poor fellow?' he asked.

'You married me to a new woman a month ago, sir,' the prisoner replied with a sigh.

'Ah, I see,' said the parson. 'And the woman was domineering and extravagant, and she drove you to desperate measures, eh?'

'No,' said the prisoner. 'My old woman turned up.'

Shortly after their return from their honeymoon they moved into their new house, and the bride was anxious to put into practice the lessons she had taken in cooking.

Returning home one evening, the husband found his wife in tears. Between sobs he managed to learn from her that something terrible had happened.

'Darling,' she said, 'it was the first meat pie I ever baked for you and the cat has eaten it.'

'That's all right, my love,' said the husband, patting her on the shoulder, 'I'll get you another cat tomorrow.'

After two months in the army, the private got his first leave, and made what he thought the best use of his holiday by getting married.

On his journey back to the camp, he gave the ticket inspector his marriage certificate instead of his railway voucher.

The official studied it carefully, and then said, 'Yes, my boy, you've got a ticket for a long wearisome journey, but it's not the one for this trip.'

'At last, my angel,' said the happy man after settling with the minister, 'we are really and truly one.'

'Theoretically yes,' said his modern bride. 'But from a practical standpoint it will be advisable to order dinner for two.'

A man who had recently married was asked by his boss how he and his wife were getting on.

'Not very well, boss,' was the reply. 'The fact is that my wife and I are separated.'

'Separated!' exclaimed the boss. 'Why, you got married only last week. You can't leave her. She's your wife and you took her for better or worse.'

'Yes, but she's worse than I took her for,' was the sad reply.

An old man in his eightieth year married a girl of twenty-two. Asked by one of his friends why he chose such a young bride, he replied, 'I decided it would be better to smell perfume for the remainder of my life than to smell liniment.'

She falls in love with a fellow
  Who swells with a foreign air;
He marries her for her money,
  She marries him for his hair!
One of the very best matches—
  Both are well mated in life;
She's got a fool for a husband,
  He's got a fool for a wife.

A widower who was married recently for the third time, and whose bride had been married once before herself, wrote on the wedding invitations, 'Be sure to come. This is no amateur performance.'

A man called at the minister's home looking as though he had something on his mind.

'I just came to ask you,' he said, 'whether it is right for any person to profit by the mistakes of other people?'

'Most certainly not,' replied the minister.

His caller brightened, and held out his hand. 'Then, if that's the case,' he said, 'perhaps you'd like to return the money I gave you last month for marrying me.'

Archibald, nineteen years old, against the wishes of his noble parents, had married a young woman of the chorus. Just after the ceremony he was instructing a friend who had offered to break the news to his mother and father. 'Tell them first that I am dead,' he advised. 'Then gently work up to the climax.'

While on her honeymoon the young bride had gone out alone one afternoon to make some purchases. Back in the hotel, she got off the lift at the wrong floor. She went down the corridor until she reached what she thought to be the door of her room. Finding it locked, and having no key with her, she knocked on it and said softly, 'Honey, oh, honey.'

There was no response. After a while she knocked again, calling somewhat more loudly, 'Honey, oh, honey.'

After this had occurred a number of times, a blatant male voice roared out from within, saying, 'Madam, this is not a beehive, it's a bathroom.'

There had been a big family row and the police had been called, Mr Jones was hauled into court for beating his wife. The magistrate rebuked him severely.

'You ought to be ashamed of yourself,' his honour began, 'for assaulting your wife like that. I never saw a nastier black eye. Do you know of any reason why I should not send you to prison?'

'If you do,' answered the defendant, 'it will break up our honeymoon.'

After three weeks of marriage, he made the mistake of taking his young wife to a nightclub that he had frequented in his bachelor days.

She got steadily more annoyed as first the cloakroom girl, then the barmaid, and then the waitress, all of whom were attractive girls, greeted him with affection. But the last straw came when a slim blonde came up to their table, kissed him fondly on the cheek and whispered, 'I'll see you another night, darling, when you're not so busy.'

The bride got up from the table and hurried out of the club, closely followed by her husband. They got into a taxi together and, as it drove away, he attempted to explain that his past was behind him and he loved only her. 'Please listen to me,' he said.

But his wife wasn't to be appeased. 'No I will not,' she shouted.

Whereupon the taxi-driver looked over his shoulder and said to the husband, 'She's no good, Harry—shall we go back and get another?'

They were leaving the church after the wedding, and the bride said, 'What's the matter, dearest; you seem flustered?'

'Oh, it's nothing,' said the groom. 'You see, this is the first time I've been married. I'll do better next time.'

HE: 'Just think, we've been married twenty-four hours.'

SHE: 'Yes, and it seems like it was only yesterday.'

Mr Newlywed rushed into the cute little kitchen and found Dearie busy with a pie that she was trying to bake.

'How wonderful!' he exclaimed as he glanced at the pie, which was about six inches wide and eighteen inches long. 'But why did you make it such a funny shape?'

'I couldn't get any shorter rhubarb,' she answered.

The height of bashfulness: they got married on Christmas Eve and he took some mistletoe with him on their honeymoon.

MR NEWLYWED: 'I married a girl who was one of twins.'

HIS FRIEND: 'How do you tell them apart?'

MR NEWLYWED: 'Her brother has a beard.'

SHE: 'Before we were married you told me you were well off.'
HE: 'But I never knew how well off.'

Before marriage Tom told his wife that nothing would be good enough for her, and after marriage he still seemed to think that it was.

Love is blind—and marriage is an eye-opener.

They had been married only a week and she was crying.
'You said that if I'd marry you, you'd be humbly grateful,' she sobbed.
'Well, what of it?' he asked.
'You're not—you're grumbly hateful.'

JIM: 'I married an adagio dancer. We've been married three weeks now and I've never kissed her yet.'
JOE: 'What's the matter—don't you love her?'
JIM: 'Of course I love her, but I can't catch her.'

JUDGE: 'You are called as a witness of the quarrel between your friend and his wife. Were you present at the beginning of the trouble?'
WITNESS: 'Certainly. I was best man at the wedding.'

One lady was talking to another at the wedding reception. 'Are you a friend of the groom?'
'Indeed not,' came the indignant reply. 'I'm the bride's mother.'

'What's a bridegroom?'
'A thing they have at weddings.'

A wealthy young man from the north of England surprised everybody when he arrived back from a business trip to London with a beautiful young bride.
'Wow!' enthused one of his friends, 'how did you manage to meet her?'
'There was nothing to it,' came the reply. 'I just opened my wallet and there she was.'

231

A young bridegroom followed his bride into their shining new kitchen. 'And what is my snookums doing in here?' he asked.

His worried bride explained, 'I rinsed the ice cubes in this hot water and now I can't find them.'

JOE: 'Ever since the honeymoon my wife has been hitting the ceiling.'

JIM: 'You're lucky that she's such a rotten shot.'

'It's not true that I married a millionaire,' said Jane to a friend after six months of marriage. 'I made him one.'

'What was he before you married him?' asked the friend.

Jane answered, 'A multi-millionaire.'

MRS NEWLYWED'S MOTHER: 'I don't think you're taking this marriage of yours very seriously.'

HER DAUGHTER: 'Well, after all, Mother, it's only my first.'

He'd been married only a month when he attended the office Christmas party and was the last to leave, having consumed more than his quota of whisky.

'What did your wife say when you got home?' asked a colleague the following day.

'The darling never said a word,' replied the wayward one. 'And I was going to have those two front teeth out, anyway.'

They'd been married three months, and she said, 'Are you satisfied with our married life?'

'Yes,' he replied. 'I've had enough of it.'

HARRY: 'What happened to you? You used to be such a dude.'

HENRY: 'I got married last week.'

HARRY: 'I see—sub-dude.'

HILDA: 'Mary married a second lieutenant last week.'

NORA: 'Why?'

HILDA: 'The first one got away.'

Mrs Newlywed was crying. 'What's the matter?' asked her friend.

'Well,' she replied, 'I didn't find out until after the wedding that he'd been married before and had five children.'

'That must have come as a shock to you,' said her friend.

'Yes,' sobbed the wife. 'And my four children weren't pleased, either.'

BILL: 'So your new wife has been married four times and you've been married twice?'

BOB: 'That's right. She's still two chumps ahead of me.'

George had been married a month and his friend commented on it.

'It's easy to see that you're married,' he said. 'No holes in your socks now.'

'No,' replied George. 'One of the first things my wife taught me was how to darn them.'

JILL: 'So you and your hubby had a runaway marriage?'

JEAN: 'Yes. He ran away, and I ran after him.'

'Darling,' she said on their honeymoon. 'Now that we are married, I want you to sack your secretary.'

'But you used to be a secretary yourself,' said hubby.

'Yes,' she replied. 'That's why I want you to sack her.'

BRIDE (tearfully): 'I'm going home to my mother.'

GROOM: 'Good. I'll come with you, then we can both get a decent meal.'

They were sitting in front of the television set after three weeks of married life when he said, 'Our marriage was a mistake.'

'I disagree with you,' said his bride.

'Yes,' he answered.

MR NEWLYWED: 'That shirt you bought me was too big.'

MRS NEWLYWED: 'Of course it was. I didn't want the shopkeeper to know that I'd married a little shrimp like you.'

HARRY: 'You say that your wife caused you to grow that long beard?'

MR NEWLYWED: 'Yes, she started choosing my neckties.'

'What were you before you were married?' asked Mrs Newlywed's next-door neighbour.

'A housemaid,' was the reply.

233

'And the change is a pleasant one?'
'What change?' answered the bride. 'I just work for nothing now.'

PAMELA: 'Well, well, I haven't seen you around here for months; are you still engaged to that sensible, thrifty young man you were telling me so much about?'
ANGELA: 'No—I married the stingy devil.'

Although they had only been married six weeks, things weren't going very well at all.
'I was a fool when I married you,' he said to his young bride.
'Yes, I suppose you were,' she replied. 'But I was so much in love with you that I didn't notice it.'

It was their first quarrel and it had started because he refused to go downstairs in the middle of the night when she heard a noise that she thought might be burglars.
'When I married you, I didn't know that you were a coward,' she said. 'I thought you were a brave man.'
'So did everybody else,' he replied wearily.

Advice to newlywed men: If you don't want your wife to know how much you earn, hide your payslip in your undarned socks.

The two bachelors were talking about their friend who had just got married.
'You've got to admire him,' said Steve. 'They were still on their honeymoon when he gave his wife a lecture on economy.'
'What happened?' asked Mike.
'He's given up smoking,' replied Steve.

STELLA: 'Since I last saw you I've been divorced, and yesterday I got married again.'
SYLVIA: 'I thought you looked like a changed woman.'

BRIAN: 'George got married yesterday.'
BRUCE: 'Good, I never liked the fellow.'

PROFESSOR: 'Do you know the two words that start the longest sentence in the world?'
STUDENT: 'I do.'
PROFESSOR: 'That's right.'

MRS NUWED: 'John, John, there's a burglar in the house.'
MR NUWED: 'What do you want me to do? Get up, and run the risk of being killed?'
MRS NUWED: 'No. But if you get up in the morning and find that someone has gone through your pockets, don't blame me.'

The newlyweds were having no luck in their search for an unfurnished flat. After another weary day, the groom said, 'Well, if the worst comes to the worst, we could always go and live with your parents.'
'Impossible,' said the bride. 'They're living with my mother's parents.'

A dentist married a manicurist and, after a week, they were scrapping tooth and nail.

CHRISTINE: 'I don't see Charlie half as much as I did three months ago.'
CAROL: 'You should have married him when you had the chance.'
CHRISTINE: 'I did.'

After three weeks of marriage she accused him of not loving her as much as he did when they were first married. 'You used to get up and light the fire every morning,' she said. 'And now you let me get up and do it.'
'Nonsense, my love,' he answered. 'Your getting up to light the fire makes me love you all the more.'

'He expects to live in clover the rest of his days.'
'Why?'
'He married a grass widow last week.'

Mrs Newlywed was really upset. 'Before we were married,' she sobbed, 'you told me that we'd be just like two birds in a nest—and now I find out that you meant we wouldn't have a roof over our heads.'

GLYNIS: 'Her father gave the bride away.'
GLADYS: 'I could have given her away, but it's none of my business.'

'You're not domesticated enough,' complained Mr Newlywed. 'Before we were married you said you would darn my socks, but you never have.'

'Well, you promised to buy me a fur coat, but you haven't,' replied the young bride.

'What's that got to do with it?' he asked.

'Well,' she replied, 'if you don't give a wrap, I don't give a darn.'

'I suppose I should have told you before,' she said: 'I can't cook.'

'That's all right, little girl,' consoled the bridegroom, 'I have a confession to make, too. I'm an out-of-work musician and there won't be anything to eat.'

After only three weeks they had their first quarrel. The groom was coming off worst until he brought his bride's family into the argument.

'Your father is an old drunkard,' he shouted: 'Your mother's a nagger, and your brother is an idle layabout.'

'Can't you say one decent thing about my family?' she asked, sarcastically.

'Yes, just one,' he replied. 'They were all opposed to our marriage.'

MR NEWLYWED: 'I'm going out after dinner.'
MRS NEWLYWED: 'Oh, darling, what will I do without you?'
MR NEWLYWED: 'The dishes.'

They were on their honeymoon and walking along the seafront, arm in arm. He gazed into her eyes and said, 'I'll love you just like I do now, if I live to be a hundred.'

'And then I suppose you'll start chasing around with women,' said the modern young bride.

'Who is that letter from?' asked the young bride over the breakfast table.

'What do you want to know for?' teased her husband.

'There you are. What do I want to know for? You're the most inquisitive person I've ever known,' replied Mrs Newlywed.

Mrs Newlywed was on the telephone and shouted to her husband, 'Darling, how would you like to talk to my mother?'

'Through a spirit medium,' came the prompt reply.

It was an embarrassing moment for George when a week after his marriage he met a former girl friend. As she had always been rather

236

moody and miserable when they had gone out together, he 'explained' his marriage by saying, 'At least I married a girl with a sense of humour.'

'Obviously,' came the cutting reply.

HE: 'Your meals aren't like my mother used to make.'
SHE: 'Well, your salary isn't like my father used to make.'

Two men were talking in a pub.

'Joe's had an unfortunate love affair,' said one.

'Why, what happened?' said the other.

'He got married yesterday,' said the first one.

'But, darling,' said the disillusioned husband after a few weeks of marriage, 'didn't that ceremony make us man and wife?'

'No, you worm!' said the equally disillusioned wife. 'It made a wife of me, but it would take more than that to make a man of you.'

'Darling,' said the old man to his young and beautiful bride on their honeymoon, 'if I could change places with Engelbert Humperdinck or Tom Jones right this minute, I wouldn't do it.'

'But,' she protested, 'you said that you would do anything to please me.'

'Have you got any photographs of your wife in the nude?' said the best man to the groom at the wedding reception.

The groom was very annoyed. 'No, I have not,' he answered sharply.

'Do you want to buy some?' asked the best man.

Jill was back at work in the typing pool after her marriage and a week's honeymoon at Blackpool.

'Jack loves me more than he has ever loved any other girl,' she said to the girl sitting at the next desk.

'Of course he does,' came the reply: 'You're the only girl who would ever go out with him more than once.'

JOE: 'I hear that you got married last week.'
JIM: 'Yes, that's right.'
JOE: 'How come?'
JIM: 'You guess '
JOE: 'O.K.—Her father got you a job.'
JIM: 'No.'

237

JOE: 'Her father's got a lot of money and looks ill.'
JIM: 'No.'
JOE: 'She's inherited a lot of money.'
JIM: 'No.'
JOE: 'Blackmail?'
JIM: 'No.'
JOE: 'I give up, what's the reason?'
JIM: 'I love her.'
JOE: 'Oh, I knew there was a catch to it.'

A month after the wedding he realised that love was just a sweet dream and marriage was the alarm clock.

'Love is the wine of life,' said the romantic office boy.
  'Yes,' agreed the newlywed clerk. 'And marriage is the morning after.'

SHE: 'Now that we are married I will share all your troubles and sorrows.'
  HE: 'But, darling, I haven't any troubles and sorrows.'
  SHE: 'Well, we've only been married an hour.'

'I don't know why your father doesn't like me,' said the groom to his bride at their wedding reception.
  'Neither do I,' she replied. 'After all, money, brains and looks aren't everything.'

'Do you think you could learn to love me?' asked the rich old man of his young bride when she confessed that she had married him for his money.
  'It's possible,' she replied: 'I learned to eat spaghetti.'

'To think that I am the first girl you have ever loved,' said Mrs Newlywed at the breakfast table one morning.
  'Yes, darling,' he replied, gazing into her eyes.
  'And to think that you believe that I believe that!' came the unexpected reply.

'Oh, darling, I love you so,' said the blushing bride.
  'So *what*?' asked her groom.

She was heartbroken when her husband was killed in a car accident after only two weeks of married bliss, and she was far from pleased when Jack, who had been the best man at their wedding, asked if he could take her husband's place.

'It all depends,' she told him.

'On what?' he asked.

'On whether you can fix it up with the undertaker,' she answered.

'Will you love me when I get old?' asked the young wife.

'Love you?' answered hubby. 'I shall idolise you. I shall worship the ground under your little feet. I shall . . . um . . . er . . . you're not going to look like your mother, are you?'

'Love is blind,' he said to his young bride on their first day together in their new house.

'Yes,' she replied, 'but the neighbours aren't, so draw the curtains.'

'How can I be sure that you love me?' teased his bride on their honeymoon.

'Why just try me,' he replied. 'Test me on something.'

'All right,' she said. 'Would you come to my rescue in distress?'

'Of course I would,' said the witty bridegroom. 'It wouldn't make any difference what you were wearing.'

'My wife gave me a rainbow kiss this morning,' said the young newlywed to his friend at work.

'What sort of kiss is that?'

'The kind that comes after a storm,' was the reply.

THE WORLD'S
Worst
PUNS

Compiled by
SIMON PHILLIPS

A

A: An expression of interrogation, usually pronounced with one hand over one ear.

ABASH: A blow with the fist.

ABERRATION: High regard; e.g., 'He compels high *ABERRATION*'.

ABET: Five bob each way.

ABILITY: Functional weakness; e.g., 'Suffering from physical *ABILITY*'.

ABROAD: A girl (Amer.).

ABSINTHE: Non-appearance; e.g., 'He was conspicuous by his *ABSINTHE*'.

ACME: A hard, inflamed pimple.

ACRE: Anything that hurts.

ADDICT: A species of fish—very nice smoked.

ADJURE: For you—generally followed by the word 'service'.

ADOLESCENT: Was taught; e.g., 'He went to a teacher and *ADOLESCENT*'.

ADONIS: Was wearing; e.g., ' *'E ADONIS* best suit'.

ADULTERY: The state of being grown up.

AFFIX: Principles of behaviour; e.g., 'State the difference between morality and *AFFIX*'.

AIRY: Possessing a well-covered chest.

243

ALAS: A girl.

ALBINO: There will not be, as in '*ALBINO* nonsense while I'm around'.

ALLEY: Used in circuses, generally followed by 'oop'.

AMATORY: Doing something for nothing.

AMITY: Void; e.g., '*AMITY* vessels make the most sound'.

AMITY: Hostility.

ANALYSE: Anna is not telling the truth.

ANEMONE: One who is hostile.

ANEROIDS: Piles.

ANOMALOUS: Without a name.

ANTENNAE: There is none; e.g., 'There *ANTENNAE* beer left'.

ANTIQUATE: Is not really; e.g., 'This *ANTIQUATE* what we are looking for'.

ANTISEPTIC: One who does not believe in spiritualism.

AORTA: Part of the regretful admission: '*AORTA* known better'.

APPARENTLY: Like a father.

APPEND: Took place.

APROPOS: A chamber utensil on approval.

ARCHERY: A blood vessel.

ARMAGEDDON: As in '*ARMAGEDDON* out of here'.

ARTICHOKE: Epitaph by a Thug on a difficult victim.

ASBESTOS: As in '*ASBESTOS* my ability'.

ASPARAGUS: That which is cast slanderously.

ASSAGAI: That's the fellow (Amer.).

ASTROLOGY: The science of walking slowly.

ATTAIN: That is not, as in '*ATTAIN* right'.

ATTENTIVE: Pertaining to a tent.

AUTO-SUGGESTION: Offering a car for sale.

AVENUE: Have you not?—as in '*AVENUE* seen me before?'

AWESOME: A proper name—as in *AWESOME* Welles.

AWFUL: Waste meats.

B

B: An insect that gathers honey.

BAILIFF: A type of leaf used in cooking.

BALDERDASH: An attack by one with less hair than his opponent.

BANDOLIER: The look musicians give a pretty girl.

BARBECUE: A line of customers at the hairdresser's.

BARBECUE: The sign from the hairdresser that it is your turn.

BARONY: Inability to bear children.

BATMAN: A cricketer.

BATTLE: A little bat.

BEACHCOMBER: Unconscious on the sea-shore.

BEADLE: A crawling insect.

BEANO: The result of rain; e.g., 'There'll *BEANO* play today'.

BEAR: Naked.

BEARSKIN: The body unadorned.

BEETLE: One who sings loudly with a wig on his head.

BEGUILE: A large island.

BELCH: Used in the current expression '*BELCH* up'—a popular phrase with Prime Ministers.

BELLADONNA: Bella does not; e.g., '*BELLADONNA* love me no more'.

BELLICOSE: Possessing a large stomach.

BELLOW: Underneath; e.g., 'He hit me *BELLOW* the belt'.

BELL-PUNCH: A blow delivered as the bell goes.

BELONG: Delay; e.g., 'Don't *BELONG*'.

BENIGN: As in 'Be home *BENIGN* o'clock'.

BIRD'S EYE: A provocative look from a girl.

BISECT: An arm muscle.

BLACKMAIL: Central African postal system.

BLOCKADE: Assistance given to a block.

BLUSTER: (Amer.) Pal or mate; e.g., 'OK, *BLUSTER*'.

BOBBIN: Enter for a short period (and then bobout again).

BOOZE: The opposite of cheers.

BRIDEWELL: A well into which brides were thrown.

BRIDLE PATH: The path along which the bride is led.

BRIDLE REIN: A thong for controlling and checking brides.

BROADSIDE: (Amer.) The haughtiness of a woman.

BROKEN-DOWN: Chopped-up duck's feathers.

BRUSQUE: Name given to a Scottish hero: 'Robert the *BRUSQUE*'.

BUFFOON: A low-pitched musical instrument.

BULLY-BEEF: To strike cruelly at cattle.

BULRUSH: The thing a toreador watches carefully.

BUOYANT: A male ant.

BURLY: Not quite, as in 'He was *BURLY* visible'.

BUTTERCUP: A drinking vessel for goats.

C

C: A bishop's jurisdiction.

CABARET: An impressive line-up of taxis.

CABRIOLET: Cabri with milk.

CADASTRAL: A nasty ghost.

CAIRN: Worrying; e.g., 'He was past *CAIRN*'.

CAJOLE: A retreat for beggars.

CAMBRIC: A curved brick.

CANNIBAL: What is his cricketing ability; e.g., '*CANNIBAL* a leg-break?'

CANONIZE: To bombard; to shell.

CANOPUS: A composition for tin-cans (Mus.).

CANTATA: Farewell to a can.

CANTILEVER: Beginning of a phrase generally directed at a screen villain: '*CANTILEVER* alone?'

CAPABLE: What the toreador does in the arena.

CAPON: How the toreador leaves the arena in cold weather.

CAPSIZE: Head measurement.

CAPTURE: Delayed you, as in 'Sorry if I've *CAPTURE*'.

CARDIGAN: A dignitary of the Roman Church.

CARESS: A plant used in salads.

CARNAL: The army rank above major.

CARROT: A room under the roof, with sloping ceilings.

CARTOGRAPHY: The art of writing things on the side of a cart.

CASHMERE: Part of what one says to the landlord over the bar, when one is short of the ready: 'Could you *CASHMERE* cheque?'

CASSOCK: A Russian horseman.

CATACOMB: An implement used for grooming cats.

CATKIN: A cat's relatives.

CELEBRATE: Unmarried.

CELERY: A stipend.

CENSUS: Conveys to us; e.g., 'Uncle Jim *CENSUS* presents every Christmas'.

CHANCERY: Risky; dubious.

CHAPLAIN: A well-known comedian.

CHASTE: Hunted.

CHAUFFEUR: Part of the phrase: 'There was little to *CHAUF-FEUR* all the work he'd done'.

CHECKMATE: A spouse in Central Europe.

CHOKER: The 53rd card in the pack.

CHOOSE: Israelis.

CINDER: Part of the slang phrase '*CINDER* bag'.

CLAMOUR: What girls have for men.

CLEEK: Chinese for 'trouble', as in 'Up the *CLEEK*'.

CLEFT: Used for marching: '*CLEFT*, right, *CLEFT*, right'.

CLOAK: Noise made by a Chinese frog.

CLOSURE: Often spoken to a child: '*CLOSURE* eyes, and go to sleep'.

COAST: A phantom.

CODA: Possessing less warmth; e.g., 'It's *CODA* today than it was yesterday'.

CODA: Part of an expletive, as in '*CODA* hell!'

CODE: Chilly.

COHABIT: Generally used by taxi passengers; e.g., 'Driver, can't you *COHABIT* faster?'

COLLECT: Free from error. (Chinese).

COMATOSE: Frostbite in the feet.

COMICAL: Tapering to a point from a curved base.

COMMODORE: An entrance shaped like a comma.

COMMUNIST: An American newspaper writer.

COMPACT: The beginning of an Irish song '*COMPACTo* Erin . . .'

COMPOUND: To throw into disorder.

CONDESCEND: One crook to another (arranging territory to be covered): 'I'll *CONDESCEND*, and you con de udder'.

CONNECT: As one actor might say of another, 'He *CONNECT* for nuts'.

CONQUER: Acquiesce; as in 'I heartily *CONQUER*, old boy'.

CONSECUTIVE: A business big-shot.

CONSONANT: The mainland of Europe.

COPPERPLATE: Crockery in the police station canteen.

COPRA: A musical drama.

COPSE: A dead body.

CORAL: Squabble.

CORONER: Used in place-names; e.g., Hyde Park *CORONER*.

CORONET: An ice-cream holder.

CORSAIR: Thick, rough hair.

COUNTERPANE: An ache in one's drinking-arm.

COUNTERPOINT: The spot where the bar bends inwards.

COYLY: Wavy (Amer.).

CREASE: What the villain usually has on his hair.

CREEK: An inhabitant of Greece.

CREPUSCULE: Found in the blood.

CROSSBOW: A curt nod.

CRUCIAL: A small pot used by chemists.

CURFEW: An imprecation of evil.

CURTAIL: A dog's appendage.

D

DAIRY: Adventurous; e.g., 'The *DAIRY* young man on the flying trapeze'.

DAIS: Part of the song title: 'When *DAIS* done'.

DALMATION: Expletive; e.g., '*DALMATION* take it'.

DAMSON: A maiden of gentle birth.

DANDELION: A well-dressed lion.

DEAD-HEAT: The temperature of a corpse.

DEAF: The extinction of life.

DEBASEMENT: The floor below ground level.

DECADE: Assistance on a passenger boat in rough weather.

DECEIT: Generally used in a train, as in 'Is *DECEIT* taken?'

DENIAL: The main river of Egypt.

DEPEND: The part of a swimming-bath holding most water.

DEPRAVE: Those that deserve the fair.

DEROGATE: A representative.

DESCANT: To pour from one vessel to another.

DESCEND: Opposite to de udder end.

DESERTER: A town in North Africa.

DESTRUCTIVE: Imparting knowledge.

DETAILED: The state of some dogs.

DETECTIVE: Lacking in something.

DETERRENT: Cleansing substance.

DETINUE: Part of the question: 'Is *DETINUE* hat you're wearing?'

DEVOUT: Not with, as in '*DEVOUT* hope'.

DEWDROP: As in '*DEWDROP* the porter for carrying bags?'

DIAGONALLY: Painful death.

DIALOGUE: A dreadful piece of wood.

DIARRHOEA: A dreadful posterior.

DIATONIC: Death through an excess of mineral water.

DIE-HARD: Change colour with difficulty.

DISAPPOINT: Italian maths:—'Join *DISAPPOINT* to dat-a-point'.

DISCORD: '*DISCORD* is better dan dat' (Mus.).

DISCREET: Part of the tune title 'On *DISCREET* where you live'.

DISGUISE: (Amer.) '*DISGUISE* crazy'.

DISLOYAL: Fuel used in Diesel engines.

DISMAL: Numbering in tens. *DISMAL* POINT, the dot between unit and tenths.

DISMAY: Generally used by dentists: '*DISMAY* hurt a little'.

DISTINCT: The smell, as in '*DISTINCT* is overpowering'.

DISTRICT: Used by Magicians; e.g., '*DISTRICT* is very difficult'.

DOGMA: A bitch with a litter.

DOMAINE: A poisonous substance.

DORMANT: A commissionaire.

DOTARD: To love with intensity.

DOUBLET: As in 'Think of a number. *DOUBLET*'.

DOUGH: The tonic in tonic-solfa.

DOUGHBOY: The choirboy who sustains the tonic in a cantata.

DOWNFALL: The moulting period of a duck.

DRENCH: A deep ditch.

DRUID: Portrayed, as in 'He *DRUID* from memory'.

DUELLER: A dealer in precious stones.

DUPLICATOR: Part of the phrase 'When she is angry *DUPLI-CATOR?*'

DYSPEPSIA: One junkie to another (offering a tablet of sorts): *DYSPEPSIA* up'.

E

EAGLE: Of the same size or number, as in 'Two and two *EAGLE* four'.

EARLDOM: Unburdened oneself of them; e.g., 'He picked up the jewels, and *EARLDOM* from him in disgust'.

EAU: An expression of pain (Fr.).

EBONIZE: Part of the parting phrase '*EBONIZE* time'.

ECHELON: Part of the song title '*ECHELON* Way to Tipperary'.

ECHIDNA: I was unable to, as in '*ECHIDNA* do it'. (Scot.).

ECRU: A ship's company.

ECSTASY: Do not like to witness, as in the famous blues tune 'I *ECSTASY* the evening sun go down'.

EFFIGY: Part of the alphabetical order: ABCDE *EFFIGY*.

EGO: Sometimes applied (*sotto-voce*) to an unwelcome guest; e.g., 'When will *EGO?*'

EGRESS: A black-faced female.

EGRET: Sorrow; e.g., 'Dear Sir, It is with great *EGRET* . . .'

EIDER: No choice necessary, as in '*EIDER* one will do'.

ELAPSE: Part of an athletics comment: '*ELAPSE* in even time'.

ELDER: To embrace, as in 'He *ELDER* tight'.

ELECT: Part of the phrase: '*ELECT* the fool if you let him'.

ELEMENT: *Not* the largest mammal.

ELF: A cockney name.

ELIGIBLE: A large airship.

ELLIPTICAL: A brief kiss.

ELSEWHERE: Part of a comment on an unreliable witness: '*ELSEWHERE* black is white'.

EMANANT: Due any moment.

EMIR: As in '*EMIR* trifle'.

EMISSION: As in '*EMISSION* free'.

EMPRISE: The eyes of an emperor.

EMPTY: Motor transport.

ENABLE: Reference to the biblical story of Cain *ENABLE*.

ENCASE: of accidents.

ENDEAR: Part of the question, 'Does this story *ENDEAR?*'

ENVELOPE: To run away with a lover.

ENVENOM: As a teacher would say to an unruly class: '*EN-VENOM* talking to you, you will please be quiet'.

EPIC: 'With this government, how *EPIC*an one be?'

ERASED: As in '*ERASED* a good point in the debate'.

ERRATIC: Like a rat.

ERROR: Ireland.

ESCALLOP: Swain (on horseback) to his lass (ditto): '*ESCALLOP* away'.

ESCARP: Fish shaped like an S.

ESCHEW: One cow to another: '*ESCHEW* the cud together'.

ESPY: The eye of a poisonous snake.

ETHERISE: A glassy stare.

ETHICS: A county in the S.E. of England.

ETONIAN: One making amends for his misdeeds.

EUPHONIUM: Ring him up.

EUREKA: As one could say to a close friend, '*EUREKA* onions'.

EVENT: '*EVENT* without giving any trouble'.

EWE: Second person plural.

EWER: As in 'Are *EWER* religious type?'

EXACT: The law relating to eggs.

EXAMINE: As the Negro cook said, 'Man, dem *EXAMINE* de pan'.

EXASPERATE: To breathe out.

EXASPERATE: Not sounding h's.

EXCEL: Roman for forty.

EXCEPT: To take what is offered.

EXCISE: Eyes of the unknown, mysterious stranger in certain films.

EXECRATE: Part of the well-worn saying, '*EXECRATE* life if you don't weaken!'

EXHORT: The part that protrudes from the rear of car.

EXPANSIVE: Costly.

EXPECTORATE: To look forward to.

EXPIATE: XP8.

EXPLAIN: An aircraft on the secret list.

EXPUGN: A utensil for eating eggs.

EXPUNGE: A sponge made from eggs.

EXTINCT: The smell of bad eggs.

EYE: First person singular.

EYEHOLE: As the villain said to the fair maiden 'Aha, *EYEHOLE* you in my power'.

EYESORE: As in '*EYESORE* you last night'.

F

FAGOTTO: Part of the famous Irving Berlin tune 'You *FAGOTTO* remember'.

FAITHLESS: Without a front part to the head.

FALTER: As in a good measure: '*FALTER* the brim'.

FANATIC: A room at the top of the house where fans are stored.

FANTAIL: Story of a fan.

FARTHER: A male parent.

FARTHINGALE (in the good old days): A small glass of beer.

FASCINATION: A method of preventing disease.

FATALITY: Animation; fullness of life.

FATEFUL: Loyal.

FATHER: A greater distance.

FATHERLESS: As in 'This is by *FATHERLESS*er of two evils'.

FATIGUE: As in the well-known song '*FATIGUE* for two'.

FAUCET: Apply strength.

FELLOWSHIP: An untilled boat.

FELON: As in 'He was dropped as a child and *FELON* his head'.

FELUCCA: As in 'I *FELUCCA* drink'.

FEMINIST: One who specialises in scarcity of food.

FERMENT: Businessman's lament: 'My *FERMENT* doing so well'.

FERRY: A small being at the bottom of the garden.

FERRYMAN: The male of the species at the bottom of the garden.

FERVOUR: More distant.

FESTAL: A kind of virgin.

FETID: As in '*FETID* up for the kill'.

FETISH: Resembling feet.

FETLOCK: Often used by a complaining wife: 'A *FETLOCK* you care'.

FEUD: Grub.

FIGURATE: A skating movement.

FIORD: A make of car.

FISSION: From the noted English dish: *FISSION* chips.

FIXTURE: Triumphal comment from one wrestler, who has effected a successful hold, to another: 'That's *FIXTURE*'.

FLATFISH: Fish small enough to be kept in a flat.

FLESH: In a good state. (Chinese).

FLIGHT: Sudden fear. (Chinese).

FLOOR: Defect.

FLY-SPECK: The bite of a fly.

FODDER: The male parent.

FOETAL: Pertaining to the feet.

FOIBLE: Fairy story.

FOIST: Number one. (Amer.).

FORCEPS: Two biceps.

FORKTAIL: Beer stirred with a fork.

FORMALIN: Part of the order: '*FORMALIN* a straight line'.

FORSAKE: Used in warnings to shipping: 'Gale *FORSAKE* expected in Cromarty, Faroes . . .'

FORTIFIES: (refers to) the limbs of a line of twenty chorus girls.

FORUM: As the harassed father said of his erring sons: 'I have done my best *FORUM*'.

FOSTER: Quicker.

FOURSOME: As in 'All right *FOURSOME*, but not for others'.

FRANCHISE: The look of a demoiselle.

FRANKINCENSE: As in 'Frank went to have a tooth extracted, and the gas rendered *FRANKINCENSE*-ible.'

FRAUD: An eminent writer on psychology.

FREE-HANDED: A trois.

FREE-LOVE: As cheaply as two.

FREE-WILL: Not using the engine.

FRENZY: A town in Italy.

FRESHMAN: An impudent male.

FRIARY: Where one buys fish and chips.

FRICTION: Not true.

FRIEZE: As in the tune: '*FRIEZE* a jolly good fellow'.

FRUSTRATE: Tip-top.

FUSELAGE: As in 'I never re-*FUSELAGE* brandy'.

G

GARBAGE: The name of a famous film actress.

GASEOUS: The first name of the former world heavyweight boxing champion – – – – – – Clay.

GASTRONOME: An instrument that beats time.

GENTRY: The tree of knowledge.

GERMINATION: The inhabitants of Germany.

GESTURE: As in 'It's *GESTURE* little joke'.

GIBBON: Part of the phrase: 'One must *GIBBON* take'.

GLOAT: A horned farm animal.

GLOW: As in '*GLOW*, and never clome back. (Chinese).

GNAW: 'Neither this *GNAW* that'.

GNU: Unused.

GODSEND: The destruction of an idol.

GOLDILOCKS: Gilded door-knobs.

GOPHER: To like, as in 'I *GOPHER* that'.

GORMANDIZE: Watch greedily.

GORSE: 'But of *GORSE*'.

GOSLING: As in '*GOSLING* your hook.'

GOULASH: A soft, sticky whip.

GRAMMAR: A parent's mother.

GRANDSON: Good boy.

GREEDY: Part of the words of the main aria in the opera PAGLIACCI: '*GREEDY* Pagliacci'.

GRENADINE: A famous regiment—The *GRENADINE* Guards.

GRIME: An unlawful act.

GROIN: As in the tune: 'Darling, we are *GROIN* older'.

GROUT: A painful affliction of the big toe.

GRUEL: Unfeeling.

GUERDON: A belt.

GUERRILLA: A great ape.

GUISE: Name of a well-known hospital.

GUNNER: Often used in 'pop' music: 'Ya *GUNNER* miss me, baby'.

GUNNING: Crafty.

H

HABERDASHER: One not afraid of taking a chance.

HALBERD: 'The boy stood on the burning deck whence *HAL-BERD* he had fled.' (One is advised to use sparingly).

HALLOW: From the scornful '*HALLOW* can one get?'

HALTER: The destination of the blushing bride.

HANDICAP: Useful headgear.

HARBOUR-BAR: The bar facing the harbour—generally situated between the Public and Saloon.

HARDIHOOD: A hood made of stout material.

HARDSHIP: A vessel difficult to manoeuvre.

HARDWARE: Clothing made of hemp.

HARELIP: A hare's impertinence.

HARMONY: As in '*HARMONY* times do I have to repeat myself?'

HARROW: The indication to keep left of a road obstruction.

HATCHWAY: A path through the jungle.

HAVOC: As in '*HAVOC*are, my friend'.

HEADBAND: The leading orchestra.

HEADSTONE: Used by David against Goliath.

HECTOR: One who performs on the stage.

HEIFER: At any time, as in the tune titled 'Did you *HEIFER* See a Dream Walking?'

HEIRLOOM: A machine for producing draughts.

HELM: As in '*HELM* I doing?'

HELPMATE: An appeal to a friend.

HENCE: From the popular dance-tune: '*HENCE*, knees and boomps-a-daisy'.

HEXAGON: Comment by a Greek waiter who has just dropped a plate of eggs 'My *HEXAGON* for six'.

HIATUS: As in '*HIATUS*ay this, but . . .'

HIAWATHA: '*HIAWATHA*-fraid of this'.

HIERARCH: The curve above.

HIGHBRED: The result of too much self-raising flour.

HIPPOCRATIC: Pretending to be what one is not.

HIRSUTE: As in '*HIRSUTE* looked very nice'.

HOMESPUN: A pun on 'homes'; e.g., 'Sherlock *HOMES*'.

HONEST: From the text '*HONEST* Soit Qui Mal Y Pense'.

HONEYDEW: As in '*HONEYDEW* really love me?' (Amer.)

HORIZON: 'She kept *HORIZON* him—wherever he went'.

HOROLOGY: The study of horror.

HOROSCOPE: A machine for projecting horror films.

HORSE-DOCTOR: A medico with a cold.

HOSIER: As in the common greeting-question '*HOSIER* father?'

HUMANIST: One who makes jokes.

HUMBUG: A buzzing insect.

HYACINTH: 'This plant is much *HYACINTH* I last saw it'.

HYGIENE: As an American youth would greet his girl Jean.

HYMN: The opposite of 'her'.

HYSTERIA: 'Beneath the rough *HYSTERIA* there beats a heart of gold'.

I

I: Signifying assent.

IAMBUS: What a bus would say if it could talk.

ICING: As, when asked to perform at a party, one says modestly, 'Yes, *ICING* a little'.

ICON: Part of the tune entitled: '*ICON* Give You Anything But Love, Baby'.

IDEAL: The start of a card game.

IDIOMATIC: foolishly.

IMITATE: As the little boy would say, denying culpability, 'It's *IMITATE* me'.

IMMATURE: As in 'You are not having *IMMATURE* party I hope'.

IMMIGRATE: As in 'We gave *IMMIGRATE* send-off'.

IMMURE: As in 'I shall give *IMMURE* best regards'.

IMPERSONALLY: As in 'I wish to see *IMPERSONALLY*'.

IMPLORE: Writing and instruction on little demons.

IMPLY: An untruth about the 'little people'.

IMPUNITY: Agreement between little demons.

INASMUCH: As in, 'I hope you are not *INASMUCH* trouble as I am'.

INCLINE: The outside edge of an ink-blot.

INCOMPLETE: As in 'He was *INCOMPLETE* control of the situation'.

INDISCREET: As in '*INDISCREET* where you live'.

INFAMY: The workman's complaint: 'The boss has it *INFAMY*'.

INGOT: Derived from the German expletive: '*INGOT*'s name, vat you do?'

INMATE: What the policeman says to the crook he has just caught.

INSPIRE: Having climbed up the steps at the top of the church.

INSTALLS: In the lower seats of the theatre.

INTENSE: The way of decimal coinage.

INTERFERE: Dread of being buried alive.

INTERSECT: A very small animal with six legs.

INURE: As in 'I love you *INURE* new hat'.

INVECTIVE: Catching (Med.).

INVERSE: Poetic.

INVEST: Prepared for cold weather.

INVITE: How most brides get married.

INVOICE: Singing well.

IRRITATE: Making an appointment—'Don't forget, be *IRRITATE*'.

ISABEL: 'When *ISABEL* not a bell, etc . . .'

ISOLATE: As in the petulant query 'Am *ISOLATE*?'

ISSUE: From the song title '*ISSUE* is, or *ISSUE* ain't My Baby?'

ISTHMUS: '*ISTHMUS* be the place we're looking for'.

J

JAMAICA: As in the question and answer: '*JAMAICA?*' No, she was willing'.

JARGON: As the harassed housewife asked: 'Where's my milk *JARGON?*'

JAVANESE: Ex-convict to another: '*JAVANESE*y time inside?'

JEERING: Loud acclamation.

JEOPARDY: From the famous song 'Roses are Shining in *JEO-PARDY*'.

JESTER: From the famous song '*JESTER* song at Twilight'.

JEWEL: Single combat.

JEZEBEL: Unit of sound.

JUBILEE: As in '*JUBILEE*ve everything you're told?'

JUDO: The tonic in Hebrew music.

JUDO: Israeli currency.

JUGGERNAUT: Dispensing beer after the match: 'A *JUGGER-NAUT* to be enough'.

JUNIOR: As one of an Arab patrol hissed to another: 'Is there a *JUNIOR?*'

JUNIPER: A little Hebrew.

JUNO: '*JUNO* what happened the other day?'

JUSTICE: '*JUSTICE*-ong At Twilight'.

JUXTAPOSE: '*JUXTAPOSE* something like this were to happen to you'.

K

KAFTAN: A ship's master.

KARMA: Quieter.

KEEL: Render lifeless.

KERNEL: The army rank above major.

KESTREL: Music for many instruments.

KETCHUP: As in 'The stragglers will have to *KETCHUP* with the main party'.

KHAKI: Very frustrating when you mislay it.

KIDDERMINSTER: A very young person from Minster.

KIDNAP: The sleep of a child.

KILT: Dead.

KINDRED: Fear of one's relatives.

KIPPER: As in '*KIPPER* stiff upper lip'.

KNAVERY: Lots of ships.

KNOUT: Nothing (North Eng.).

KOBANG: 'Does this firework *KOBANG*?'

KOPECK: As in '*KOPECK* to the beginning'.

L

L: The place to which the wicked go.

LACKADAISICAL: Failing to possess a daisy.

LACTIC: As in 'Do you possess a gas or *LACTIC* fire?'

LADYBIRD: A smart girl.

LAGGARD: Hooligan.

LAGOON: The idiot (Fr.).

LAPSE: What dogs sit on.

LARGESS: Capital S.

LASTING: As in putting the cat out *LASTING* at night.

LATENT: A tent set up for the laity.

LATIN: As in '*LATIN* the dog—his barking will arouse the neighbours'.

LAXITY: Loosening tea.

LEAVEN: The hour between ten and twelve.

LETTUCE: As in '*LETTUCE* pray'.

LEVER: The examination instruction: '*LEVER* space for marginal notes'.

LEVITY: A toilet.

LIONISE: The optics of a great cat.

LITERAL: Relating to refuse.

LITTER: Caused to burn, as in 'He *LITTER* cigarette'.

LOOFAH: The subdominant (mus.) when sung in the smallest room.

LORGNETTE: Generally heard when the wife's voice awakes one from a sofa-slumber: 'George, have you mown the *LORGNETTE*?'

LOVABLE: What one expects a cow does sometimes.

LOVELORN: A stretch of grassland used by lovers.

LOW-SPIRITED: Appertaining to a pub that delivers short measures.

LUBBER: An amorous swain.

LUBRICATOR: One who detests brick-built toilets.

LUNACY: A 'sea' expanse on the moon.

LUNATIC: A face-twitch caused by the moon.

LYMPHATIC: Highly stressed.

LYNX: Parts of a chain.

LYRA: One who tells falsehoods.

M

MACCABEES: Insects found at the Mohammedan shrine.

MAGNESIA: Forgetfulness.

MAJOR: As in 'That *MAJOR* think'.

MALICE: The classic—'*MALICE* in Wonderland'.

MALINGER: Stay awhile, as in '*MALINGER* (ma)longer'.

MALTREAT: Buying a friend a drink in the Mall.

MANDATE: What girls often agree to keep.

MANDRILL: What a girl bears in mind at a mandate.

MANURE: Part of the song title '*MANURE* Smiling'.

MARGIN: A drink for mothers.

MARMOSET: A child's query on hearing the door open— '*MARMOSET* you?' (Amer.)

MARQUEE: As the American (feeling in his pockets) asked, 'Where's *MARQUEE*?'

MARQUETRY: Shopping.

MARSUPIAL: 'I've spilled *MARSUPIAL* over the place'.

MARTYR: The title of a well-known song . . . '*MARTYR*, Rambling Rose of the Wild Wood'.

MATRICE: An under-bed.

MEANDER: As the young man said: '*MEANDER*, we're going steady'.

MECCA: As in 'Let's *MECCA* foursome'.

MEDDLING: Moderate.

MEDICATION: Continued thought.

MEDIOCRE: Slightly yellow.

MELANCHOLIC: Stomach pains induced by too much melon.

MELODY: Disease.

MERE: As in 'Get *MERE* a drink, old chap'.

MESSUAGE: The salary paid to ship-stewards.

METEOR: As in 'I should like to *METEOR* friend'.

MICROBE: Broadcasting dress.

MIGRATE: As in '*MIGRATE* friend, etc . . .'

MINARET: A slow, graceful dance.

MISDEED: The daughter of Mr & Mrs Deed.

MITRE: Could have, as in 'You *MITRE* let me know'.

MODERNISE: Sporting false eyelashes.

MOORISH: Deserving of repetition.

MORPHIA: As one housewife might say to another: 'I always shop at X's . . . you get *MORPHIA* money'.

MUSHROOM: The parlour 'with dimmed lights', as a rule.

MUSKETEER: As the ensnared heroine might say: 'My hero *MUSKETEER* by midnight or I am lost'.

MUSLIN: According to one-time Chicago racketeer: 'I won't let no bum *MUSLIN* on my territory'.

MUSQUASH: One *MUSQUASH* the lemon to get the juice.

MUSTANG: As the sheriff said to the posse: 'Billy the Kid *MUST-ANG*'.

MUSTARD: As in 'He *MUSTARD*riven like the wind to get there on time'.

MUTINOUS: A trumpet is generally played with a *MUTINOUS*oft passage.

MYRMIDON: 'As the ship approached the source of the seductive music, the sailors espied a *MYRMIDON* the rocks'.

MYSIS: As the little boy said: '*MYSIS* is ever so pretty'.

MYSTIFY: An example of future in the past from a golfer 'I shall have *MYSTIFY* don't hit the ball'.

MYTH: A female moth.

N

NAIVE: As the plumber said 'I could have finished the job *NAIVE* I'd brought the right tools'.

NANNY: As in 'There is *NANNY* left'.

NANNY: Part of the song title '*NANNY* body Here Seen Kelly?'

NARRATE: There is not; e.g., '*NARRATE* much to do around here'.

NARROW: Part of the poem: 'I shot '*NARROW* high in the air'.

NAVIGATE: The site entrance for the labourers.

NECTAR: One who performs on the stage.

NEUROSIS: As the gardener said: 'I have planted *NEUROSIS* in my garden'.

NEUTER: As the novice said: 'This is all *NEUTER* me'.

NIBLICK: Moistening the working end of a new pen.

NICETY: As in 'X's café serves *NICETY* than Y's café'.

NICHE: Desire to scratch, as in 'I've got a *NICHE*'.

NIGHTMARE: The female of a nighthorse.

NISI: Second (to battered boxer): 'That's a *NISI* he's given you'.

NITRATE: Basis of pay for night work.

NITRE: As in 'He has a *NITRE* better things'.

NOBBY: Contraction of 'not be'; e.g., 'I will *NOBBY* hurried'.

NOGGIN: As Uncle Tom said, 'Oo dat *NOGGIN* at de door?'

NOMINAL: Part of the hymn 'Sed *NOMINAL* tua de glorium'.

NOMINEE: Not many; e.g., 'There are *NOMINEE* people in'.

NONDESCRIPT: As when the producer insisted on being i.*NON-DESCRIPT*.

NOOSE: Information.

NORSE: 'A-*NORSE*, a-*NORSE*, my kingdom for a-*NORSE*' (Shakespeare).

NOSE: 'Who *NOSE*?'

NOTABLE: An incomplete dining-suite.

NOXIOUS: A drop of the 'hard stuff' *NOXIOUS*ideways.

NUDITY: A recent composition.

NUMEROUS: Funny.

NURTURE: Mother (to unwilling son at the dentist's), 'Now Johnny, the man wo*NURTURE*'.

O

OAKUM: The doctor's stand-in: *OAKUM* Tenens.

OAT: '*OATo* be in England, now that April's there'.

OBLIVION: As the rebel said: 'I'm tired *OBLIVION* under these conditions'.

OBSCURITY: We all desire the feeling *OBSCURITY*.

OCCIDENT: Mishap.

OCCUR: A dog, as in 'Sire, you are *OCCUR*'.

OCTAGON: As in 'I *OCTAGON* ages ago'.

OCTOBER: As in 'He tripped, an' *OCTOBER* all the glasses'.

ODE: From the famous song '*ODE*ar, What can The Matter Be?'

ODIUM: As the tired lady said at the Ball: '*O-DIUM*ind if we sit this out?'

ODYSSEY: Difficult to see . . . 'If was *ODYSSEY* in the dim light'.

OFFAL: Dreadful.

OFFICE: As one might say of the author 'I'm tired *OFFICE OFFAL* puns'.

OFFICIAL: Contrary to general belief, no amount *OFFICIAL* improve one's intelligence.

OFFICIATE: 'He hoped to become quite brainy, with the amount *OFFICIATE*'.

OHM: What there is no place like (The late Will Hay).

OIL: From the song '*OIL* See You in My Dreams'.

OLIVER: Heard at the butchers': 'Half-a-pound *OLIVER* please'.

OLYMPIAN: As the injured athlete said, 'I'm tired *OLYMPIAN* all the way home'.

OMINOUS: From the hymn 'Sed *OMINOUS* tua da gloriam'.

OMNISCIENCE: Small American boy to another: '*OMNI-SCIENCE* have you got?'

ONEROUS: As in 'Do *ONEROUS* with a visit'.

ONYX: From the proverb '*ONYX* Soit Qui Mal Y Pense'.

OOLITIC: Master (opening dormitory door) '*OOLITIC*andle after light out?'

OOZE: '*OOZE* there?'

OOZY: '*OOZY*?'

OPERATIC: The attic above this attic.

OPPOSE: As in 'His demeanour is a lot *OPPOSE*'.

OPTIMISE: 'I'm *OPTIMISE* in trouble'.

ORATE: As in 'He attempted it seven *ORATE* times'.

ORGANISE: The holes at the bottom of organ pipes.

ORGANISM: As in 'The *ORGANISM* easy instrument to play'.

ORGANIST: 'This *ORGANIST*erribly out of tune'.

ORIENTATE: 'The *ORIENTATE* what it's cracked to be'.

ORIFICE: 'I don't care if a man is white *ORIFICE* black'.

ORIGIN: One drunk to another: 'Let'sh 'ave an *ORIGIN*'.

ORPHAN: Many times, as in, 'I go there *ORPHAN*'.

ORTHODOX: Unloaded. As the fruit-barrow boy would say: 'Luvly fresh bananas—just *ORTHODOX*'.

OSCULATE: Win an Oscar.

OSPREY: Heard in church 'Let *OSPREY*'.

OTTER: The opposite of colder.

OUTLAST: The final wicket to fall in an innings.

OUTSTRIP: To take off more clothes than anybody else.

OVA: Called by the umpire after six balls.

OVERBEARING: Twins, triplets, or quadruplets.

OVERDOSE: As in 'One must get *OVERDOSE* obstacles'.

OVERHEAD: Egg-shaped head.

OVERHEAR: The reverse of 'over there'.

OVERRATE: The extra drink one should not have.

OVERSTAY: A stiffened bodice worn outside the clothes.

OVERWORK: The efforts of a bowler.

OVOID: Shun.

OVUM: As in '*OVUM*y dead body'.

OWL: Cry of distress.

P

PANIKIN: As in, 'There was *PANIKIN* the kitchen'.

PANTRY: A stand for hanging up pans.

PARAPHRASE: 'I can't think of a *PARAPHRASE* than this'.

PARISH: The (hic!) capital of Fransh.

PARSE: A move in card games, 'I *PARSE*' (meaning 'on to the next player').

PARSNIP: Dad's quick one before dinner.

PARTISAN: As the actor said, on reading a new script, 'This *PARTISAN*atural'.

PATHOS: One of the Three Musketeers.

PATRIARCH: The bower under which the paymaster sits when dishing out the troops' pay.

PATRONIZE: Wherewith waiters in a French café are kept under surveillance.

PATTER: A little bit of, as in 'A *PATTER* butter'.

PAUCITY: A city low in funds.

PAUNCH: The boxer's stock-in-trade.

PAUSE: What dogs use for feet.

PAX: In which wolves roam and hunt.

PEACEMAKER: One who drops crockery.

PEARLY: As in 'I am always u*PEARLY*'.

PEDANT: A walking ant.

PELTER: A king of geist.

PENANCE: Copper coins.

PENCHANT: What one receives in one's old age.

PERIPATETIC: Arousing the deepest sympathy.

PERISH: The area of ministration allotted to a vicar.

PERUSE: Belonging to Peru.

PHEASANT: From the well-known opera by Suppé—Poet and *PHEASANT*.

PHLEBITIS: Illness caused by an insect bite.

PICCANINNY: Choose a ninny.

PILLORY: Where pills are made.

PIMPERNEL: A small red pustule on the skin.

PING PONG: The smell of a ping.

PITCHER: A painting.

PITEOUS: Have mercy upon us.

PLACENTA: A place for children to play in.

PLAYMATES: Instruction from a Cockney umpire for the game to start.

PLOVER: A soft-voiced lover.

PLUMBING: Picking plums.

PLUMB-RULE: A gadget for measuring plums.

PNEUMATIC: Like a new mat.

POLYGAMY: Marriage between parrots.

POPCORN: Well-meaning (but not with-it) advice from father.

PORTEND: The end on the left.

PORTRAY: A shore radar beam for shipping.

PREAMBLE: A short walk before opening time.

PRECEDENT: The head of a republic.

PRISM: Jail.

PROFILE: A catalogue of professionals.

PROPAGANDA: A very correct male goose.

PUNISH: Resembling a pun.

Q

Q: Famous gardens.

QUADRILLE: Exercise in the school quadrangle.

QUARTZ: Served in pubs to the very thirsty.

QUENCH: A young woman.

QUILT: As in '*QUILT* thou take this woman, etc.?'

QUIVER: As the Cockney father said of his wayward daughter: 'I must 'ave a tor*QUIVER*'.

QUOIT: Entirely, as in 'I *QUOIT* agree'.

R

RACIAL: Jacob's wife.

RANSOM: As in 'Gordon Pirie *RANSOM* good races in his day'.

RAPTURE: As the shop assistant said, 'I've *RAPTURE* purchases for you, madam'.

RATTAN: Sunburn on a rat.

RATTLING: A small rat.

RAVISH: A salad vegetable.

REALISE: Not false ones.

REASSURE: Opposite to foreshore.

RECEDE: As in, 'I *RECEDE* your letter today'.

RECONNOITRE: Policeman (to himself, on seeing milling crowd ahead): '*RECONNOITRE* go and see what's up'.

RECONQUER: A repeat of a game played by schoolboys.

RED-LETTER: A letter, the contents of which have been scrutinised.

RED-LETTERS: L-plates.

REDUCE: A further levelling of the score at tennis.

REFLEX: Applies to a voyager who has mastered the art of walking on reefs.

REFUSE: Employment of a referee.

REPROACH: As in 'One can *REPROACH* this from another angle .

REPTILE: A tile with a ribbed surface.

REPUBLICAN: Concerning the inn-keeper.

RESCUE: Used in billiards when the cue-ball is too far for the ordinary cue.

RESPITE: The hole in which a navvy can take a breather.

RETICULE: Contemptuous laughter.

RETINA: The publishers expressed their deep reg*RETINA* letter of refusal.

RETORT: Further consideration.

REVENUE: The old tune, 'I *REVENUE* I Could Love Anybody Honey Like I'm Lovin' You'.

REVERIE: As in 'I feel younge*REVERIE* day'.

REVIVE: As in 'Sorry *REVIVE* offended you'.

REVUE: As in 'All my thoughts are *REVUE*'.

RHEUMY: Spacious.

RIGID: The famous film actress, *RIGID* Bardot.

RIOTER: Author.

RISIBLE: As in 'The ship was barely *RISIBLE* on the horizon'.

RIVETS: 'I'd like this one, *RIVETS* all the same to you'.

ROVER: As in 'My wandering days are *ROVER*'.

RUBICAN: Trusting mother: '*RUBICAN* take care of herself'.

RUDENESS: An uncivil promontory.

RUMPUS: Buttocky.

RUSTIC: Degeneration through exposure to air.

S

SACBUT: As in 'He'd have got the *SACBUT* for my intervention'.

SAGO: As in 'Start when I *SAGO*'.

SALARY: A salad vegetable.

SALIVA: A flower.

SALUTE: Question: 'What's that old-fashioned looking instrument?' Answer: '*SALUTE*'.

SAMOVAR: As in '*SAMOVAR* best friends are Russians'.

SANCTUM: 'When we left their house after the party, we *SANTUM* very much'.

SANITY: Every Christmas little children receive presents from *SANITY* Claus.

SARDONIC: Resembling a very small fish.

SATIATED: 'She did not *SATIATED* it'.

SATURANT: '*SATURANT*?' 'No, 'smy cousin'.

SAUCER: As in 'I've had enough of your *SAUCER*'.

SAVANT: One, two, three, four, five, six, *SAVANT*.

SAVOUR: In the first line of the National Anthem: 'God *SAVOUR* gracious Queen'.

SAWBONES: Aching in every limb.

SCANDAL: Open footwear.

SCANTY: Large shrimps.

SCEPTRE: As in 'All *SCEPTRE* few had left by midnight'.

SCHEDULE: 'In the *SCHEDULE* find the tools'.

SCHEMER: A ship.

SCIENCE: 'Be quiet!'

SCURF: Waves on the shore.

SECEDE: 'Persevere and you'll *SECEDE*'.

SECT: 'For his insolence he was *SECT* on the spot'.

SEIZURE: Perceives you, as in 'If he *SEIZURE*, that's your lot'.

SELFISH: Edible molluscs.

SELLABLE: What one would try to do in the cattle-market.

SEMAPHORE: As in '*SEMAPHORE* Labour, others for Liberal'.

SEMIBREVE: Half an inhalation.

SEMICOLON: Half-way down the tummy.

SENSUAL: As in '*SENSUAL* insist, 'I'll sing you a song''.

SENSUALISE: The 'come hither' look.

SEQUIN: From the proverb '*SEQUIN* ye shall find'.

SESAME: As in 'So 'e *SESAME*, 'e sez'. (cockney).

SEWER: Plaintiff.

SHADDOCK: As in 'Fre*SHADDOCK*'.

SHALLOT: From the French war-cry: 'They *SHALLOT* pass'.

SHALT: A loud cry.

SHAMROCK: A counterfeit diamond.

SHEKEL: From the Novel: 'Dr *SHEKEL* and Mr Hyde'.

SHOFAR: And no further.

SIESTA: As King Ahasueras may have ordered: '*SIESTA* gets all she wants'.

SIGNET: For catching sigs.

SILICATE: A silly girl.

SLATE: As in 'Let's go, '*SLATE*'.

SLITHER: A long piece.

SOBERSIDES: Cricket teams captained by Sobers.

SORCERY: Resembling crockery.

SOUSE: Opposite Norse.

SPHERE: 'Superstition is *SPHERE* of the unknown'.

SPIRIT-LEVEL: Above which the crystals turn green.

SPOKESHAVE: A session with a garrulous barber.

STATUE: Generally used when answering the 'phone: 'Hello *STATUE*?'

STELLAR: From the tune '*STELLAR* by Starlight'.

STERNMOST: Very severe.

STRATAGEM: A precious stone from a certain rock formation.

STURGEON: A doctor who operates.

STYX: Adheres.

SUBDIVISION: A direct hit on target by a depth-charge.

SUBMISSION: Sailing orders for a submarine.

SUBSTANCE: The angle at which a submarine travels.

SUB-TITLE: U boat.

SUCCOUR: One who is easily swindled.

SUFFRAGE: Enduring hardship.

SUICIDE: The side of the road under which a sewer runs.

SUMMARILY: Open-neck shirt and flannels.

SUNDRY: The week-end.

SUNNY: Little boy.

SUPERFICIAL: Relating to the earlier dishes in a meal.

SUPERTONIC: A jolly good swig.

SURPLICE: Excess.

SWAIN: Trees in the breeze.

SWARM: It's hot.

SWEETSTUFF: Furniture covering.

SWINERY: Bad behaviour.

SYMBOL: A percussion instrument.

T

T: A popular beverage.

TABBY: As in Shakespeare's Hamlet: '*TABBY* or not *TABBY*, that is the question'.

TACTIC: The noise of a clock.

TAFFRAIL: The rail around the bar in Welsh pubs.

TAINT: It is not.

TALLYMAN: The chap who services your T.V. set.

TANKER: As in '*TANKER* very much'.

TARTAR: So-long.

TAUT: As in 'Just like *I TAUT*' (Amer.)

TAVERN: From the song: '*TAVERN* glorious *TAVERN*'.

TAXIDERMY: A skin affliction peculiar to taxi-drivers.

TENDRIL: An exercise for a platoon of ten men.

TEUTON: A teacher.

TEXT: As in '*TEXT* a long time to sort some of these out'.

THEME: As in, 'Things don't *THEME* the thame any more'.

THERAPEUTIST: 'Is *THERAPEUTIST* in the house?'

THESIS: As in, '*THESIS* what I want you to do'.

THINGAMY: From the old Irving Berlin tune: 'Do you ever *THINGAMY*?'

TIARA: The old song: '*TIARA* Ra Boom-De-Ay'.

TIBIAL: Of little account.

TITAN: What one does to one's belt in times of hardship.

TOADY: As in 'One has to *TOADY* line sometimes'.

TOKAY: 'Is tha*TOKAY*?'

TOMBOLA: As in, 'I watched *TOMBOLA* maiden over'.

TORQUE: As in '*TORQUE* of the Town'.

TORTOISE: As in, 'History has *TORTOISE* much'.

TOURNIQUET: 'One had to *TOURNIQUET* to unlock a door'.

TOWNSHIP: An amphibious vessel.

TRAIPSE: Curtains.

TRIALOGUE: When ordinary arithmetic won't do.

TRIPOD: As one might hear in a North Country restaurant, 'Isn't this *TRIPOD*?'

TRITON: As in, 'Here's a new jacket—*TRITON*'.

TROTH: A feeding vessel for animals.

TROW: To cast: cause to fall (Irish).

TRUCE: Reality.

TURNKEY: Christmas fare.

TWINGE: Two born at the same time.

TYMPAN: *TYMPAN* Alley: Where songs are published.

U

U: Second person plural.

UDDER: The second of two; not this—the opposite.

UNABASHED: Unmarked; Cassius Clay after a fight.

UNCHASTE: Left in peace.

UNDERBRED: The bottom of a loaf.

UNDERWORLD: Australia.

UNEATEN: A town near Leicester.

UNIT: An expression of contempt.

U.N.O.: You are in possession of the facts.

UNWIND: Not given wine at dinner.

USANCE: That which annoys.

USURY: As in, '*USURY*magination'.

V

VAGRANT: Diffusing an agreeable odour.

VALET: *VAL, -ET* had to happen sometime!

VANITY: 'I shall be glad *VANITY* comes along—I'm parched'.

VAPID: 'I'll take it—*VAPID* up'.

VARICOSE: 'It's *VARICOSE*y here'.

VARLET: Produced by mixing blue and red.

VATICAN: As in, 'I'm sure he'll do *VATICAN* for you'.

VEHICULAR: From the Italian tune: 'Vehiculee *VEHICULAR*'.

VENAL: A kind of schnitzel.

VENOM: 'Look at me *VENOM* talking to you'.

VENTILATE: 'He never *VENTILATE*, and it's only a quarter past now'.

VENUE: '*VENUE* hear de vistle—off you go'.

VERSATILE: (Foreign builder): 'Dat is a *VERSATILE* dan dis one'.

VERTIGO: As in 'There is not *VERTIGO* now—we are nearly there'.

VESPER: What the lover does in the ear of his lass.

VESTAL: Like a vest.

VICIOUS: 'Ye gods and little *VICIOUS*'.

VIEWER: 'A—*VIEWER* a match, please?'

VIGOUR: Mozart's '*VIGOUR-O* here, *VIGOUR-O* there'.

VILIFY: 'I *VILIFY* can find the time'.

VIMINAL: '*VIMINAL* always have the last word'.

VINTRY: Very cold

VIOLENCE: Orchestral Strings.

VIRAGO: '*VIRAGO* you go'.

VIRGIN: Approaching to the edge.

VIZIER: 'Bring de vife *VIZIER*'.

VOCAL: As in '*VOCAL* point'.

VOGUE: A vuffian.

W

WADDLE: From Irving Berlin's famous tune: '*WADDLE* I do?'

WAFER: 'Make *WAFER* his lordship'.

WANTON: As in 'I shall not be *WANTON* any lunch today'.

WARFARE: The atmosphere around the wharf.

WASHTUB: 'She *WASHTUB* after dinner'.

WASTAGE: Measurement around the middle.

WAZIR: 'He *WAZIR* a short while ago'.

WEAL: '*WEAL* fight and *WEAL* conquer again and again'.

WEAVER: '*WEAVER* long way to go yet'.

WELL-BRED: Brought up in a well.

WELTER: 'It's as *WELTER* be prepared'.

WENDY: From Bing Crosby's famous tune: '*WENDY* moon comes over de mountain'.

WHARFINGER: The finger that presses the button.

WHIRRING: 'The bride was *WHIRRING* white'.

WICKET: Evil.

WIELD: As in '*WIELD*eal with that later'.

WINNOW: '*WINNOW* all about that'.

WITHER: '*WITHER* hey and a ho, and a nonny-no'.

WOODEN: As in 'She *WOODEN* do as I asked'.

WORSE: '. . . or *WORSE* to that effect'.

WREAK: Of onions?

Y

Y: For what reason.

YAM: '*YAM* what I *YAM*'.

YAOURT: '*YAOURT*o know better'.

YARDARM: An arm three feet in length.

YASHMAK: (Inebriate, accepting an offer of a drink): '*YASH-MAK*, I'll have another'.

YAWN: From the song entitled: '*YAWN*obody Till Somebody Loves You'.

YCLEPT: 'The conductor came and *YCLEPT* our tickets'.

YESTERDAY: As in '*YES,TERDAY* is my birthday'.

YOGA: '*YOGA* you way, I'll go mine'.

YOKE: The yellow part of an egg.

YOKEL: Egg-like.

YONDER: As in 'Be*YONDER* Blue Horizon'.

YORE: Belonging to you.

YORKIST: (Poetic) '*YORKIST*ells me you love me'.

YOU: A female sheep.

YOUTH: Serviceability; 'What'th the *YOUTH*?'

Z

Z: As in 'Zimple Zimon *Z*'.

ZANY: As the Frenchman might say: '*ZANY*d it more zan we do'

ZINC: Where the washing-up is done.

ZITHER: 'He ran a *ZITHER* pack of dogs were at his heels'.

ZOON: *ZOON* and *ZOON*.

ZOUNDS: '*ZOUNDS* alright to me'.

ZUNA: '*ZUNA* him than me'.

BEST
Medical
JOKES

Compiled by
GRAHAM REED

A professor of medicine asked a student what dosage of a particular drug should be administered to a patient. 'Five grains, sir,' replied the student confidently. But a minute later he raised his hand diffidently.

'Professor,' he gulped, 'About that last question of yours . . . I think the answer should have been ——'

'Don't bother, young man,' broke in the professor, glancing at his watch. 'Your patient has already been dead for thirty-five seconds.'

Just as they were about to leave on their summer holiday, the G.P. announced that he had been unable to find a locum and thus would be unable to accompany his wife. However, he insisted that this need not spoil her holiday plans and that she should go away on her own for a fortnight.

The next day, as the doctor drove his wife to the station, his attractive young receptionist found a basket on her desk. It contained fourteen apples.

The consultant had spent a long time trying to convince an anxious but perfectly healthy businessman that he was not suffering from heart disease.

'You must stop worrying, my dear fellow,' he beamed, edging his patient towards the door. 'Your heart will last you as long as you live.'

There is something ominous about the fact that doctors are usually described as practising . . .'

A doctor advised his patient to drink warm water an hour before every meal. At his next appointment, the patient reported that there had been no improvement in his condition.

'Did you follow my instruction to drink warm water an hour before every meal?' enquired the doctor.

'I'm afraid not,' admitted the patient ruefully. 'I've tried, but I can only keep it up for about fifteen minutes.'

A consultant physician, who believed in being absolutely frank with his patients, found it necessary to inform a financial magnate that he was critically ill.

The financier took the news bravely, but offered to donate £15,000 to the hospital if he pulled through. Six months later the two met in the street, and the doctor asked him how he felt.

'One hundred per cent,' beamed the financier. 'Never felt better.'

'That's splendid,' the doctor nodded, 'Now, about the donation—'

'What donation?' enquired the financier.

'You remember—you promised to donate £15,000 to the hospital if you pulled through.'

'I did? I *must* have been ill. . . .'

PATIENT: 'Doctor, I'm afraid I've brought you on a long journey.'

G.P.: 'Oh, don't worry about that. I had to visit a neighbour of yours, so I thought I'd kill two birds with one stone.'

PHYSICIAN: 'Why did you operate on Mr Smithkins?'

SURGEON: 'Two hundred and fifty guineas.'

PHYSICIAN: 'No, I mean what did he have?'

SURGEON: 'Two hundred and fifty guineas.'

'Your husband has contracted a very mild infection, Mrs Lucre,' said the doctor reassuringly. 'I think it will be sufficient to paint his throat with nitrate of silver.'

'Silver, doctor!' cried rich, social-climbing Mrs Lucre. 'What's wrong with nitrate of gold?'

A cold is like a committee meeting: sometimes the eyes have it, and sometimes the nose.

A lissom young lady brought an under-weight baby to be examined by the doctor.

'Hmmm,' said the doctor, after looking at the baby, 'Very under-nourished I'm afraid. Excuse me, madam . . .'

He undid the girl's blouse and examined her breasts with care.

'Just as I thought!' he announced. 'You're not producing any milk!'

'I should hope not, doctor!' she beamed. 'I'm his aunt.'

An expensive boarding school had an arrangement whereby a local doctor treated the pupils privately, when necessary. At the end of one winter term, the mother of one boy rang up the doctor.

'I must say,' she complained, 'Your bill seems very steep. After all, Charles only had measles.'

'Come, come, Mrs Montmorency,' remonstrated the doctor, 'Don't forget that I had to visit him several times.'

'Perhaps so, doctor—but don't *you* forget that he infected the whole school.'

A rather pompous surgeon was in the middle of a long speech after a medical club dinner.

'Let it never be said,' he intoned, 'That our profession receives its full due in the eyes of society. Indeed, we have many critics in this world.'

'Not to mention' muttered a sardonic colleague, 'those in the next.'

CONSULTANT: *A colleague who is called in at the last moment to share the blame.*

The patient walked into the surgery wearing a very tall hat. When he took it off, there was a rose bush growing out of his head.

'You see my trouble, doctor, don't you . . .' he began.

'Of course, my dear chap,' said the doctor, soothingly. 'And don't worry about a thing. We'll have that rose bush off in no time.'

'Don't you dare!' shouted the patient. 'You just leave my rose bush alone! I've had it all my life . . .'

'My dear fellow, calm down,' said the doctor. 'If it's not the rose bush, what *have* you come to see me about?'

'Call yourself a doctor!' screamed the patient. 'Can't you see I'm covered in greenfly?'

During an insurance examination, the physician was enquiring into a patient's family history.

'And did your father die a natural death, Mrs Brown?' he asked.

'Oh, no!' replied Mrs Brown, 'He had a doctor.'

'Bloggs has built himself quite a reputation as a surgeon, but really he should have been in business,' said one jealous colleague to another. 'He's the sort who is quite capable of taking a small operation and making it into a major undertaking.'

A fashionable doctor asked a young colleague to act as his locum while he went on holiday.

'I'm not sure that I could manage it,' replied the other dubiously,

'I've not been at it very long, as you know, and I've no experience at all of your sort of practice.'

'Don't worry about that, old boy,' the society doctor reassured him. 'You'll have no difficulty at all with the sort of patients I get. Tell all the men to play more golf, and pack all the women off to the Continent.'

Then there was the young man who was studying to be a tree surgeon. He had to give it up—he just couldn't stand the sight of sap.

After the birth of her first child, a young housewife became pre-occupied with cleanliness and hygiene. She had always been very house-proud; now she went to inordinate lengths to disinfect or sterilise everything with which her baby might come into contact.

Her friends' remonstrances were met with peremptory assertions about the criminal negligence most parents displayed in their lack of concern for their children's health.

One day she announced that her baby was cutting his first tooth and asked what she should do.

'Don't worry,' advised an older friend soothingly. 'Just put your finger gently into his mouth ——'. She broke off, noticing the young mother's horrified expression, then added hastily: 'Naturally, you boil the finger first. . . .'

The doctor had tried for years to persuade a very obese patient to do something about his weight. One day the man came to see him to ask if he could recommend something to stop him sleeping with his mouth open.

'Certainly I can,' said the doctor gravely. 'It's your old problem—you must get your weight down.'

'My weight?' the fat man protested, 'What's my weight got to do with it?'

'Everything, my dear sir. Your skin is now so tight that every time you close your eyes your mouth opens.'

The doctor crawled wearily into bed in the early hours of the morning after being called out on an emergency. Hardly had he dropped off to sleep when the telephone rang insistently.

'Is that you, doctor?' wailed a voice at the other end. 'I can't get off to sleep!'

'Hold the line,' grated the doctor bitterly. 'Hold the line and I'll hum you a ruddy lullaby.'

The young wife, eager to impress the neighbourhood, had planned a dinner party to which she had invited all the local celebrities, including the doctor. Unfortunately, his reply was quite illegible.

'What shall I do?' she asked her husband anxiously. 'I must know exactly who is coming. But I don't like to ring the doctor up and admit that I can't read his letter.'

Her husband had a brainwave. 'Take it round to the chemist,' he suggested, 'He must be familiar with the doctor's scrawl.'

The young lady duly took the note round to the chemist, who took one look at it and disappeared into his dispensary without a word. Two minutes later he returned.

'There you are, madam,' he said, pressing a large bottle into her hands. 'One tablespoon before every meal.'

After having lunch at the vicarage, the local doctor took a stroll in the churchyard nearby. One of the other guests enquired where he had gone.

'Oh, he's just popped out,' twinkled the vicar, 'to visit some of his old patients.'

A choleric old G.P. was seeing one of his patients for the first time.

'Funny you haven't been to see me before!' he barked. 'Have you consulted any other doctor about your condition?'

'No, sir,' stammered the patient. 'Only the chemist.'

'Good heavens, man,' snorted the doctor, 'Have you no sense? This just shows how stupid people can be! The chemist isn't medically qualified—you had no right to consult him. And what nonsense did he tell you?'

'He told me to come and see you.'

DOCTOR: *A professional man who suffers from good health.*

The doctor had been called out to see a rich, self-willed old lady. After completing his examination he shook his head reproachfully.

'This won't do at all, Miss Darrimond,' he said. 'I asked you to call me at once if your symptoms returned. Now, how long have you been like this?'

'Oh, weeks,' snapped Miss Darrimond. 'But I've never seen much point in calling you in. As you know, I haven't the slightest faith in doctors!'

'Well, don't let that worry you in the future,' smiled the doctor placatingly. 'I'm here to put you right. After all, a donkey hasn't much faith in veterinary surgeons, but they can cure him just the same.'

Many people call a doctor when what they really want is an audience.

A self-important young physician was haranguing an elderly family doctor about modern developments in medicine.

'The days of the non-specialist are over,' he declaimed. 'To keep abreast with modern medical science one must specialise intensively. Even the old so-called specialities were far too broadly based. Take ear, nose and throat work, for instance—nowadays that represents far too wide and complex a field of investigation for one man to cover scientifically. I intend to concentrate only on the nose. . . .'

'Really?' murmured the old doctor. 'Which nostril?'

Henry was becoming alarmed about his girth, but sheer indolence, coupled with a liking for beer, had prevented him from accomplishing any noticeable reduction in weight. So he was filled with envy and respect when one evening he encountered a friend who told him that he had shed two stones in weight during the previous six weeks.

'Look at that, Fatso,' bragged his friend, beating his abdomen. 'Flat as a board!'

'True—you've certainly lost it,' admitted Henry. 'Strict dieting, I suppose?'

'Not at all—eat what I like!'

Henry eyed him suspiciously. 'What then? Fifteen mile runs and thousands of press-ups? I just couldn't keep up that sort of thing.'

'Wrong again,' beamed his friend. 'I haven't had to do a thing. It's all the result of a new drug that Doctor Needle gave me. One dose at bed-time and off it rolls!'

'Sounds miraculous!' Henry gasped. 'But how does it work?'

'Oh, it's one of these psychological things. Very pleasant, actually. Every night I dream that I'm on a desert island surrounded by hordes of dusky beauties. All night I chase them round and round the island. Wake up cheered and refreshed, having sweated off another pound or two. Marvellous! The best slimming method I've ever come across.'

The next morning Henry rushed round to see the doctor; he started the new slimming treatment that very night. But within a week he was back at the surgery.

'What's the matter now?' demanded Dr Needle. 'It looks as though the tablets are working already—you've lost weight, haven't you?'

'Oh yes. I lost seven pounds in the first four days . . .'

'Well then?'

'Well, the friend who told me of your new treatment was enjoying it,' complained Henry miserably. 'Every night he dreamed of chasing all these lovely girls ——'

'So?'

'I dream of the desert island every night. But it's inhabited by gangs of horrible cannibals, who chase *me* round and round the island all night long!'

'It's quite simple. Your friend is a private patient of mine,' explained the doctor. '*You* are on the National Health Service.'

QUERULOUS PATIENT: 'Do I have to have one of these anaesthetics?'
DOCTOR: 'Yes, you do.'
PATIENT: 'Will it hurt?'
DOCTOR: 'No, of course not.'
PATIENT: 'Will it make me sick?'
DOCTOR: 'I don't think so. Now please stop worrying—'
PATIENT: 'How long will it be before I know anything?'
DOCTOR: 'This is an anaesthetic, not a miracle drug.'

The doctor called to see eccentric Uncle Albert and found him sitting up in bed, stuffing tobacco up his nose.

Putting on his most diplomatic bedside manner, the doctor began: 'Your niece asked me to drop by if I was passing. And here I am. Now then . . . how can I be of help?'

'For a start,' said Uncle Albert, pushing more tobacco up his nose, 'you can give me a light.'

The clinical lecturer pointed at the projection screen.

'It is clear from this x-ray that one of this patient's legs is shorter than the other, which accounts for his limp. Now, Mr Simpson—what would you do in a case like this?'

The student brooded for some time, and then replied earnestly: 'I suspect, sir, that I might limp, too.'

VOICE ON TELEPHONE: 'Please come at once, doctor. My little boy has swallowed a razor blade!'
DOCTOR: 'Don't panic—I'm on my way. But what have you done so far?'
VOICE: 'I've used my electric razor.'

A doctor was taking a walk with his wife when a vivacious young blonde waved to him.

'Who was your friend, dear?' enquired his wife.

'Oh, just a young woman I met professionally,' he explained airily.

'Professionally, heh?' cooed his wife. 'Yours or hers?'

ST JOHN'S INSTRUCTOR: 'Outline the steps to be taken in the rescue and resuscitation of a drowning man.'

KEEN PUPIL: 'One—get the man out of the water. Two—get the water out of the man.'

The doctor gazed at the harassed, stout lady who sat at the other side of his desk.

'I was right, Mrs Trubshaw,' he announced. 'You are definitely pregnant again.'

'This'll be the fifteenth, doctor,' said Mrs Trubshaw grimly. 'You'll have to help me—enough is enough. I want one of these hearing aids!'

'A hearing aid?' frowned the doctor. 'Surely you mean a contraceptive device?'

'I mean a hearing aid, doctor. You see, it's like this. Every Saturday night my old man comes in drunk. When we get into bed he says: "Now then—are we going to sleep or what?" And every blasted time I say: "What?"'

A minor operation is one undergone by somebody else.

An anxious young mother was continually summoning the family doctor to investigate what usually turned out to be imaginary symptoms. One night the telephone roused him from his bed.

'Please come at once, doctor,' gasped the young woman's voice, 'It's my little boy——'

'Does he feel ill?' yawned the doctor.

'No, that's the odd thing. But I took his temperature as usual—and it's 125!'

'In that case, madam,' growled the doctor, 'I suggest you call the fire-brigade.'

The doctor walked into the bedroom, leaving the husband standing nervously outside.

In two minutes he was out again, asking if he could borrow a carving knife. The husband obliged and the doctor disappeared back into the room.

Soon he was out again, this time asking for a hammer and chisel. The husband rushed downstairs, returned with a hammer and chisel, but by now was in a fearful state of nervous agitation.

The doctor went back into the room, only to return five minutes later.

'I'm sorry,' he said. 'But I'm afraid I need a crowbar.'

'A crowbar!' screeched the poor husband. 'For goodness sake, doctor, can't you get my wife in hospital for something as drastic as this? What's wrong with her, anyway?'

'I haven't a clue,' said the doctor. 'I'm still trying to get my bag open.'

DOCTOR (outside sick-room): 'I'm rather worried about your wife's condition, Mr Partridge. I don't like the way she looks.'
 HUSBAND: 'I haven't liked it for years.'

An unduly health-conscious woman, who was always taking up new fads, consulted her doctor about an article she had been reading.
 'Tell me, doctor,' she gasped excitedly, 'Is it true that insomnia can be cured by sleeping outdoors?'
 The doctor looked at her closely.
 'Quite true, madam,' he replied at last. 'But sleeping indoors does it just as well.'

He was the kind of doctor who diagnosed your condition by feeling your purse.

A man rushed into the doctor's surgery, looking very agitated.
 'It's my wife, Doctor!' he gasped. 'There's something very wrong with her. Her face seems to have seized up, and she can't speak!'
 'Hmmm . . . It could be lockjaw,' replied the doctor.
 'Could it really? . . . In that case, doctor, if you happen to be in our neighbourhood during the next few weeks, perhaps you could drop in and have a look at her. . . .'

The family doctor was called out to see an elderly man who lived with his married daughter.
 'What seems to be the matter with your father?' he asked as he arrived.
 'I don't know, doctor,' replied the daughter. 'He just keeps groaning that he wants to die.'
 'Aha,' said the doctor, 'Then you were right in sending for me.'

PHYSICIAN (after completing examination): 'I have some good news for you, Mrs Brown——'
 YOUNG LADY: '*Miss* Brown, Doctor.'
 PHYSICIAN: 'In that case, Miss Brown, I have some bad news for you.'

The son of a general practitioner had recently qualified in medicine, and his father took him into partnership. A few months later, the old doctor went away on holiday, leaving the youngster to look after the practice. On his return his son informed him smugly that during his absence he had effected a complete cure of the back pains which had troubled an elderly private patient for years.

'You did a grand job there, son,' smiled his father. 'Especially as it was those back pains which put you through medical school.'

A Wiltshire farmer dropped in to see the doctor one market day and asked him if he would examine his wife the next time he happened to be near.

'Certainly' said the doctor, 'Is she ill?'

'No—not exactly ill, doctor.'

'What seems to be the trouble then?'

'Hard to say,' replied the farmer. 'Yesterday morning she got up as usual about four o'clock, milked the cows, made the lads' breakfasts, did the weekly wash, churned the milk, did her housework, made dinner, stooked corn all afternoon, made the supper . . . Then along about ten o'clock at night she started complaining she was tired, I reckon she needs a bit of a tonic. . . .'

'This may hurt a little,' said the doctor as he stepped forward with the syringe.

Suddenly the patient let out the most agonised howl.

'What's the matter with you?' said the doctor. 'I haven't touched you yet.'

'Not with the syringe, you haven't,' said the patient, 'but you're standing right on my corn.'

PHYSIOPTHERAPIST: 'It's going to rain today—I can feel it in your joints.'

CONSULTANT: 'If I considered an operation to be necessary, would you have the money to pay for it?'

PRIVATE PATIENT: 'Let's put it the other way, doctor—if I didn't have the money to pay for it, would you consider the operation to be necessary?'

A man went to see his doctor, complaining of a steady deterioration in his hearing. After a careful consideration of all aspects of the case, the doctor advised him to refrain from drinking alcohol. This he did, and at his next appointment he was able to inform the doctor that, much to his surprise, his hearing had shown an immediate improvement.

However, three months later he presented himself at the surgery again and reported sadly that he had become almost totally deaf.

'You haven't started drinking again, have you?' demanded the doctor.

'Yes,' admitted his patient, 'I'm afraid I have.'

'Why?'

'Well, doctor, I suppose it was because I liked what I was drinking much more than what I was hearing.'

SPECIALIST: *A doctor whose patients are supposed to be ill only during office hours.*

A young husband taking his wife to the maternity hospital mistimed their departure. After a series of traffic hold-ups they arrived at the hospital just in time for her to give birth to a fine baby at the hospital entrance.

Subsequently, the husband received the hospital bill, to discover that it included the item: 'Delivery room, services and equipment—£28.'

Much annoyed, he wrote a strong letter to the hospital bursar, pointing out that he was certainly not liable for that particular charge as his wife had been delivered of her child on the lawn outside the hospital.

Two days later he received an amended bill which included the item: 'Green fee—£28.'

A portly and lethargic young man visited the doctor to complain of insomnia.

'Don't you sleep at all at night?' asked his doctor.

'Oh, I sleep like a top at night,' admitted the sufferer, 'And I sleep fairly soundly during the mornings. But I often have difficulty dropping off in the afternoons.'

A doctor went round to his local garage to query his bill. The foreman assured him that there had been no mistake.

'But it seems a fantastic amount for a routine service,' complained the doctor. 'You people have begun to charge more per hour than we members of the medical profession do!'

The foreman regarded him stolidly. 'Look at it this way, doc— you lot have been servicing the same old model ever since Adam. *We* have to study up on a new one practically every month.'

SURGEON'S WIFE: 'Hector has had to rush off to do an emergency operation, I'm afraid.'

FRIEND: 'A risky one?'

SURGEON'S WIFE: 'Very. He's not even sure that he'll be paid at all.'

The restaurant was not nearly so salubrious as it had appeared from outside, and the doctor was further put off by the fact that the waitress kept scratching her nose.

'Tell me my girl,' he said sharply, 'Have you got eczema?'

'Naw,' snuffled the waitress, 'Only what you see on the menu.'

PATIENT: 'I'm much better now, doctor. Please let me have your bill.'

DOCTOR: 'Come, come, my dear sir. I don't think that you are quite strong enough for that yet.'

'I can find nothing organically wrong with you,' announced the doctor. 'Your problem is nerves.'

'In that case,' said the patient, 'I'd better not go home on the bus, had I? I wonder whether you'd be good enough to lend me enough to get a taxi? Oh, and while you're at it, a few more bob for some tonics would come in handy.'

'On second thoughts,' said the physician, 'my original diagnosis was incorrect. There is nothing wrong with your nerve whatsoever. You simply have an enlarged gall.'

A wealthy patient insisted upon being treated privately by a top rank specialist who, after a lengthy treatment, succeeded in curing him. The patient's gratitude was somewhat marred by the size of the medical man's bill, and he told him so at a follow-up examination.

'You wouldn't grumble at a bill five times as great, said the specialist blandly, 'if you knew how interesting your case was medically . . . and how tempted I was to let it go to post-mortem.'

'So you're suffering from fatigue in the evenings?' nodded the doctor. 'That's common enough. Have a couple of brandies before your dinner—they'll set you up!'

'Right you are!' beamed his patient. Then his face fell. 'But wait a minute, doctor. You told me I was to cut alcohol right out, when I consulted you before.'

The doctor waved airily. 'Oh, that was last August, my dear fellow. Medical science has developed enormously since then.'

The best doctor is the one you run for and cannot find.

—DIDEROT.

A young lady asked her doctor if he could recommend an absolutely safe method of contraception.

'The only sure method I know of, Miss Brown,' the doctor replied coldly, 'is a glass of unsweetened lemon juice.'

'Thank you so much, Doctor,' fluted the girl. 'Just a glass of lemon juice? Before or after?'

'Instead of!'

The old physician was wont to impress upon his young partner the importance of common-sense and close observation. 'There's more to medicine than physiology and materia medica, my boy,' he would say. 'There's a lot of general detection work about it—comes with experience.'

One day, to demonstrate his point, he took the young physician with him on his rounds. At the first call he made a cursory examination of the patient, wrote out a prescription and told the sufferer to cut down on his smoking. As the two colleagues got into the car outside, the younger man asked:

'How on earth did you know he was a heavy smoker? Cardiac signs? Teeth? Tongue?'

'No, my boy,' smiled the old doctor. 'Didn't you notice all the cigarette ash on the counterpane?'

The next patient was advised to cut down on her consumption of sweets.

Afterwards the young doctor grinned ruefully. 'All right—what put you on to that?'

His old partner was triumphant. 'Easy—caught sight of a pile of toffee wrappers behind the bed-side table. Get the idea? You try it at our next stop.'

The next patient was a rather agitated lady. The young doctor took her pulse, listened to her heart and solemnly advised her to cut down on her church activities. Back in the car the old doctor expressed his reluctant admitation.

'But how did you twig that? I've got to admit *I* didn't notice anything special.'

'Remember when I dropped my stethoscope?' asked the young doctor. 'When I picked it up I couldn't help noticing the vicar under the bed.'

'So your son is an undertaker? I understood you to say he was a doctor.'

'No—I said he followed the medical profession.'

Dyspepsia is the remorse of a guilty stomach.

—A. KERR.

PATIENT: 'And when my arm is quite better will I be able to play my trombone?'

DOCTOR: 'Oh yes—you'll have no trouble at all.'

PATIENT: 'That's splendid, doctor—I could never play it before.'

The family doctor had got to bed when he was roused by the phone.

'Doctor, doctor,' squeaked a female voice. 'I think I've developed water on the knee! 'What can I do?'

'Come and see me tomorrow,' the doctor yawned.

'But this is urgent, surely, doctor,' wailed the voice. 'What do I do meanwhile?'

'If it will make you feel safer, madam,' snarled the doctor, 'Try wearing pumps.'

'I do like your uniform,' prattled the young charmer, 'Tell me, what do you do, exactly.'

'I'm a naval surgeon, miss.'

'Really?' the young lady replied, wide-eyed. 'How you doctors specialise. . . .'

'No, I'm not officially off work sick. But I am taking a sort of rest cure.'

'How do you mean?'

'Our G.P. has a very large practice. Every day I just sit for about three hours in his waiting room.'

The G.P. was making his rounds. 'Good morning, Mrs Kelly,' he said briskly, 'Your husband's no worse, I hope? Did you take his temperature, as I suggested?'

'I did that, doctor,' beamed Mrs Kelly. 'I stuffed the barometer under his blankets. It said "Very Dry", so I popped out and got him a couple of pints of bitter and he's just staggered off to work.'

A physician was well-known locally for his sour disposition and dubious diagnoses. One day he stopped for some time to watch a bricklayer at work.

'Ha!' he snorted eventually, 'I see there are many errors covered up with a trowel!'

'Aye,' said the bricklayer reflectively, 'But more with a spade. . . .'

A patient took his place in the queue in the doctor's waiting room. He was flushed, his eyes and nose were streaming and he was sneezing explosively.

'Godder bad cold,' he explained to the man next to him, between sneezes.

'Hard luck, mate,' commiserated the other. 'You should have had pneumonia. They know what to do for that.'

302

A man who had been found unconscious in the street was rushed to the local infirmary. There, the nurses were about to strip him for examination when the casualty officer found a note pinned to his jacket:

'*Dear Doctor,*

    I am just dead drunk. Kindly allow me merely to sleep it off. In any case do not attempt to remove my appendix. You've already done that twice.'

DOCTOR *to call girl*: 'You look run down. My advice is that you stay out of bed for a week or two.'

'I've tried every diet I can think of, doctor,' said the obese patient, 'and I still can't get any thinner. It's driving me crazy.'

'Now, now,' said the doctor, 'we mustn't get in a state, must we? Take these tranquillisers three times a day after meals.'

'And will they make me thin, doctor?'

'No—but they'll stop you worrying about being fat.'

A small boy was admitted to a hospital ward. After he had been settled in he took stock of his surroundings, to find that the boy in the next bed was regarding him with patronising curiosity.

'What you got?' enquired the veteran.

'Dunno,' admitted the new boy.

'Well, are you medical or surgical?'

'Dunno that either.'

'You dunno whether you're medical or surgical?' squeaked the interrogator. 'Well—were you sick before you came in, or did they make you sick after?'

DOCTOR: 'Did you tell that beastly young man of yours my opinion of him?'

DAUGHTER: 'Of course, Daddy.'

DOCTOR: 'Good. And what had he got to say to that?'

DAUGHTER: 'Nothing much. Just that your diagnosis was as bad as ever.'

The society lady was discussing with a friend her daughter's imminent operation.

'Money's no consideration, of course,' she confided. 'Henry and I aren't worried about the hundred guineas. But the idea of our little girl's life being in danger . . .'

'I shouldn't worry, dear,' said her friend, consolingly. 'There can't be much danger if the surgeon is only asking a hundred guineas.'

This is a bit subtle, but did you ever hear about the army doctor who said to the other army doctor: 'And what did you do in civvy street?'

Live according to nature, be patient, and to hell with the doctors.
—ROUSSEAU

The local doctor, who was a church sidesman, had seen fit to complain to several fellow parishioners about the sexton's drunkenness.

'I'm disappointed in you, doctor,' the sexton reproached him. 'You're the last person I would have thought would have publicised my little weakness. Think of all *your* blunders I've had to cover up.'

'You are certain to make a complete recovery,' the doctor assured his patient. 'I have no doubt about it whatsoever.'

'But how can you be so sure, doctor?' asked the patient; 'I thought that this was a very serious disease, with a pretty poor outlook?'

'So it is,' replied the doctor heartily, 'The text-books state that nine out of every ten patients with your condition die . . .'

'Well then, how can you be so optimistic in my case?'

'Just a matter of statistics,' beamed the doctor. 'You are the tenth case I have treated . . . and the other nine are already dead.'

DOCTOR: 'You look much better this week.'

PATIENT: 'I certainly am, doctor. I reckon it's because I followed the directions on that bottle of medicine you prescribed for me last time.'

DOCTOR: 'Splendid. Er—what directions?'

PATIENT: 'It said: "Keep this bottle tightly corked".'

Two registrars at the bedside of a patient, who had been admitted to hospital in a coma, were trying to take his pulse. They fumbled under the sheets, and each doctor found the other's wrist.

'Nothing much wrong with him,' pronounced the first.

'True,' agreed the second. 'He's probably drunk.'

The doctor was busy and noted, anyway, for his impatience. When the girl was shown into his surgery he wasted no time.

'Clothes off,' he snapped, 'and lie down on the couch.'

'But doctor,' protested the girl.

'Clothes off, I said—and be quick about it! I haven't got all day!'

The girl took off her clothes and lay, stark naked, on the couch. The doctor gave her a thorough examination, looking more and more exasperated.

'What the devil are you playing at!' he barked. 'There's absolutely nothing wrong with you!'

'I know,' said the girl. 'I only came in to clean the 'phone.'

The village doctor had attended the parson privately throughout the winter and was having trouble getting settlement of his bill. Finally he pointed this out to the worthy cleric and insisted that he should pay his dues.

'I have a suggestion, old friend,' said the parson. 'You go on doing your best to keep me out of heaven. In return, I'll try to keep you out of hell. Is it a bargain?'

Grandma was very old and in poor health. But she was an imperious, strong-willed person, who had always steadfastly refused to be seen by a doctor. Eventually her daughter summoned the family doctor. She requested him to ignore the old lady's protestations and give her a complete check-up. She then ushered him into the bedroom and left without a word of explanation to her mother.

After the doctor's departure, Grandma summoned her daughter.

'Emily, what was that young lawyer's name?' she demanded, her eyes sparkling.

'That wasn't a lawyer, I'm afraid, mother,' admitted the daughter uneasily. 'He was the doctor.'

'A doctor?' asked Grandma, disappointedly. 'Well, that explains it. I thought he was a little familiar for a lawyer.'

The captain of the football team was disturbed to find that he was developing a painfully sore throat a few days before an important match. He hastily took himself off to see the G.P. who had just moved to the area. The doctor's door was opened by his pretty young wife.

'Is the doctor in?' the young man asked in a bronchial whisper.

'No,' whispered the young wife, looking quickly up and down the street, 'Come on in.'

SURGEON's WIFE: 'Did the operation go all right, dear?'

SURGEON: 'Yes, I managed to do it in the nick of time—another few hours and the patient would have recovered without it.'

'How is this patient getting on?' the doctor asked the new nurse. 'Have you kept a chart of his progress?'

The nurse blushed prettily. 'Not exactly, doctor,' she replied. 'But I can show you my diary.'

The nubile young blonde had just had her appendix removed.

'Will the scar show, doctor?' she asked.

'That depends,' answered the surgeon gravely, 'on your discretion and the demands of fashion.'

A very cheerful young man strode into the doctor's surgery.

'I just dropped by, doctor, to thank you,' he announced. 'I'd like you to know how much I've benefited from your treatment.'

The doctor regarded him puzzledly. 'Er—are you one of my patients?' he asked.

'No,' beamed the young man, 'But my uncle was, and I've just heard his will read.'

Paddy had just had a major abdominal operation. He came round from the anaesthetic, to find himself back in the ward.

'Praise be to the Lord!' he cried. 'It's over with, is it?'

The man in the next bed shook his head lugubriously. 'Don't be so sure, mate,' he warned. 'They had to open me up again after my op—they'd left a swab inside me!'

'That's nothing!' bragged the man on Paddy's other side, 'They left a scalpel in me!'

The surgical registrar bounded into the ward.

'Sister!' he called, 'has anybody seen my golf clubs?'

It took them half an hour to revive Paddy. . . .

PATIENT: 'And will just one course of these tablets cure me?'

DOCTOR: 'Let's put it this way—none of my patients has ever come back for a second one. . . .'

'You certainly seem in excellent health,' said the young physician to the octogenarian. 'What's your secret?'

'I've kept off drink and women, doctor,' said the old man firmly. 'Never gone out with a girl or touched a drop in my whole life.'

Just then there was a crash and a terrified female scream from the adjoining room.

'What on earth is that?' asked the doctor in alarm.

'That'll be father chasing the maid,' snapped the greybeard. 'He's drunk again.'

The desire to take medicine is perhaps the greatest feature which distinguishes man from animals.

—SIR WILLIAM OSLER

SURGEON: 'I'm afraid your condition is critical. I shall have to remove half your large bowel.'

PATIENT: 'That's all right, doctor—better a semi-colon than a full stop.'

Does a doctor's doctor doctor the doctor according to his own doctoring or does the doctor doing the doctoring doctor the other doctor according to the doctored doctor's doctoring doctrine?

The consultant was doing a hospital round. He stopped at the bed-side of one gloomy-looking patient and examined the charts and case notes, nodding wisely.

'You are progressing very well indeed, my man,' he announced at last. 'I see that your neck is still very swollen, but I'm not too worried about that . . .'

'I dare say you're not!' burst out the patient. 'And if yours was swollen don't kid yourself that I'd be shedding any tears either.'

Happy the physician who is summoned at the end of the illness.
—FRENCH PROVERB

A forward young man had been tended during his stay in hospital by a very attractive nurse. As his health improved he claimed to have developed a passion for her, and his advances became pro-gressively more daring.

'Nurse, nurse! I have fallen desperately in love with you!' he declared one day. 'I don't want to get better.'

'You probably won't,' said the nurse amiably, 'The houseman saw you trying to kiss me last night. And he's my husband.'

A chic model girl was being examined by her doctor, after com-plaining of abdominal pains.

'There's no doubt about it,' said the doctor, pursing his lips, 'You have acute appendicitis.'

The model yawned ostentatiously.

'Thank you, doctor, but I came here to be examined, not admired.'

RESIDENT: 'Is this the sympathetic chain, sir?'

SURGEON: 'Why not pull it and see if the patient flushes?'

An Irish physician once submitted a bill headed:
'To curing your husband till he died . . .'

307

An apprehensive hospital patient had been the subject of a pro-longed bedside clinical conference. Subsequently, he showed such anxiety and tension that the sister summoned the senior registrar.

'Now, what's all this about then?' demanded the registrar, heartily. 'We do seem to have got ourself worked up, don't we?'

'It was that conference, doctor,' panted the ill man. 'There must be a lot of doubt about what's wrong with me.'

'Not at all,' asserted the registrar. 'Where did you get that idea?'

'Well, there was all that argument about the diagnosis. All the other doctors disagreed with you, didn't they?'

'To some extent,' said the registrar, consolingly. 'But I'll bet you the post-mortem proves I was right.'

SENIOR PARTNER: 'You seem to have cured the patient. What's worrying you now?'

JUNIOR PARTNER: 'I filled him up with so many medicines I don't know which one worked.'

DOCTOR (*approvingly*): 'You are coughing much more easily this morning.'

PATIENT (*bitterly*): 'So I should. I've been practising hard all night.'

The patient was a lanky, solemn individual; he was trying to describe his symptom to an impatient physician.

'It's a sort of jabbing pain in my right shoulder, doctor. I get it when I lean forward, stretch out one arm, then the other, raise my elbows, hunch my shoulders and then stand straight up.'

'Is that so?' said the doctor, sneering. 'I don't suppose it's occurred to you that you could avoid this mysterious pain, simply by not carrying out such an absurd series of movements?'

'It did occur to me, doctor,' the patient assured him earnestly, 'but I couldn't think of any other way of getting into my overcoat.'

The stout lady burst into the doctor's surgery.

'Doctor,' she gasped, 'What should I take when I'm run down?'

'The licence number, madam,' the physician replied absently, 'and the make of car.'

'I'm getting more and more worried about Grandma,' said the young woman. 'She's smoking very heavily and insists on inhaling.'

'It's not unusual, you know,' replied the doctor, soothingly. 'Most heavy smokers inhale.'

'Yes, but this is different—you see, Grandma doesn't *exhale*.'

PROFESSOR: 'What would be the appropriate steps to take in the case of a patient eating poisonous fungi?'
STUDENT: 'Advise a change of diet.'

Two doctors were sun-bathing on the beach.
'What wonderful legs that girl had!' exclaimed the first.
'I didn't notice,' replied the other. 'I'm a chest man myself.'

'Jasper will be in hospital a long, long time.'
'How do you know—did you see the doctor?'
'No—the nurse.'

The doctor had just given one of his male patients a routine check-up and reported favourably upon his general condition.
'Several of my relatives have lived until they were ninety, doctor,' said the patient wistfully. 'What are my chances?'
'How old are you now?' asked the doctor.
'I'm just forty.'
'How much do you drink?'
'I don't—I'm a teetotal.'
'How many cigarettes do you smoke?'
'I don't touch tobacco, doctor.'
'Do you make excessive demands on yourself—fast driving, gambling, undue sexuality . . .'
'Nothing like that, doctor. I live a very orderly life, and I can honestly say I have no vices whatsoever.'
'Then why,' asked the doctor, 'do you want to live another fifty years?'

Doctors are men who prescribe medicines of which they know little to cure diseases of which they know less in human beings of whom they know nothing.
—VOLTAIRE

*PLEASE HELP
OUR NEW NURSES HOME*
—HOSPITAL POSTER

'Deep breathing kills germs.'
'Yes, but how do you make them breathe deeply?'

A very old doctor died in surprisingly straitened circumstances. A group of his friends decided to set up a fund to give him a funeral of distinction. Their collection was not going well until they called on an eccentric old gentleman, who pricked up his ears when the word 'doctor' was mentioned.

'How much were you hoping for from me?' he demanded.

The members of the delegation looked at each other quickly. 'Er—five guineas?' suggested their leader. The old gentleman brought out his wallet.

'Here,' he said, 'here's sixty. Bury a dozen of 'em.'

'That osteopath swore he'd have me walking within six months.'

'And did he?'

'He certainly did. He's sent me three bills so far and I've had to sell my car.'

Jones hurried round to see his friend Smith after hearing he had been in an accident. He found Smith lying gloomily in bed, swathed in bandages.

'My dear fellow!' cried Jones. 'What a ghastly mess! You must be in terrible pain. A state of shock, too, no doubt?'

'Not exactly shock,' replied Smith morosely. 'More wonderment at the ironies of life.'

'What on earth do you mean?'

'My present condition is entirely due to the fact that this morning I went to see my doctor because I had a slight headache.'

'How does that account for the mess you're in?'

'I was given an emergency abdominal operation by mistake. I was only there in the first place because I rolled off the stretcher as I was being put in the ambulance; I broke my leg and three ribs.'

'Ambulance? For a headache?'

'The doctor had said I needed more fresh air and advised me to take up riding. I went off to the riding school and got on a horse. He was frightened by the district nurse's motor scooter, and I fell off and sprained my ankle. And that's why I'm like this.'

FIRST PARTNER: 'We seemed to have far more patients at this time last year than we have now. I wonder where they've all got to?'

SECOND PARTNER: 'We can only hope for the best.'

An eminent physician was seated at dinner next to an awed but talkative young woman.

'You'll never guess where I went last summer,' she babbled.

'You are perfectly correct, miss,' replied the great man coldly, 'I shall never guess. I don't go in for guessing.'

'Oh, get away with you, doctor,' giggled the girl, 'Why, everybody knows that you are a famous diagnostician.'

At the medical ball a young houseman had the temerity to ask the glamorous daughter of the local senior consultant for a dance. She was a haughty creature, several inches taller than he was. She looked down at him superciliously and snapped:

'I prefer not to dance with a child, thank you!'

'I am so sorry, miss,' replied the houseman in a loud, clear voice. 'I had not observed your condition.'

NERVOUS PATIENT: 'Is this operation very dangerous, doctor?'

SURGEON: 'That, my dear sir, is what we are about to find out.'

An established general practitioner was talking shop with a young colleague who had just taken over an adjoining practice.

'How's it going, laddie?' he enquired kindly.

'Not too badly, thank you,' replied the new man nervously, 'At least—the medical side seems straightforward. But, to tell you the truth, I haven't quite managed to get the right *tone* yet. But I've been practising looking over the top of my spectacles and grunting a bit.'

'That's the stuff,' said the older doctor, encouragingly. 'And I tell you what—I'll lend you a few 1926 magazines for your waiting room.'

'Give it to me straight, doctor,' said the very sick man. 'How long have I got?'

'It's hard to say,' said the doctor; 'but if I were you, I wouldn't start reading any serials.'

DOCTOR: 'I haven't seen your husband for some time, Mrs White. The last time I saw him he told me he was a martyr to dyspepsia. Is that still so?'

MRS WHITE: 'Well, yes and no, doctor. He has the dyspepsia. I am the martyr.'

Telegram to famous physician:

MOTHER-IN-LAW AT DEATH'S DOOR STOP. CAN YOU PULL HER THROUGH?

From a Parish magazine:

'*Unfortunately Mr K——fell heavily and injured his right shoulder. The sympathy of all of us went out to him, for he was obliged to call in Dr T——.*'

PHYSICIAN: 'I see you've had this throat irritation for some time. Have you ever gargled with salt water?'

PATIENT (*eagerly*): 'Oh yes, doctor—I was nearly drowned on the Costa Brava last August.'

A patient rang up his doctor at two in the morning.

'I do hope I didn't disturb you, doctor,' he began, apologetically.

'Not at all,' replied the doctor, 'I had to get up to answer the 'phone anyway.'

DOCTOR: 'Now, miss, I want you to say "Ah".'

DOLLY: 'That's a change—most men want me to say "Yes".'

Heard about the sensitive young doctor who refused to visit the farmer any more until he gagged his ducks?

'Dear me, you *are* in a bad way,' said the casualty officer, 'How on earth did you manage to break both your legs?'

'Pure habit,' groaned the patient; 'I threw my cigarette down a man-hole and stepped on it.'

PATIENT: 'Yes, I feel much better, thank you, doctor. But I'm still having trouble with my breathing.'

DOCTOR: 'I see ... Well, I shall have to give you something to stop that.'

The doctor put the fat girl on a diet of nuts and bananas. A month later she came in beaming happily—but still as fat as ever.

'Dear me,' said the doctor. 'The diet doesn't seem to have affected your weight at all.'

'Perhaps not,' said the girl, 'but you should see me climb trees.'

'I was called to a most unfortunate case this morning,' the doctor told his wife. 'A patient of mine died after drinking half a pint of varnish.'

'What a dreadful end!' gasped his wife.

'Yes,' agreed the doctor, 'but a glossy finish.'

The doctor was summoned by a fenland farmer to attend to his son-in-law. He arrived at the remote farm, and was taken to see a dreadfully battered and still only semi-conscious young man.

'This man appears to have been grievously assaulted with a blunt instrument,' said the doctor.

'True,' nodded the farmer.

'Have you any idea who was responsible?'

'Aye,' said the farmer complacently. 'Me.'

The doctor stared at him incredulously. 'But my dear man, how on earth could you administer such a brutal thrashing to your own son-in-law?'

'He weren't my son-in-law then.'

Then there was the very advanced medical researcher who discovered a cure for which there was no known disease.

Referral letter from G.P. to specialist:
This patient, Mrs H—— has been married for two years but has never achieved satisfaction. I wonder whether you can help her?

'Grandpa won't live much longer. You might say he has one foot in the grate.'

'Don't you mean one foot in the grave?'

'No—he wants to be cremated.'

A man recovered consciousness after an operation, to find himself back in his hospital room; the surgeon was sitting by the bedside. The patient smiled weakly and looked round him.

'Why are the curtains drawn, doctor?' he enquired, 'It's not night-time already, is it?'

'No,' beamed the surgeon. 'There's a fire across the road and I didn't want you to wake up and think the operation hadn't been successful.'

The doctor was cleaning out his medical bag, and asked his receptionist to boil some of his instruments. A few minutes later he noticed her poking among them with a fork.

'What are you doing with that fork, Gladys?' he asked.

Gladys coloured prettily, 'I was just prodding them, doctor,' she explained, 'to see if they were done.'

A curvaceous young beauty groped her way in to the young opthalmologist's surgery.

'I've lost my spectacles,' she reported, 'Must I be examined all over again?'

'No,' said the young man, wistfully: 'Just your eyes.'

The physician was also a family friend who rallied round in time of need. He sent the following telegram to the man of the house, who was away on business:

'Regret inform you your mother-in-law dead. Do you wish her buried, cremated or embalmed.'

He received the following reply:

'All three. Take no chances.'

'Well, Dad, I've decided to try to set up in private practice like you,' announced the young physician. 'Any suggestions to offer?'

The old man thought for a while, before replying: 'Only two, son. Always write your prescriptions illegibly, and always write your bills clearly.'

A man presented himself at his doctor's surgery with his face covered in green blotches. The doctor had only recently qualified and was completely mystified by the symptom: even reference to his textbooks provided no enlightenment. He felt his status as a diagnotician to be in jeopardy.

'Tell me,' said the doctor, 'have you ever had this before?'

'I certainly have, doctor,' the patient replied, impatiently. 'I got it seven or eight times last year.'

'In that case,' announced the doctor, 'I reckon you've got it again.'

A patient discovered that the surgeon had left a sponge inside his stomach. He didn't suffer any pain, but he was intolerably thirsty.

PATIENT: 'Doctor, is it true that uncooked lobsters are healthy?'

DOCTOR: 'I imagine so. I've never heard of any complaining.'

The burly patient had been off work for some time with a variety of vague complaints. One morning the doctor gave him an intensive examination and reviewed his medical history.

'Give it to me straight, doc,' begged the man at the end of the proceedings, 'What's wrong with me? I'd sooner know the truth. Skip the jargon—tell me in plain English, will you?'

'In plain English,' said the doctor calmly, 'you are just bone idle!'

'Thanks a lot, doc,' gasped the patient in relief. 'Now if you'll give me the posh, scientific name for it, I can go home and tell the missus.'

DOCTOR: 'And how often does this terrible pain come on?'

PATIENT: 'Every three minutes, doctor.'

DOCTOR: 'And how long does each attack last?'

PATIENT: 'Oh, at least twenty minutes.'

'Is the doctor treating her for being run down?'

'No, she can afford to go to a psychiatrist privately and have a psychoneurosis.'

'Oh, doctor, I'm in a terrible state!' groaned the stout gentleman histrionically, 'Every night at twilight the ghosts of the departed come and perch on the fence posts round my garden—waiting, waiting, waiting . . . What can I do?'

'Hard to say,' grunted the psychiatrist. 'You might try sharpening the tops of the fence posts.'

'I'm troubled by dreams, doctor,' said the aristocratic chinless wonder. 'Every night I dream about playing cricket.'

'Indeed,' said the doctor, 'and who do you play for?'

'Eton, of course,' said the young man scornfully. 'Who else?'

'Yes, yes,' said the doctor, realising he would have to try another approach. 'But tell me, don't you ever dream about girls?'

'What!' exploded the young man. 'And miss my innings?

MENTAL NURSE: 'There's a man on the telephone who wants to know if any of our patients have escaped recently.'

MEDICAL SUPERINTENDENT: 'What does he want to know that for?'

NURSE: 'Somebody has run away with his wife

'I'm very jumpy at the moment. Can't face a dog biscuit,' confided the first Pekinese to the second, 'And I'm not sleeping well, I get spots before my eyes, I'm terrified of cats ——'

'Look here,' said his friend, 'shouldn't you go to see a psychiatrist?'

'That wouldn't work,' squeaked the first, 'I'm not allowed on the couch.'

'You are suffering from nervous exhaustion,' pronounced the specialist. 'It will be a long job, but I think I can cure you for about five hundred guineas.'

'I see, doctor,' the patient reflected. 'And will my nerve be as strong as yours then?'

People who live on their nerves often live on other people's too.

'I suspect that your son's peculiarities are congenital, Mrs Hoosis,' said the doctor gently. 'It may be hereditary in your family.'

Mrs Hoosis was scandalised.

'You must be wrong, doctor,' she protested. 'I can assure you there's never been anything in the slightest hereditary in *my* family.'

A young man went to see his doctor, complaining that he was suffering from continuous fatigue and lassitude. After examining him thoroughly, the doctor announced that he could find nothing organically wrong.

'I suspect that this problem of yours is merely functional,' twinkled the doctor. 'The best advice I can give you is that you cut down on your love life by half.'

The patient considered this for some moments. 'Fifty per cent, heh?' he said at last. 'Which half do you suggest I cut out—thinking about it, or talking about it?'

The general practitioner had just finished his examination of a nervous young man who had a morbid fear of death.

'Why can't you be honest with me, doctor?' gasped the patient. I'm not going to live, am I?'

'Of course you're going to live!' snapped the G.P., who was not noted for his patience. 'As I have just told you, you are suffering from a mild bout of influenza.'

'But are you sure, doctor?' his patient persisted. 'I've heard of people who have died of double pneumonia after their doctors had wrongly diagnosed influenza.'

'Rubbish,' barked the physician. 'When I diagnose influenza, that's what they die of.'

Heard about the lady patient who wanted her doctor's assurance that his new treatment would not affect her complexion? He refused to make any rash promises.

A very stout man was advised by his doctor to take up golf. A few weeks later he came back to see the doctor and asked if the latter could recommend some other form of exercise.

'In heaven's name, why?' demanded the doctor. 'Golf is the finest game in the world!'

'Maybe so,' replied the corpulent patient. 'But it's not for me. If I put the ball where I can see it, I can't hit it. And if I put it where I can hit it I can't see it. . . .'

DOCTOR: 'Was that slimming diet I recommended to your wife satisfactory?'

HUSBAND: 'Very. Three weeks ago she disappeared completely.'

An attractive young brunette was about to undergo a minor operation. She had been prepared for the operation, and wheeled along to the theatre door where the nurse left her to find out if the theatre staff was ready.

Hardly had the nurse departed when a young man in a white coat came up to the trolley, lifted the sheet, examined her closely and walked away, nodding reflectively. He was succeeded by another, who also left without comment.

When a third appeared and drew back the sheet, the young lady demanded pettishly: 'Isn't it about time you got on with the operation? I don't see the point of all this last-minute observation. Is the theatre ready?'

'No idea, lady,' replied the young man. 'We're just painting the corridor.'

PHYSICIAN (*excitedly*): 'A most unusual condition! My dear fellow, your case will enrich medical science!'

PATIENT: 'Not likely—I'm on the National Health Service.'

Two lugubrious northern housewives met in the village street.

'How's your George, then?' enquired the first. 'Taken a turn for the better for the time being, has he?'

'He has not,' replied the second. 'Turn for the worse, more like. I doubt he'll see the winter out, the way he's going on.'

'Eee, poor lad!' gasped the first. 'But I thought doctor said he were on the mend last week?'

'So he did. Got over the other all right, he did, but seems from what doctor says he's got convalescence now.'

'I've received your wife's audiogram,' the family doctor told the nervous little man. 'Perhaps you'd tell her that mild deafness of hers is nothing to worry about? It's merely a sign of her advancing years.'

'I'm sure that will be a relief to know,' said the little man. 'But—er—doctor, I wonder if you'd like to break it to her yourself?'

PRETTY NURSE: 'Each time I take this patient's pulse it gets faster. Should I give him a sedative?'

DOCTOR: 'No—a blindfold.'

The chronic alcoholic was told by his doctor to cut out drink.

'I can't cut it out just like that, doctor,' wailed the drunk. 'It would kill me!'

'Hmmm ... you've probably got something there,' said the doctor. 'We'll compromise, then, and do it gradually. For the next week you can drink four double scotches a day and no more. The following week we'll cut it down to three, and the week after down to two.'

The patient staggered off, and was back in a week—absolutely blotto.

317

'What do you think you're playing at?' demanded the doctor. 'I told you to cut down to four double scotches a day.'

'I did, doctor, honeshly,' said the drunk.

'Well how is it that you're in this dreadfully inebriated condition?'

'Well, doctor, ish like thish. After I left you last week, I called in on another doctor down the road for a second opinion—and he prescribed the same treatment. . . .'

Then there was the millionaire who went into the private nursing home for a gallstones operation. He had a different surgeon for every stone.

You couldn't really call the handsome young locum egotistical—but every time he took a woman's pulse he subtracted ten beats for the effects of his personality.

PATIENT: 'I've got a pain in my left foot.'

DOCTOR: 'Don't worry. It's just old age.'

PATIENT: 'In that case, why doesn't my right foot hurt—I've had it just as long.'